Apple Pro Training Series
Color Correction in Final Cut Studio

Michael Wohl / David Gross

Apple
Certified

Apple Pro Training Series: Color Correction in Final Cut Studio
Michael Wohl, David Gross
Copyright © 2010 by Michael Wohl and David Gross

Published by Peachpit Press. For information on Peachpit Press books, contact:

Peachpit Press
1249 Eighth Street
Berkeley, CA 94710
(510) 524-2178
Fax: (510) 524-2221
http://www.peachpit.com
To report errors, please send a note to errata@peachpit.com.
Peachpit Press is a division of Pearson Education.

Apple Series Editor: Serena Herr
Project Editor: Stephen Nathans-Kelly
Production Coordinator: Kim Wimpsett, Happenstance Type-O-Rama
Technical Editor: Alexis Van Hurkman
Technical Reviewer: Robert Sliga
Copy Editor: Dave Awl
Compositor: Chris Gillespie, Happenstance Type-O-Rama
Media Producer: Eric Geoffroy
Indexer: Valerie Haynes Perry
Cover Illustration: Kent Oberheu
Cover Production: Happenstance Type-O-Rama

ISBN 13: 978-0-321-63528-0
ISBN 10: 0-321-63528-0
9 8 7 6 5 4 3 2 1
Printed and bound in the United States of America

Acknowledgments Special thanks to Lachlan Milne, *www.lachlanmilne. com,* for his help with the planning and execution of the book, his generous sharing of his experience with both traditional color grading and digital intermediates, and, of course, his award-winning cinematography.

Thanks to our generous footage providers, Hugh Miller, *www.hughmiller.com.au*; Nathan Tomlinson, *www.xtremefreelance.com.au;* Leverage Holdings; Anthony Rose, Caroline David, and Paul Friedmann of Flying Fish, Sydney, *www.flyingfish.co.nz;* Ben Blick-Hodge and Jo Sudol of Definition Films, *www.definitionfilms.com;* Mark Furmie and Carl Robertson, *www.filmgraphics.com*; Anne Robinson of Cutting Edge Post in Sydney, *www.cuttingedge.com.au*; and Ben Briand and Pip Smart of Cherub Pictures, *www.cherubpictures.com.au.*

Thanks for technical assistance and equipment to Warren Lynch of Intercolour Australia; Stuart Harris, Peter Belton, and Michael Frew of Apple Australia; Peter Sintras of Sony BMG Music Australia; Greg Clarke of Channel Seven Sport; Paul Saccone, Steve Bayes, Kirk Paulsen, and Patty Montesion of Apple; Olivier Jean, Peter Mousis, and Arthur Pennas of Powermedia Systems, Sydney; and Roger Savage, Bruce Emery, and Jennifer Lum of Soundfirm Sydney, Fox Studios Australia, *www.soundfirm.com.au.*

Contents at a Glance

Table of Contents

Getting Started

Welcome to the official Apple Pro Training course for Color Correction in Final Cut Studio!

This book is a comprehensive guide to color grading with Final Cut Pro 7 and Color 1.5. It aims to broaden your skills as a post-production expert, adding color correction and grading to your arsenal of tools.

The book uses real-world footage from the hit TNT series *Leverage* as well as beautiful HD footage shot around the world to demonstrate the software features and practical techniques you'll use every day. While you work through the exercises, you'll learn not only the many correction and grading features in both Final Cut Pro and Color, but also how to perform those tasks in real-world situations.

Whether you're an expert or a newcomer to the Final Cut Studio suite, this book will help you master color grading in Final Cut Pro and Color while improving your workflow and technique. So let's get started!

The Methodology

This book takes a hands-on approach to learning the software. The lessons are project-based and designed to teach you the color grading techniques and workflows most commonly encountered in a professional setting. Every exercise aims to get you performing professional-quality color grades in Final Cut Pro and Color as quickly as possible.

Each lesson builds on previous lessons, methodically introducing the interface elements and guiding you through their functions and capabilities until you can comfortably use the standard workflows of both applications.

The lessons are self-contained, so if you're already familiar with these powerful tools, you can go directly to a specific section and focus on that topic. However, each lesson is designed to support the concepts learned in the preceding lesson, and newcomers to color grading should go through the book from start to finish. The first six lessons, in particular, teach basic concepts and are best completed in order.

Course Structure

The book begins with the fundamentals of color grading, using the Final Cut Pro color correction filters and a variety of sample clips to explain the basics of contrast, color, and scene-to-scene corrections.

Once the essentials are covered in Final Cut Pro, you'll start working with Color. Most editors who use Final Cut Studio will employ this workflow, where projects are edited in Final Cut Pro, sent to Color for grading and finishing, and then returned to Final Cut Pro for final output.

The Color interface is divided into eight "rooms." The most common workflow moves clips through the rooms in more or less sequential order. This is also the organizational model for the rest of the book, which walks you through each of the main rooms in Color and goes into detail on how to use the controls as well as which tools and techniques to apply given the specific circumstances of your projects.

The lessons are grouped into the following categories:

▶ Lessons 1-3: Color Grading in Final Cut Pro

The first three lessons utilize the Final Cut Pro color correction tools and interface. They introduce you to the most important aspects of color grading, familiarize you with the common scopes and gauges, and facilitate a deeper understanding of the color grading process.

▶ Lessons 4-5: Introduction to Color

Lesson 4 is an overview of the entire Color workflow, taking a project round-trip from Final Cut Pro to Color and back to Final Cut Pro. Along the way, you'll get a brief introduction to each of the rooms in Color and the types of tasks typically performed there. Lesson 5, Basic Grading, covers the most common color-correcting tools and techniques you'll use to improve the look of virtually every clip in your project.

▶ Lessons 6-9: Secondary Color Grading and Effects

Lessons 6 and 7 cover secondary grading, where you really customize the look and style of each shot. You'll learn how to affect different parts of the image discretely and apply multiple grades simultaneously. Lesson 8 introduces you to Color's flexible effects tools, and teaches you how to build your own unique effects using the built-in presets as your starting point. Finally, Lesson 9 covers scene-to-scene color matching and how to re-apply or batch-apply grades—because while learning to grade individual shots is essential, in the real world you'll encounter projects with multiple shots that require grade matching.

▶ Lessons 10-13: Advanced Techniques and Finishing

Once you master the basic tools Color has to offer, you can explore the additional control made possible by employing keyframes, pan and scan motion effects, and motion tracking, covered in Lessons 10 and 11. Lesson 12 covers rendering and final output decisions, including workflows for professional environments with stringent delivery requirements. Finally, the Bonus Lesson contains a set of recipes for creating popular and useful effects and "looks" that are sure to wow your clients.

Using the DVD Book Files

The *APTS Color 1.5* DVD (included with the book) contains the project files you'll use for each lesson, as well as media files that contain the video content you'll need for each exercise. After you transfer the files to your hard drive, each lesson will instruct you in the use of the project and media files.

Installing the Color Lesson Files

On the DVD, you'll find a folder titled Color_Book_Files, which contains individual sub-folders for each lesson in the book. Each subfolder contains a lesson file (either a Final Cut Pro or Color project file) and a Media folder containing all the clips required for that lesson.

To install the lesson files automatically:

1   Insert the *APTS Color 1.5* DVD into your DVD drive.

2   Double-click the installer on the DVD. The files will be copied to the Users > Shared folder on your startup drive, and an alias to that folder will be created on your desktop.

To install the lesson files manually:

1   Insert the *APTS Color 1.5* DVD into your DVD drive.

2   Drag the Color_Book_Files folder from the DVD to the folder Macintosh HD > Users > Shared. The Media folders contain about 3 GB of media in total.

Reconnecting Media

When copying files from the DVD to your hard drive, Color may lose the link between the project files and the associated media. This will result in the clips appearing "offline" in the Color project. Each lesson contains specific steps to remedy this, but here are the basic steps you'll apply whenever you open a new Color project and the media appears offline.

1   After opening each Color project, the Timeline will show all the clips in red with a red X across the clip icon. Choose File > Reconnect Media.

    A Choose Media Path dialog opens.

2   Navigate (using the Parent Directory button in the upper left) to the media folder for the current lesson and click Choose.

    You don't need to select an individual file; just choosing the directory that contains the media is sufficient.

    When the link between the project file and the media file is reestablished, Color will be able to access the media within the project.

System Requirements

Before using *Apple Pro Training Series: Color Correction in Final Cut Studio,* you should have a working knowledge of your Macintosh and the Mac OS X operating system. Make sure that you know how to use the mouse and standard menus and commands; and also how to open, save, and close files. If you need to review these techniques, see the printed or online documentation included with your system. For the basic system requirements for Color, refer to the Final Cut Studio documentation or check Apple's web site, www.apple.com/finalcutstudio.

Large Monitor Needed

Although you can operate Final Cut Pro satisfactorily on a screen as small as 1024x768, Color requires a much larger canvas. The minimum screen resolution for Color is 1600x1024. Launching Color on a system with a smaller screen resolution will elicit a warning dialog. The interface will be squished, and text sizes will be reduced to an extent that will make it very difficult to work.

For best results, you should work on a system with three monitors: two computer screens and an external preview monitor in NTSC, PAL, or HD, depending on the footage you most commonly work with.

Three-Button Mouse Required

Color makes extensive use of a multi-button mouse, and many functions and tasks are impossible or at least very inconvenient without a right mouse button and a middle-mouse button/scroll wheel. Although you can almost always use Control-click as a replacement for a right-click, there is no keyboard equivalent for the middle-click or the scroll wheel.

The Apple Mighty Mouse is an excellent multi-button mouse to use with Color, although many third-party mice will work as well. Regardless of the mouse you use, be sure that the Keyboard & Mouse settings in your System Preferences are configured so the right button is set to "Secondary Button" and the middle button is set to "Button 3."

About the Apple Pro Training Series

Apple Pro Training Series: Color Correction in Final Cut Studio is both a self-paced learning tool and the official curriculum of the Apple Pro Training and Certification Program.

Developed by experts in the field and certified by Apple, the series is used by Apple Authorized Training Centers worldwide and offers complete training in all Apple Pro products. The lessons are designed to let you learn at your own pace. Each lesson concludes with review questions and answers summarizing what you've learned, which can be used to help you prepare for the Apple Pro Certification Exam.

For a complete list of Apple Pro Training Series books, see the ad at the back of this book, or visit www.peachpit.com/apts.

Apple Pro Certification Program

The Apple Pro Training and Certification Programs are designed to keep you at the forefront of Apple's digital media technology while giving you a competitive edge in today's ever-changing job market. Whether you're an editor, graphic designer, sound designer, special effects artist, or teacher, these training tools are meant to help you expand your skills.

Upon completing the course material in this book, you can become an Apple Certified Pro by taking the certification exam at an Apple Authorized Training Center. Certification is offered in Final Cut Pro, Motion, Color, Soundtrack Pro, DVD Studio Pro, Shake, and Logic Pro. Certification as an Apple Pro gives you official recognition of your knowledge of Apple's professional applications while allowing you to market yourself to employers and clients as a skilled, pro-level user of Apple products.

For those who prefer to learn in an instructor-led setting, Apple offers training courses at Apple Authorized Training Centers worldwide. These courses, which use the Apple Pro Training Series books as their curriculum, are taught by Apple Certified Trainers and balance concepts and lectures with hands-on labs and exercises. Apple Authorized Training Centers have been carefully selected and have met Apple's highest standards in all areas, including facilities, instructors, course delivery, and infrastructure. The goal of the program is to offer Apple customers, from beginners to the most seasoned professionals, the highest-quality training experience.

For more information, please see the ad at the back of this book, or to find an Authorized Training Center near you, go to training.apple.com.

Resources

Apple Pro Training Series: Color Correction in Final Cut Studio is not intended as a comprehensive reference manual, nor does it replace the documentation that comes with the application. For comprehensive information about program features, refer to these resources:

▶ The Reference Guide. Accessed through the Color Help menu, the Reference Guide contains a complete description of all features.

▶ Apple's website: www.apple.com

1

Lesson Files	Lesson Files > Lesson 01 > Contrast.fcp
Media	Dance Correction Exampcle
Time	This lesson takes approximately 60 minutes to complete.
Goals	Break down a video image into its components
	Incorporate video scopes in the grading process
	Use the Color Corrector 3-way filter
	Modify the contrast of an image
	Understand contrast, blacks, mids, whites, highlights, and grayscale

Color Correcting Basics: Controlling Contrast in Final Cut Pro

In the world of film and television, the tasks of editing, sound design, and special effects are fairly well understood, and even casual fans know that those jobs are necessary parts of the process. But the colorist still dwells largely in the realm of voodoo or magic.

Welcome to voodoo-land.

It's a somewhat under-appreciated fact that the look of a film has an enormous impact on the tone and mood of the piece, and a correspondingly significant (if unconscious) impact on the audience's interpretation of the material. If the colorist creates a high-contrast look, he may be signaling that the stakes within the story are high and urgent; if he opts for a palette of many grays, it might be a way to inform the audience that the situation is more nuanced and complicated. A warm cast (where the colors are shifted toward orange and away from blue) might indicate a happier or more nostalgic tone, whereas a shift toward blue or cyan might suggest a more clinical, scientific feel. And of course, talented colorists often combine or confound such conventions to create entirely new and unique looks.

Ultimately, the colorist's job is about storytelling. You must work with the producer, director, cinematographer, and editor to interpret the story in a consistent and deliberate way. This is just as true for casually shot news B-roll as it is for carefully storyboarded special effects sequences. In the end, the audience doesn't care how the footage got on the screen in front of them. The subtle choices you make in grading that footage will affect how they absorb the content within it.

You also have to fix mistakes. The colorist's task is often described as color *correction*, which rightfully implies that something needed fixing. In fact, a great deal of the colorist's job will include tasks, such as matching clips that were shot at different times or in different locations so they look like they're part of the same scene; overcoming obstacles from the production (such as an overexposed window, mixed light color temperatures, or an unwanted color cast); or just trying to fix general exposure, white balance, and even framing problems that occurred during shooting. These tasks can rightfully be called corrections, but there is a great deal more that colorists can (and should) do to make the most of the footage they're handed. For that reason, this book will use the more general term color *grading*.

The colorist's tools are deceptively simple: contrast and color. But there are infinite varieties and combinations based on these simple attributes, and even within those categories the image can be examined in many ways, such as shadows, midtones, and highlights; red, green, and blue; hue, saturation, and lightness; and so on.

There are powerful and effective color grading controls available in Final Cut Pro that allow you to perform a wide range of manipulations and create a variety of looks. Final Cut Studio also includes a separate application, Color, which offers an expanded control set as well as supplemental tools that are helpful for advanced color grading jobs (such as tracking, masking, and keying). The basic controls and the various scopes used to guide your progress work the same in both programs.

This book begins by addressing the fundamentals of color grading in Final Cut Pro and then moves on to perform some of the same tasks in Color. The time and effort you take to learn the tools in the first few lessons are not wasted—they provide an important foundation that makes the migration to Color a more gradual and comfortable transition.

We'll start with contrast. Professional colorists spend years honing their skills and their eye for color. It's essential to learn to really *see* the video image—to grasp subtle color nuances and appreciate the subconscious effects of manipulating color balance and contrast.

Understanding Contrast

The term *contrast* is thrown around a lot and means different things to different people. For the sake of simplicity, consider that contrast represents the number of steps from the darkest to the lightest tone in your image.

Regardless of the colors involved, an image can range from deep, solid blacks, through varied mid-gray tones, to light, pure whites.

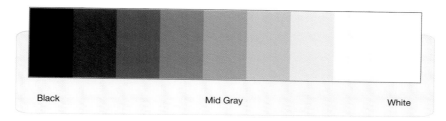

Black   Mid Gray   White

Getting Started

In this exercise, you'll examine the contrast in two different images, with the help of the Final Cut Pro video scopes.

1   Open Lesson Files > Lesson 01 > **Contrast.fcp**.

2   Choose Window > Arrange > Color Correction to change the window layout and automatically open the Video Scopes tab.

In the Video Scopes window, you can control the brightness of both the *traces* (the representation of the video data) and the scales.

3 In the upper-left corner of the Video Scopes window, click the Traces Brightness button (on the left).

Traces Brightness button

Scales Brightness button

A slider appears beside the two buttons.

4 Drag the slider to brighten the display.

5 Click the Scales Brightness button.

The slider now changes the brightness of the scales.

6 Adjust the brightness to your liking.

In the real world, you'll make occasional adjustments to these two values, based on the specific needs of the content you're color correcting.

7 Click the Scales Brightness button again.

The slider disappears.

8 Click the Layout pop-up menu and choose Waveform to switch to that view.

9 Make sure that the View pop-up menu is set to Current Frame.

10 Open the Exercise 1 – Evaluating Contrast bin and double-click the *Evaluating Contrast* sequence.

Evaluating the Values in an Image—Highlights Versus Shadows

First, you need to break down the image into shadows, midtones, and highlights. In the Final Cut Pro color correction controls, these regions are referred to as *blacks*, *mids*, and *whites*.

This may sound obvious, but learning to perceive which color values of an image fall into which of these zones is the basis for all the color correction work to follow, and it is a valuable skill to develop.

1 Scrub through the first clip in the Evaluating Contrast sequence.

To focus on the brightness levels in the image, you can eliminate the color.

2 Select the **Dance_Club.mov** clip, then choose Effects > Video Filters > Image Control > Desaturate.

The image is *desaturated*. In other words, the chrominance of the image has been eliminated, conveniently leaving the luma for your evaluation.

3   Scrub through the desaturated image, and pay careful attention to the darkest and lightest areas of the image.

The different levels of brightness should really leap out at you. In particular, notice how some areas that may have seemed darker because of their colored tint, like the almost sepia glow in the windows and interior highlights, are now revealed to be very close to white.

Judging Contrast Ratios

For purposes of color correction, one of the most important characteristics of an image is its *contrast ratio*: how much difference there is between the blackest black and the whitest white. You can quickly judge the contrast ratio by looking at the height of the graph displayed in the Waveform Monitor.

1   Scrub through the desaturated image again, this time watching the graph in the Waveform Monitor.

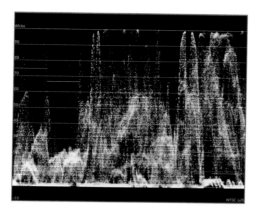

As you can see, there are large portions of the image that fall into the blacks down around 0 percent, but there are also numerous graph spikes up in the whites at 100 percent luminance. This is the widest possible contrast ratio, and it accounts for the crispness of the image.

2   Move the playhead to the **Skier.mov** clip, and play through it to get a sense of the colors and brightness.

3   Select the **Skier.mov** clip, and choose Effects > Last - Desaturate.

TIP ▶ Because the Desaturate filter was the last one you applied, it appears at the top of the Effects menu in case you want to apply it again.

4   Move the playhead to 01:00:04:11, and look at the Waveform Monitor.

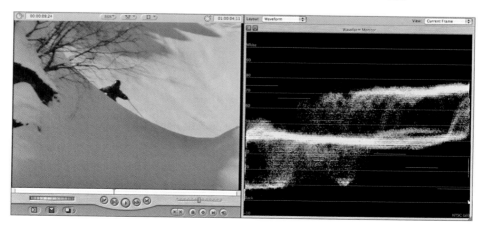

You may already have noticed, and the waveform confirms, that the whitest white in the image tops out at around 80 percent, landing it firmly in the mids. Also, the darkest black (the rocks at the left of the frame), doesn't really fall all the way to 0 percent.

The result is an image that looks somewhat murky, with washed-out shadows and lackluster highlights. This is the result of a narrow contrast ratio.

5   Press the Down Arrow key to navigate to the next cut, which is actually both clips superimposed using a split screen.

Once again, look carefully at the areas of light and shadow in the image, and try to imagine what it looks like without any color.

6   Select both clips, and choose Effects > Last - Desaturate.

Although you may have had difficulty seeing the difference between both images' contrast ratios when jumping between the two clips, the split screen makes that difference readily apparent.

The blacks in the **Skier.mov** clip aren't nearly as deep as those in the **Dance_Club.mov** clip, nor are the whites as light. The graph in the Waveform Monitor shows this more dramatically.

NOTE ► You may need to adjust the traces brightness, as described earlier, to see all the detail in the Waveform Monitor.

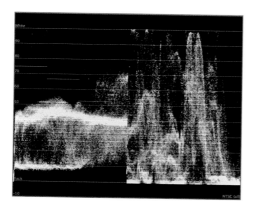

The graph in the Waveform Monitor is split just like the image in the Canvas, and you can see that the graph on the left side is not nearly as tall as the one on the right side.

Higher contrast ratios are not only more visually appealing; a low contrast ratio can limit your ability to manipulate color in an image.

Comparing Low- and High-Contrast Images

Another way to view contrast is to consider how much of an image is found within the mids compared to how much of the image is in the blacks and whites. The balance between midtones and blacks-plus-whites is probably the most conventional way to describe contrast.

Images with large regions in the mids are considered *low contrast.* Low-contrast images tend to be fairly neutral, but in extreme cases, this color distribution may result in an image that looks somewhat washed out.

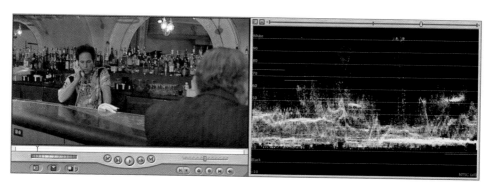

When the majority of the luminance values in an image are located in the whites and blacks, with few pixels in the mids, the image is considered *high contrast*.

The borders between dark and light areas are usually perceived by viewers as edges, so higher-contrast images may be perceived as "sharper" than low-contrast images. On the other hand, extremes of black and white in very high-contrast images are typically harsher than we're used to seeing with the naked eye, so creating high-contrast images can lend a stylized look to a scene.

Whereas the *contrast ratio* of an image may be considered a simple qualitative issue (with higher contrast ratios able to bring out more image detail), whether or not the *perceived* contrast described in this section should be high or low remains primarily a matter of preference and artistic license.

Comparing High- and Low-Key Images

Another way to describe contrast is in terms of the lighting strategy used to shoot the image. Terms such as *high-key* and *low-key* (originally used to describe methods of lighting on the set) have carried over to color correction to distinguish different methods of lighting a scene for dramatic effect.

High-key generally describes images that are brightly and evenly lit. The lighting tends to be softer, with *fill light* eliminating harsh shadows. High-key images also happen to be low-contrast (although this doesn't automatically imply a low contrast ratio). There may be black in the frame, but a look at the Histogram (which plots the bright and dark pixels of an image on a horizontal graph) will reveal that most luminance values are spread throughout the mids and the whites.

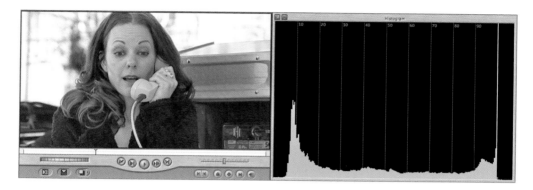

High-key images are often used to convey a light mood: The characters are happy, and all is well with the world.

Low-key images are the opposite. They are generally underlit, with deep shadows and plenty of them. As you've probably guessed, low-key images are also high contrast. Highlights tend to be harsh and bright compared to the blackness of the image. A look at the Histogram will often reveal large, wide swaths of values in the blacks, with low mids and perhaps a spike or two in the whites (though not in this example). Low-key lighting is often used to portray night, or a serious, dramatic moment. Think *film noir*.

Why use these different ways to describe contrast? The description depends on who you're talking to, and what aspect of the image they're trying to describe. The director of photography may try to impress upon you the importance of preserving a high-key look, but the producer (who happens to be an amateur photographer) may counter that she thinks it should be low contrast. In reality, they're both describing a desire for the exact same look, they're just using different ways to describe it.

It's also worth pointing out that an image with a high contrast ratio may not necessarily be a high-contrast, low-key image. Because the perceived contrast of an image is often dependent upon the amount and average levels of brightness and visible detail in the midrange of an image, it's completely possible to have a relatively low-contrast image with a high contrast ratio.

Now that you understand the basics of contrast, you're ready to manipulate it to achieve specific goals.

Controlling Contrast Using the Color Corrector 3-Way Filter

The Final Cut Pro Color Corrector 3-way filter is the workhorse for all of the following exercises. It is one of the few filters (along with the more simply named Color Corrector filter) that have a custom graphical interface with specific controls optimized for color correcting images.

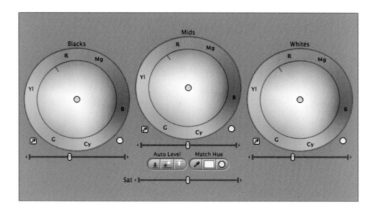

For now, you'll ignore the color wheels. With the three sliders underneath, you can push and pull the luminance values within an image using separate controls to target the image's black level, mids distribution, and white level.

In the following exercises, you'll use these three sliders to achieve complete control over the contrast in your images.

Adjusting the Black and White Points

Among its many virtues, the Color Corrector 3-way filter is able to play to an external monitor in real time, depending on your computer's configuration. Remember, you should *always* view the image you're manipulating on a broadcast monitor when preparing a program for broadcast.

1   In the Browser, open the Exercise 02 - Controlling Contrast bin.

2   Double-click the Controlling Contrast - Basics sequence.

The first clip in the sequence is a gradient generator. You'll notice that the default gradient is a ramp from 100 percent luminance (white) to 0 percent (black), with a direct correspondence to the diagonal graph shown in the Waveform Monitor.

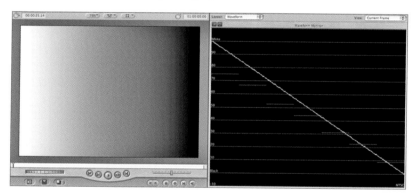

This is an ideal test image to see how changes you make with the Color Corrector 3-way filter manipulate the balance of luminance in an image.

3   In the Timeline, select the **Gradient** clip, then choose Effects > Video Filters > Color Correction > Color Corrector 3-way.

4   In the Timeline, double-click the **Gradient** clip to open it into the Viewer.

Even though you've added a filter, you'll notice an additional Color Corrector 3-way tab at the top of the Viewer.

This tab contains a custom interface for the Color Corrector 3-way filter, providing explicit control over the characteristics of your image.

5 Click the Filters tab.

The Color Corrector 3-way filter is listed.

6 Click the disclosure triangle to the left of the filter name to view the filter's parameters.

A tall stack of parameters appears. Don't worry if you don't initially understand their functions. Every one of these parameters is represented by a graphical control in the Color Corrector 3-way tab.

Later, when you know what each parameter affects, you can adjust the sliders and dials in the Filters tab if you feel you need to make more finely detailed changes to the image than the graphical interface allows.

Also, color correction filters such as the Color Corrector 3-way filter cannot be removed—or their order rearranged—directly within the Color Corrector 3-way tab. Instead, these operations need to be performed in the Filters tab just as with any other video filter.

7   Click the disclosure triangle to close the parameters list, and click the Visual button to the right of the filter's name, or click the Color Corrector 3-way tab, to go to the Color Corrector 3-way graphical interface.

   NOTE ▸ In the visual Color Corrector 3-way tab, you can click the Numeric button to go back to the Filters tab.

With the Color Corrector controls in view, and the Viewer, Canvas, and video scopes open side by side in the Final Cut Pro default Color Correction layout, you have all the tools you need for analyzing, adjusting, and monitoring your images.

Even though the three color wheels may be the biggest, brightest things on the screen, simply screaming to be manipulated, leave them alone for now. In this lesson, you're going to focus on the three slider controls beneath the wheels. These are the controls you'll use to manipulate contrast.

Each slider corresponds to one of the color wheels in providing control over the black level, mids distribution, and white level. These sliders adjust the luminance of the image independent of the chrominance levels.

8   Drag the Whites slider to the left to lower the level of the whites.

Two things happen. The light part of the image darkens to a deeper gray, and the graph redraws itself so the diagonal line lowers.

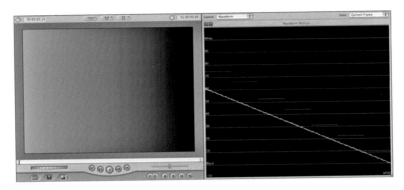

Notice, however, that the bottom of the graph didn't move. This is a vital characteristic of the three luminance controls in the Color Corrector 3-way filter. Changes to the whites leave the blacks untouched.

9   Drag the Blacks slider to the right to raise the level of the blacks.

This time, you lightened the levels of the darkest parts of the image, which redraws the graph to reflect the new luminance distribution. Notice that, despite this second change, the whites level remains unchanged.

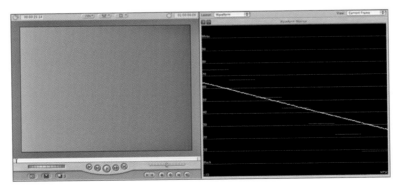

Incidentally, because you've just decreased the height from the blackest black to the whitest white, you've successfully lowered the contrast ratio of this image.

Changes you make to the blacks and whites levels are fairly easy to understand, because they essentially scale all of the image's luminance values linearly, relative to the opposite end of the graph.

Adjusting the Mids

The Mids slider provides control over the distribution of all values falling between the black and white points of your image.

1   In the Color Corrector 3-way tab, Shift-click any one of the Reset buttons to reset all of the parameters to their default values.

Ordinarily, clicking a Reset button resets only the parameters associated with that control, but Shift-clicking any color correction Reset button in the top control group resets everything except for the Limit Effects controls (which appear in the collapsed section at the bottom of the Color Correction tab). As a result, the image and the graph in the Waveform Monitor return to their original states.

2   Drag the Mids slider to the left.

Immediately, you'll notice a far different effect. The whites and blacks remain, for the most part, where they are (although more extreme changes do move the white point), but the range of grays in the middle of the image appear to move toward the left as the image progressively darkens.

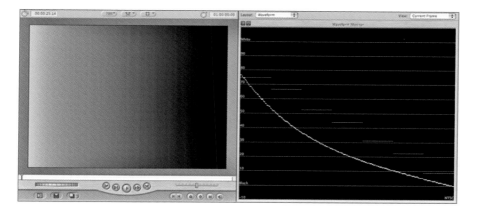

The result in the Waveform Monitor is even more dramatic. Changes to the blacks and whites resulted in a straight line in the graph, but lowering the mids had two effects: reshaping the graph into a downward curve, and moving down the white point.

3 Drag the Mids slider to the right.

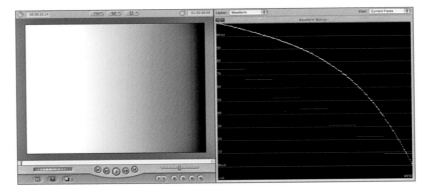

Predictably, this has the opposite effect, with the distribution of gray tones moving to the right as the image lightens, and the graph curving upward.

Basically, changes made to the mids redistribute the midtone values falling between the white and black points of the image so the image can be lightened or darkened without muddying the blacks or whites. This change is nonlinear (as shown by the slope of the curve), which allows for subtle changes across the range of the image.

You can also see that the relationship between the mids and the whites is tricky. Changes made to one may require you to interact with the other.

Next, you'll see how adjusting the contrast in these three regions will enhance a real-world image. You'll also learn the proper sequence in which to approach these contrast corrections when using the Color Corrector 3-way filter.

Stretching Contrast in a Video Clip

The contrast sliders give you total control over the contrast ratio of any image by allowing you to adjust the distance from the brightest to the darkest value in the picture using the Blacks and Whites sliders. You can also control whether your image is high-contrast or low-contrast by redistributing the midtones that fall between using the Mids slider.

In the following exercise, you'll deal with one of the most common issues in video: murky-looking source footage with a low contrast ratio. You'll see how this is easily curable using the Blacks, Mids, and Whites controls.

1   Press the Down Arrow key to move to the first frame of the **Ski_Jump.mov** clip.

You've seen this image before. It's the one with the blacks that are too high, and the whites that are too low, resulting in murky shadows and lackluster whites. You've probably already guessed what needs to happen based on the last exercise, but methodically going through this process will help you develop good habits for approaching the color correction process.

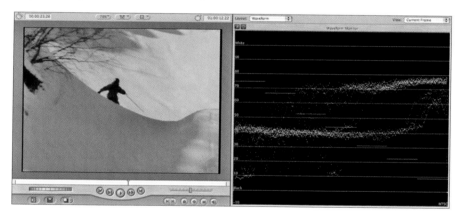

2   In the Timeline, select the **Ski_Jump.mov** clip, then choose Effects > Video Filters > Color Correction > Color Corrector 3-way.

3   In the Timeline, double-click the **Ski_Jump.mov** clip to open it into the Viewer.

NOTE ▶ Either the Timeline or Canvas must have focus in order to see the changes you make being updated in real time on an external monitor.

4   Click the Color Corrector 3-way tab to display the color correction controls.

NOTE ▶ If the Color Corrector tab from another clip is already open in the Viewer, opening a new clip into the Viewer leaves the Color Corrector tab open, as long as the new clip has one color correction filter applied to it. This saves you from having to constantly click the Color Corrector tab in the Viewer as you adjust numerous filters.

The first step in any color correction process is to set the black levels. As you saw in the preceding exercise, the black point is unaffected by changes made to the whites or mids, so it serves as the baseline for all changes you make to the image.

TIP ▶ Get in the habit of setting the blacks first. If you make a change to the mids or whites first, and adjust the blacks last, the change in the blacks will definitely affect the distribution of mids and whites, resulting in more fiddling around on your part.

5   Examine the image in the Viewer.

You need to determine which parts of the image correspond to absolute black (0 percent) to make this adjustment. Typical images have at least a few pixels located at 0 percent. This results in deeper, richer blacks, which makes the lighter values pop out more by comparison.

One of the tricky things about this image is that the lighting is fairly diffuse, and the shadows of the trees aren't supposed to be that dark. However, there are some very dark shadows in the rocky outcropping at the left of the screen.

6   Look at the lower-left corner of the Waveform Monitor.

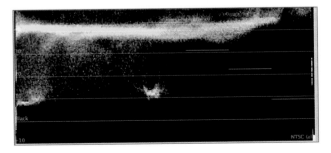

You can see a dip in the waveform graph that corresponds to the rocks. These levels seem low enough to qualify as the absolute black of the image, and, in fact, some of these pixels seem to be touching 0 percent black. Still, this image could benefit from a slightly deeper black level, although you don't want to make a big change.

7   To make a very slight reduction to the blacks, click the small arrow to the left of the Blacks slider five or six times.

TIP ▶ There are two good ways to use the mouse to make incremental adjustments with any effects slider: Click one of the little arrows at either end of the slider to nudge it in one-point increments, or if you have a mouse with a standard scroll wheel, position the pointer at a slider and scroll upward to slide left or scroll downward to slide right. The scroll wheel technique is actually more accurate than dragging the slider itself. You can also use a two-finger swipe gesture on a multi-touch trackpad to move a slider. Swipe right to increase the value and swipe left to decrease the value.

You can also press the Command key while using a slider, forcing it to move more slowly, allowing finer adjustments.

As slight as this change is, you can see the graph in the Waveform Monitor stretch downward.

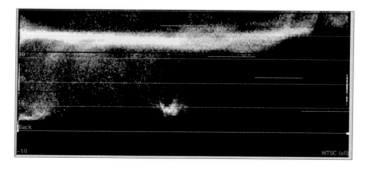

Although it's difficult to see, the dots at the bottom of the graph begin to bunch up at the black line. As more and more of the graph hits the bottom, the result is typically referred to as *crushing the blacks*. Crushing the blacks increases the deepness of the shadows, which can be pleasing, but comes at the expense of losing detail.

8   To see the result of severely crushed blacks, drag the Blacks slider farther to the left.

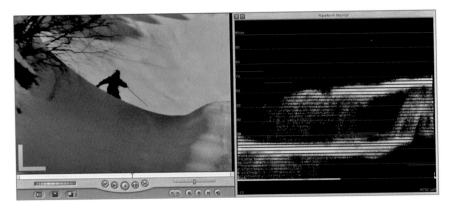

Notice that the dark areas of the image go completely black, and the bottom of the waveform graph bunches up. This is the best way to tell if your blacks are crushed when it's difficult to determine in the Canvas.

Notice that the black levels never go below 0 percent. A value of 0 percent is the absolute bottom of the digital luma scale. There is no way to create values that are "blacker than black." This is a very good thing when readying the video for broadcast because broadcast formats such as NTSC or PAL have regulations about black levels being lower than a certain amount. When working in Final Cut Pro, the values are simply digital percentages, so you don't have to worry about blacks being *unsafe*. This is true regardless of whether or not the source video was from a digital or analog format. Once digitized, all video is measured on a digital scale.

NOTE ▶ You need to be concerned with only IRE black levels when outputting your program from digital to an analog NTSC Beta format—and then it's simply a matter of properly setting up your video output hardware (and the software drivers that control it, if necessary) to the appropriate standard—0 or 7.5. There are no IRE settings internal to Final Cut Pro, and digital video output to SDI or HD-SDI always puts the black point at 0 percent, corresponding to 0 IRE or 0 mV. The bottom line: When color correcting in Final Cut Pro, regardless of the system or format, always set blacks to 0 percent in the video scopes.

9   Press Command-Z to undo the last change.

Next, you'll address the biggest problem in this image—those dismal-looking whites in the snow. Adjusting the whites is generally the second step after adjusting the blacks, especially when the white level is so low.

10 Drag the Whites slider to the right to boost the whites until the top of the graph in the Waveform Monitor hits 100 percent.

The difference is huge, much more noticeable than the slight adjustment made to the blacks. The results of expanding the contrast ratio of this clip are immediately visible, almost as if you wiped a layer of grime off the monitor screen.

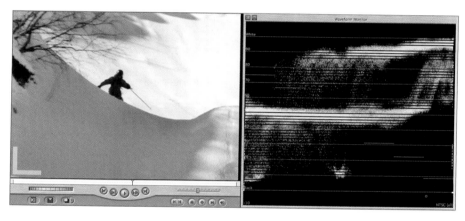

Incidentally, as you work it may be tempting to boost values into the super-white range (from 100 to 109 percent). Resist this urge. Although it may make your brights "whiter than white," you will also run into problems when you want to output your program to a broadcast format. Remember that when setting whites for broadcast, the levels should never rise above 100 percent.

Furthermore, even though the details are faint, there's still a lot of texture and detail in the bright regions of this image, and you want to avoid clipping them off and "flattening" the image.

Now that the black and white points of the image are set, check to see if you need to make any changes to the mids.

11 Play the clip.

As you get a third of the way though the clip, you should notice an immediate problem. The whites are practically glowing, and they appear strangely flat. Stopping playback reveals that the whites in the frame you were balancing were far too dark, but other whites later on in the clip are much brighter. In fact, the later whites are being clipped off at the top of the Waveform Monitor.

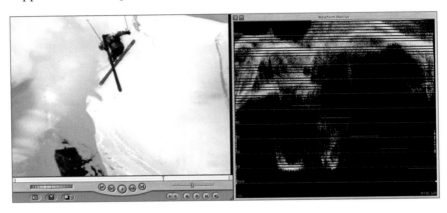

Unfortunately, the previous setting does not work throughout the entire clip, which brings up an important point. When you pick an image to color correct, you must evaluate it over its entire duration to account for changes in lighting that might happen later on in the shot.

12 Drag the Whites slider to the left to bring the white levels back to 100 percent.

This brings the white level back very near to its original level, and the whites, although legal, lose their snap. Because you've now determined that this is the widest possible contrast ratio for this shot, it's time to adjust the Mids to make this a higher-key shot.

13 Drag the Mids slider to the right.

This gives the desired whiter-looking whites, by making the midtones brighten up.

As you saw in the previous exercise, however, the whites have been pushed up, which you'll need to fix.

14 Drag the Whites slider to the left to bring the top of the graph back to 100 percent.

Ironically, this brings the Whites slider back to its default position. All of this effort illustrates that, oftentimes, adjusting the mids and whites is an interactive process of push and pull.

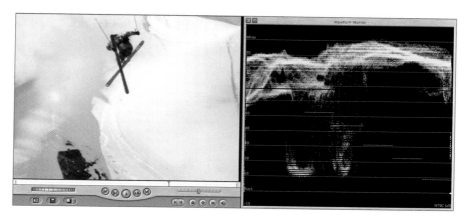

After all that, if you find yourself wondering whether this meddling has made any real improvement, you can perform a simple test to get a fast before-and-after look at the clip, to make sure you prefer the end result.

15 At the top of the Color Corrector 3-way tab, select and deselect the Enable Filter checkbox to toggle it on and off, comparing the two results.

As you've worked through this exercise, your eyes have gotten accustomed to the new contrast settings. Toggling the Color Corrector filter on and off is a good comparative tool you can use to see how much you've changed the initial look of the video.

Adjusting contrast is always the first step of color correction, and it comes before *any* changes you make to the clip's color. The process almost always begins by adjusting the blacks, then interactively making adjustments to the whites and mids until you've achieved the desired quality of contrast.

Setting Mood with the Mids

Adjusting the blacks and whites to establish the contrast ratio of an image is a fairly straightforward process. You want to provide the greatest contrast range for your image, and the only questions are which parts of the picture to map to absolute black, and which to absolute white.

Adjustments to the midtones, on the other hand, are much more subjective. Do you want a high-contrast look, or a low-contrast look? Is the picture supposed to be high-key, or low-key? There are no right or wrong answers, just what you and your client prefer.

The majority of the pixels in an image are generally found in the midtones. This is the luma region with the most detail, and if the image is well-lit, it is also where faces are exposed. As a result, the distribution of midtones in an image goes a long way toward defining the feeling of a shot.

For instance, by making simple adjustments to the midtones, you can influence the perceived time of day—is it midday, afternoon, or evening? Or, you can make sunlight look bright, or dark and overcast. These are all looks you can begin to define by adjusting the mids.

In this exercise, you'll make mids adjustments to a generally well-exposed image, in order to change the apparent time of day.

1 Open the Controlling Contrast - Grading sequence.

2 Scrub through the **Dance_Club.mov** clip and examine how the waveform changes over time.

> **NOTE ▶** The best way to see how the video scopes change over the course of the clip is to scrub through the image by dragging the playhead in the Canvas or Timeline. While the clip is playing, the resolution of the scopes is reduced.

As you can see, the contrast ratio of this clip is already as high as it can be, with many values at 0 percent, and several spikes at 100 percent.

3   Select the **Dance_Club.mov** clip, and choose Effects > Video Filters > Color Correction > Color Corrector 3-way.

4   In the Timeline, double-click the **Dance_Club.mov** clip to open the color correction filter into the Viewer. The Color Corrector 3-way tab updates to reflect the settings of the filter you just added.

As it is now, the quality of light in the image indicates afternoon, or an extremely well-lit evening. You'll first try to make this scene look more like an evening shot.

5   Drag the Mids slider to the left to lower the levels in the image.

This darkens the image, but now the highlights look dimmer. The Waveform Monitor confirms this observation by showing that the top of the graph has fallen to about 90 percent.

6   Drag the Whites slider to the right to return the top of the waveform graph to 100 percent.

It's a small change, but it puts the snap back into the highlights of the image, while keeping the rest of the room darker.

7   To compare the before-and-after results, select and deselect the Enable Filter checkbox.

Next, you'll reset the color correction controls and make the same clip look like it was shot closer to midday.

8   In the Color Corrector 3-way tab, Shift-click any of the Reset buttons to reset the default values.

9   Drag the Mids slider to the right to boost the levels and create the illusion of more light coming into the room.

As you make this adjustment, pay particular attention to the quality of the light in the background—this is the darkest area you need to boost.

As you've seen before, boosting the mids also boosts the highlights, and in this case, the mids adjustment is making the whites blow out well above 100 percent.

10 Drag the Whites slider to the left to bring the top of the waveform graph back down to 100 percent.

Now the image looks brighter, and the whites aren't blowing out any more.

It's not a bad range of options for using two simple sliders. Later on, you'll learn to combine contrast adjustments with color balance adjustments to create even more sophisticated looks. The important thing to remember is that adjustments to the contrast are the first, and sometimes only, adjustments you'll need to make.

Creating Artificially High Contrast

So far, you've been adjusting the contrast to create a natural look. However, you can use these same controls to create extremely stylized, high-contrast images. You might do this for a number of creative purposes: to enhance the separation of different elements within the frame, to hide a flaw in the exposure, or simply to create a distinctive look.

Creating a High-Contrast Look

In this exercise, you will treat the image you've been working with as high-contrast.

1 In the Browser, open the Exercise 03 - High Contrast bin and double-click the *Higher Contrast - Finished* sequence.

In order to create high contrast in an image, you need to push up the midtones toward white and down toward black, and away from the center, as you see in this image.

2   Open the *Higher Contrast - Beginning* sequence.

3   Select the **Winner.mov** clip, and choose Effects > Video Filters > Color Correction > Color Corrector 3-way.

4   In the Timeline, double-click the **Winner.mov** clip to open the color correction filter you've just added into the currently open Color Corrector 3-way tab in the Viewer.

The original image is very well exposed, with a high contrast ratio and detail throughout the entire range of luma.

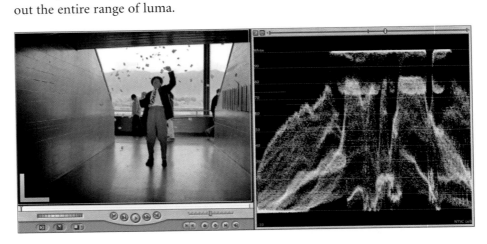

The first step you'll take toward creating a high-contrast look is to crush the blacks.

5   Move the Blacks slider to the left.

The farther you drag left, the more values get crushed to the bottom of the waveform graph, and the darker your image gets.

It's not high-contrast yet; it's just dark. For truly high contrast, you need to boost the highlights back up. However, you're not going for a realistic look, so you can take a shortcut and crank up the mids first, without regard for where the highlights fall.

6   Drag the Mids slider to the right to redistribute the midtones up toward the whites. Don't be shy.

The result is definitely high contrast, but with whites that are outrageously overblown. Stylized or not, you can't allow whites to go above 100 percent.

7   Drag the Whites slider to the left, until the top of the waveform graph sits at 100 percent.

Now you have an extremely high-contrast image, with broadcast-legal luma, and as an added bonus, you were able to retrieve some pleasing detail from the background.

Although this is not something you'd do to every image, it's good to know how to push the contrast to create more stylized effects.

However, suppose you didn't want to bring the whites back down in step 7. What if you wanted to blow out the whites, and leave them blown out? In the next exercise, you'll learn how to safely manage illegal values in an image—values that aren't broadcast-safe—while getting the results you want.

Applying the Broadcast Safe Filter

Let's say you want to deliberately clip the whites in the previous exercise. Leaving illegal levels in a clip is never good practice, because they can cause innumerable problems later. In these instances, you can use the Broadcast Safe filter.

The Broadcast Safe filter limits the maximum allowable luma and saturation levels. In this case, it's the perfect tool to help you extend the contrast of the clip by compressing the highlights to a broadcast-legal level.

1   Still working on the **Winner.mov** clip in the *Higher Contrast – Beginning* sequence, drag the Whites slider to the default center position, so that the whites blow out once again.

An examination of the Waveform Monitor confirms that the white levels are completely illegal.

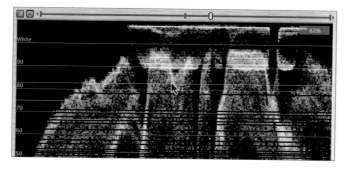

2   Select the **Winner.mov** clip in the Timeline, and choose Effects > Video Filters > Color Correction > Broadcast Safe to add the Broadcast Safe filter to the clip.

Instantly, you'll see that the illegal levels displayed in the Waveform Monitor have been compressed to a safe 100 percent, although the whites in the Viewer are still blown out.

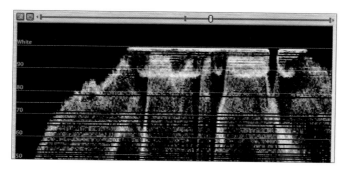

If you look at the image in the Canvas, you can see that a bit of detail has crept back into the image. You can just make out the faint outline of the mountain in the background.

This is because the broadcast monitor is *compressing* the illegal levels, or squeezing them all together, rather than *clipping* them, or cutting them off. The end result is still quite bright, but the effect is a little more pleasing.

3   Click the Filters tab.

Notice that the default mode of the Broadcast Safe filter is Conservative. This setting is recommended for most situations.

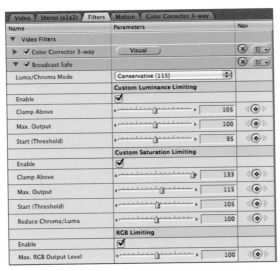

4   Click the Color Corrector 3-way tab.

5   Drag the Whites slider to the right so you can see how the Broadcast Safe filter is limiting the increased values.

As you continue to drag to the right, the values in the graph climb to 100 percent and then compress and bunch up.

The Broadcast Safe filter is good to use whenever you want to make a range of light values brighter but don't want to worry about going into unsafe luma ranges.

6   Click the Filters tab.

7   In the Broadcast Safe filter tab, click the Luma/Chroma Mode pop-up menu to see the available choices.

As a rule of thumb, you can use the default choice, Conservative, which limits values to 100 percent. The other choices, including the Custom option, set the top end of the luma scale to better suit your needs.

NOTE ▶ When you're working in Custom mode, these controls are all manual. In choices other than Custom, the sliders have no effect.

A Note About Contrast and Video Noise

What is the result of all this pushing and pulling of the contrast? Whenever you expand the contrast range of an image, you're stretching a limited amount of color information across a wider range. Depending on the image format, and the amount of data in the original image, you may be able to make your changes without creating any discernable artifacts in the image.

However, in cases where you need to make extreme corrections, such as with underexposed or overexposed images, making contrast adjustments can result in unsightly artifacts. This is especially true when attempting to lighten underexposed shots captured with highly compressed video formats such as HDV that also lack color information.

In these cases, the process of increasing contrast can also bring out certain elements of the image that you would rather conceal. One of the most common problems is that increased contrast can make the image appear more noisy, by accentuating its grain (with film) or noise (with video). In these cases, you'll have to strike a compromise between the level of correction you need to make and the amount of image noise you're willing to tolerate.

▶ Correcting, Timing, and Grading: A Word on the Language of the Colorist

The task of changing the contrast and color properties of a film or video image has a variety of names that can be somewhat confusing.

Although "correction" implies fixing mistakes, the term *color correction* is widely used to refer to any work affecting the color, whether it is to correct a mistake, alter the mood, create special effects, or any other related task. However, the overly broad application of the term led to colorists describing all their work as "correcting," which implied that the directors of photography (DPs) who shot the material had—in all instances where a colorist intervened—made some kind of mistake.

To help clarify this potential confusion (and protect some egos), some began using the term *color timing* as a way of differentiating elective changes from required fixes, but quickly that term also evolved into a general term for the whole process including correcting mistakes.

The term color timing actually refers to the specific job of determining for how much time celluloid film is exposed to different color lights, which has the overall result of controlling the contrast and color attributes of the printed film. Professional color timers resented lowly video engineers calling their work "timing" and so colorists were again stuck with inadequate terminology.

More recently, many have begun using the term *color grading* to refer to any color modifcation work, and this is becoming the most popular term today. After all, one colorist's correction is another's elective change.

In this book, we use all three terms—correcting, grading, and timing—somewhat interchangeably. However, with Color, Apple makes a significant differentiation between "corrections," which refer to settings applied in any one room, and "grades," which refer to the combination of effects across multiple rooms.

Lesson Review

1. What does *contrast ratio* describe?

2. What do the *mids* describe?

3. What's better, a higher contrast ratio or a lower contrast ratio?

4. Does a high contrast ratio automatically create a high-contrast image?

5. How do you maximize the contrast ratio of a clip using the Color Corrector 3-way filter?

6. How would you adjust the Mids slider to make an image seem like it was shot in the late afternoon?

7. What are two ways you can eliminate illegal whites in an image?

Answers

1. The distance between the blackest and lightest values in an image.

2. The range of values that falls within the middle tones of the image, between shadows and highlights.

3. Higher contrast ratios are generally better.

4. No. Contrast ratios and perceived contrast are different.

5. Adjust the Blacks slider so that the blackest part of the image is around 0 percent, and then adjust the Whites slider so that any highlights in the image are around 100 percent.

6. Drag the Mids slider to the left to lower the mids distribution.

7. You could use the Color Corrector 3-way filter and lower the whites, or you could apply the Broadcast Safe filter.

2

Lesson File Lesson Files > Lesson 02 > Color.fcp

Media Color Correction Examples

Time This lesson takes approximately 60 minutes to complete.

Goals Identify color using a color wheel

Manipulate color with hue, saturation, and luma controls

Incorporate color effects during grading

Use video scopes to identify and manipulate color

Use the Color Corrector 3-way filter

Use color balancing to enhance the final scene

Describe the color terms hue, saturation, color wheel, color space, primary, secondary, and complementary

Controlling Color

Lesson 1 was entirely focused on luma and contrast. Once you've graded the contrast, the next step in the color correction process is to work on the color balance of the image.

Choosing the color balance is a creative, as well as corrective, endeavor. You may find yourself wanting to manipulate color to enhance an image, to alter the mood of a scene, or perhaps to create highly stylized color schemes for a title sequence or motion graphics segment.

Whatever your goals, you need to understand how to judge colors and which controls to use to create the desired effect. This lesson focuses on how you evaluate and manipulate color in Final Cut Pro. You'll learn how to read and understand the color balance of an image and then use color correction to alter the color balance in that clip with total control.

Understanding Color Balance

Color balance refers to the relative amounts of red, green, and blue in an image. As the name implies, by controlling the balance of each color in relation to the others, you can change the hue and saturation of all the colors found within an image.

Final Cut Pro goes further by providing you with separate controls over the balance of the colors found in each of the three zones of luma in an image, which allows you to make separate changes to the colors found in the blacks (such as shadows), those found in the mids (most of the image), and those in the whites (the bright areas and highlights). Each color balance control consists of a color wheel, at the center of which is a handle that allows you to make the necessary adjustments.

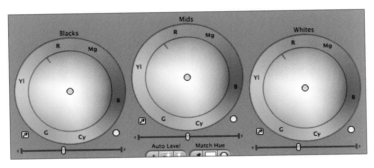

The contrast controls (the sliders beneath each wheel) help you ensure that the video is broadcast legal, but the color balance controls help you ensure that the colors in the image *look right*. For example, by manipulating the color balance within an image, you can make video shot with unnaturally orange lighting look more natural by neutralizing the tint.

Removing Color Casts

Ideally, color grading is an extension of the original cinematography. As a colorist, you are a collaborator in one step of the artistic process, and your ideas and contributions help shape the final look of the program. You may work with the director of photography (though not always) to establish a starting point for the color correction process, and the two of you may continue to finesse the images into their final form. It's also likely that the director or producer will have a say about the look of the program, and this input will weave its way into the creative process.

At other times, color grading may take the form of damage control, as you attempt to rescue footage that was shot under less than ideal conditions, or footage that was shot using an aesthetic that is no longer compatible with the project goals. Furthermore, the client may be relying on color grading to implement ideas that are too difficult or costly to execute on location.

In this lesson, you'll evaluate an image to determine *color casts* (inappropriately strong color channels that tint an image), one of the most common color issues you'll have to address. For example, this image may seem, at first glance, to be fine, but a closer examination will reveal a subtle blue cast from the shadows through the highlights.

Once you learn to identify a color cast in a clip, you'll work toward correcting it to create a clean, neutral look, where whites are pure and blacks are solid.

Understanding the Color Balance Controls

Before you start pushing and pulling the color balance in your shots, take a few minutes to get a better understanding of the color wheel that's at the heart of the color balance controls. In doing so, you'll also learn how to better understand the Vectorscope, which displays a graph of the colors in your image against a backdrop of targets that are directly analogous to the color wheel.

In its various forms, the color wheel is an effective way to provide independent, yet unified, control over hue (color) and saturation (intensity of color). Once you understand how the color wheel represents the fundamental components of color, you can reliably predict and control the results of color adjustments.

Learning About the Color Wheel

The color wheel displays all of the possible hues around the outside of a circle. If you follow the edge of the color wheel, you can find the three *primary* colors: red, green, and blue.

The pure primaries are equally distant from one another, and they divide the color wheel into thirds.

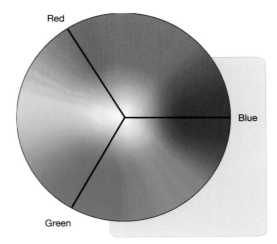

Video systems, regardless of the format, create color in an additive fashion, by mixing the three primaries together. The primary colors found on the color wheel correspond to the red, green, and blue components of a video signal; the red, green, and blue phosphors of a CRT display; and the red, green, and blue components of the pixels on a flat-screen monitor.

(Incidentally, film also records color in three layers, or substrates, each of which is sensitive to red, green, and blue.)

By mixing these primary colors, any color of the rainbow can be displayed, and you can see this happening in the color wheel. As the primary colors blend together around the outer edge of the wheel, you can see other hues emerge.

An equal mixture of any two primaries creates the *secondary* colors on the color wheel. The three secondary colors are cyan, magenta, and yellow. For example, yellow (a secondary color) is a combination of green and red (both primaries).

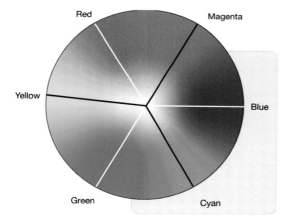

Notice that each secondary color falls directly opposite a primary color. Any two colors that are opposite one another—such as yellow and blue—on the color wheel are considered to be *complementary*.

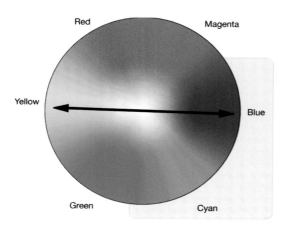

Combining any color with its complementary color on the wheel neutralizes it, effectively *desaturating* it. You can see this phenomenon represented in the color wheel—the outer edge of the wheel represents each hue at 100 percent saturation, and the center of the wheel has 0 percent saturation, which is represented by white.

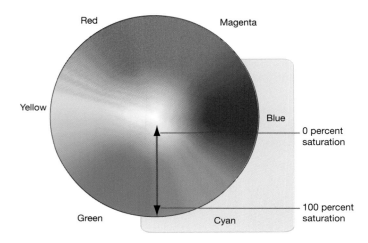

NOTE ▶ Even though 0 percent saturation is represented in the color wheel by white, it's important to remember that 0 percent saturation simply means an absence of color. Removing all saturation from an image does nothing to alter the luma of the image, which may then consist of any shade of gray.

To effectively control colors with the Final Cut Pro color correction filters, you must understand the relationship between complementary colors, and the neutralizing effect of blending them together.

Manipulating Color Channels with the Color Balance Control

This simple exercise will help you understand the color wheel's effect on an image and how those effects are displayed in the video scopes.

1   Open Lesson Files > Lesson 02 > **Color.fcp**.

If you haven't already done so, set up your workspace to include the video scopes in the Tool Bench window.

2   Choose Window > Arrange > Color Correction to open the Video Scopes tab.

3   In the Layout pop-up menu, choose All to ensure all four scopes are visible.

4   Open the Exercise 01 - Color Wheel Basics bin.

5   Open the *Color Wheel Basics* sequence.

6   Double-click the first **Custom Gradient** clip in the sequence to open it into the Viewer. Then, at the top of the Viewer, click the Color Corrector tab.

The first clip in the sequence is a custom gradient generator that's been set to a low, neutral gray. A Color Corrector filter has been applied to the clip, but all the parameters are still at their defaults, so it isn't affecting the image.

The first thing you should notice in the Vectorscope is the lack of any graph whatsoever, which means that the image is completely desaturated. The second thing you should notice in the Parade scope is that each color channel is equally strong. This latter graph shows the additive nature of the red, green, blue primary color system—adding equal amounts of each color results in a neutral gray.

7   Click anywhere in the color balance control and drag toward the R (red) target.

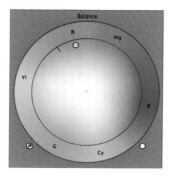

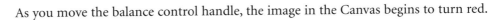

As you move the balance control handle, the image in the Canvas begins to turn red.

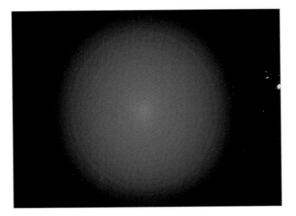

8 Control-click the Vectorscope and choose Magnify from the shortcut menu.

Because most adjustments you'll be making to an image happen close to the center of the Vectorscope, the Magnify setting lets you see the results in more detail.

As you adjusted the color balance control, the graph in the Vectorscope stretched out in the same direction as the adjustment you made. The red channel, represented by the red graph in the Parade scope, also increased in intensity relative to the green and blue channels.

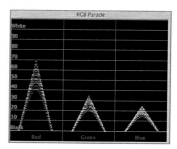

9   Click the color balance control and drag around the edge of the wheel toward the Cy (cyan) target. Watch the video scopes while you make the adjustment.

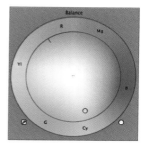

You can see the graph in the Vectorscope change to mirror the new direction of the balance control indicator. At the same time, you can see the three color channels in the Parade scope individually shift as you push and pull colors in each channel.

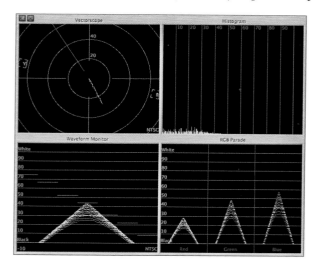

No matter what you do with the color balance control, and no matter how much the individual channel levels change in the Parade scope, the overall luma of the image stays the same, as represented by the Waveform Monitor. This is an important concept. As its name implies, the color balance control lets you change the balance of colors in the red, green, and blue channels of an image, but the end result always has the same overall luma.

More importantly, the color balance controls let you simultaneously rebalance the levels of all three color channels. This is an extremely powerful, and extremely fast, way to work.

NOTE ▸ Final Cut Pro works in the native $Y'C_bC_r$ colorspace of broadcast video, so contrast adjustments to the luma component can be made independently of color adjustments to the C_b and C_r color components; one does not affect the other.

As you'll see in later chapters, Color works natively in the RGB colorspace, so there's a much more interactive relationship between the contrast and color balance controls.

10 Take a minute to make additional changes to the color balance controls, observing the changes in the picture and in the video scopes.

Adjusting Saturation and Neutralizing Colors with Their Complementary Colors

In this exercise, you'll use the color balance control to modify the saturation of a color and to neutralize any single color by adding it to its complementary color.

1 Press the Down Arrow key to navigate to the second clip in the *Color Wheel Basics* sequence. Double-click the second **Custom Gradient** clip to open it into the Viewer.

This clip also has a Color Corrector filter applied.

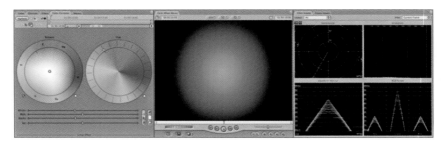

This clip is a circular gradient, just like the first clip. However, this clip already has a clear green cast, which you can see by the off-center graph in the Vectorscope, and the signifigantly higher green channel of the RGB Parade scope.

2   In the viewer, click the Color Corrector tab.

3   Click the color balance control, and drag toward a point somewhere between the Mg (magenta) and B (blue) targets, so that the spike in the green channel of the Parade scope diminishes, while the blue and red spikes remain roughly the same height relative to one another.

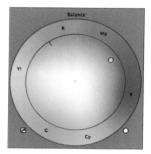

4   Stop dragging when the green has diminished but not quite faded completely, and look at the video scopes.

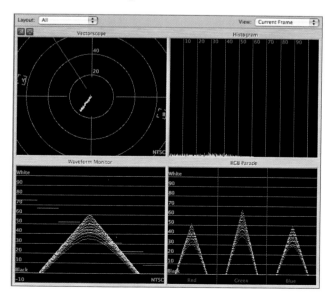

It's a little tricky to maintain the balance between the red and blue graphs in the Parade scope, while pulling down the green channel, but keep at it until you have roughly the result shown in the preceding figure.

By moving color balance in the opposite direction from the original green color, you've begun to desaturate the image, as you can see by the shortening of the graph in the Vectorscope. Because the balance between the red and blue spikes in the Parade scope is roughly equal, you can be sure that you're moving in the direction of purely neutralizing the image, rather than tinting it another color.

5 Immediately after you start to drag the balance control indicator to the right, hold down Shift and resume dragging, ever so slightly, until the three graphs in the Parade scope are the same height, and the graph in the Vectorscope is as close to the center as possible.

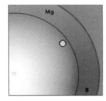

By Shift-dragging, you lock the angle of your adjustment. Because every hue is represented by an angle around the perimeter of the wheel, locking the angle lets you move the balance control indicator in and out from the center of the wheel to the edge, without changing its angle. This allows you to make saturation adjustments without also changing the hue of the image.

When you've made the adjustment, the gradient should appear almost completely gray.

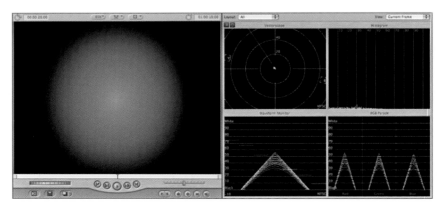

If the image isn't gray, the channels as displayed in the Parade scope weren't balanced equally enough when you made the last change. Keep working at it until you've completely neutralized the color.

Feel free to continue experimenting with this last image until you get the hang of the technique. The most important thing to learn is that by moving a color balance control you can adjust all three color channels of your image at once.

Even more important, the direction in which you rebalance colors with the color balance control is mirrored by the direction in which the graph moves in the Vectorscope. This direct relationship is a key element in your ability to predict necessary changes in color balancing.

Identifying and Correcting Color Casts

Have you ever taken a picture with a digital camera, or shot some video on vacation, only to get home and find that your footage is inexplicably orange, or blue, or green? What you're seeing is an incorrect white balance, often referred to as a *color cast*.

Every light source has a different *color temperature*. Each of the three types of light sources you'll typically encounter—incandescent (tungsten), fluorescent, and sunlight—produce light with strengths in different parts of the visible spectrum. Most of the time, you don't consciously notice these color temperatures, because the human eye is extremely adaptive, automatically doing the equivalent of white balancing everything you see after a moment. Also, your perception of what is white and what is black is relative to the surrounding colors.

Film and video cameras are not usually so forgiving. Color casts are a result of the recording device not being correctly adjusted to interpret the color temperature of the dominant light source. With film, the film stock wasn't intended for the light source in use. With video, the white balance control was incorrectly set, or the automatic setting wasn't quite so automatic.

The results are sometimes obvious (the whites look orange!) and sometimes subtle (what's wrong with his face?); but, in any event, the colors in the image are not what was expected. No matter what your creative goals are for the color of an image, you generally want to begin with an image where the whites look white, the blacks look black, and faces look the way they're supposed to, instead of orange, or green, or blue.

For this reason, you must learn to spot a color cast, determine which color channel is creating a problem, and neutralize the cast using the color balance controls.

Identifying Color Casts

Colorists need to perceive nuances in color and color casts in an image, and know how to alter the colors to create a natural appearance. Although every colorist has subjective viewpoints on the use of color, finding a natural balance is often the first step to creating the final look of the video.

1   In the Browser, open the Exercise 02 - Auto Balance bin and double-click the *Auto Balance Exercise* sequence.

> **NOTE** ▶ This lesson assumes that you're working on a calibrated external NTSC monitor. A computer monitor does not provide a true representation of the actual NTSC broadcast image. If your system is PAL, or you don't have an external monitor, you may complete this exercise using your computer's monitor, but be aware that it's not accurate for finishing purposes, and the resulting images won't look the same when output to broadcast video. If you have an SDI out from your video card and a DVI-D display, with the right adapter/converter, you can get a pretty reliable monitoring solution, although it won't be 100 percent accurate.

2   In the Video Scopes tab, make sure that the Layout pop-up menu is set to All.

3   Before you do anything else, take a close look at the image in the Canvas.

Your first impression is extremely important. The longer you look at any image, the more your eyes adapt to the relative differences between the colors in the frame, and the less sensitive you'll be to a color cast in the picture.

You need to get into the habit of asking the following three questions:

▶ Do the shadows seem pure black, or are they slightly tinted?

▶ Do things that should be pure white seem properly desaturated?

▶ Do people's faces look healthy and natural, or do they look faded, tired, or motion-sick?

If the answer to these is a collective no, as it should be for this image, you need to quantify the problem. In this case, you may have noticed that the image has a slightly blue, cool quality to it. To confirm your suspicions, it's time to look at the video scopes to determine exactly what the problem is.

4   Look at the video scopes.

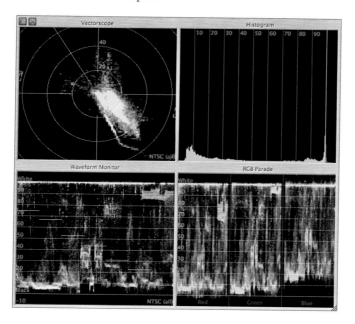

You'll notice by looking at the Waveform Monitor that the image is well exposed, with a wide contrast ratio that stretches from 0 percent (black) all the way to 100 percent (white). Furthermore, there is an enormous amount of detail throughout the mids. From the clustering at the top of the Waveform Monitor, however, you can surmise that there's a bit of overexposure, and the huge spike to the right of the Histogram at the 100 percent line confirms that there's an excess of white in the image.

As far as color casts go, however, the scopes reveal two telltale signs that the image is too blue. Before going on to the next step, see if you can guess what they are.

5 From the Layout pop-up menu, choose Parade.

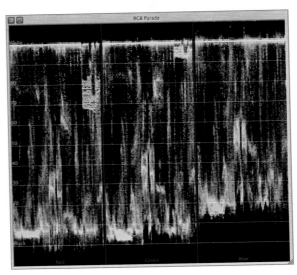

In many cases when there are abundant blacks and whites in the image, the three graphs that represent the red, green, and blue channels in the Parade scope look somewhat similar, in terms of their overall shape. Clearly, the mids will vary considerably, but because blacks represent an absence of all three colors, and whites represent the presence of all three colors, the tops and bottoms of each of the three graphs should fall roughly in the same places and be of equal value.

6 Carefully examine the top of the blue waveform.

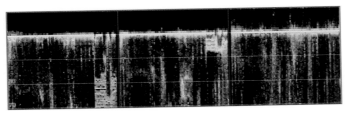

This confirms the problem. While the Waveform Monitor shows you the average luma of all three color channels together, the Parade scope shows you that the blues in this image are considerably stronger than the reds and greens. The bottom of the Parade scope shows that the blue channel is lighter in the blacks, which explains why the blacks seem somewhat washed out, even though parts of the Waveform Monitor extend all the way to the bottom.

7 From the Layout pop-up menu, choose Vectorscope. Control-click the Vectorscope and deselect Magnify in the shortcut menu.

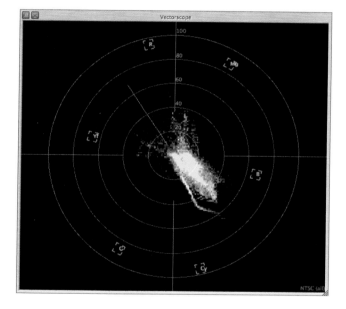

If you didn't have enough proof already, here's the smoking gun. In an image featuring three people, there are no traces clustered around the Flesh Tone line (the diagonal line in the upper-left quadrant) in the Vectorscope.

Furthermore, even though there is a lot of color in the Canvas (the reds and yellows in the clown's outfit and on the phone signage) the entire graph within the Vectorscope seems oddly uncentered, and in fact is offset in the direction of blue and cyan.

Although you can oftentimes identify a color cast by sight, the Parade scope and the Vectorscope are your best tools for correctly identifying the type, and severity, of a color cast in any image. Even though you may train your eye to accurately spot the hue of a color cast, the scopes are still useful for revealing just how much correction you need to make, based on the numbers.

Correcting Color Casts with the Auto-Balance Eyedroppers

Now that you've identified an improper color cast, you'll want to eliminate it before taking any other steps. To expedite the process, the Color Corrector 3-way filter provides three Select Auto-balance Color buttons that can automatically rebalance an image to make the blacks and whites neutral and rich.

1   Open the **Phone_Call.mov** clip into the Viewer and click the Color Corrector 3-way tab.

2   In the Video Scopes tab, choose All from the Layout pop-up menu.

You're now set to start correcting this clip. You'll notice a small eyedropper button at the bottom left of each color balance control in the Viewer. These are the Select Auto-balance Color buttons—one corresponds to each zone of luma.

The most important of these buttons corresponds to the blacks and whites. Whenever you use the automatic balancing controls in Final Cut Pro, you want to start where the color cast is most noticeable. In this case, it's in the blacks.

3   Click the Blacks Select Auto-balance Color button so that it's highlighted.

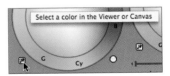

When you click the button, a tooltip appears with an instruction. What the instruction doesn't tell you is that you need to select an area that's supposed to be pure black.

This is an important decision, and it's not as easy as it may seem. You want to select an area that you think corresponds as closely to solid black as possible. In particular, because there's a color cast, you want to select an area that is *supposed* to be black, even if it doesn't appear to be so at first. In this image, there are several candidates: the woman's black dress, the shadow in the phone kiosk, or the color of the man's trousers. Each of these black areas is slightly different, however, and will yield different results.

4 Click the shadows of the phone kiosk.

Immediately, three things happen. The most noticeable event is that the image immediately looks more natural.

If you look in the Color Corrector tab, you'll see that the balance control indicator in the Blacks color balance control has moved to the left, toward yellow. As you learned earlier, yellow is the complementary color of blue, so this small adjustment neutralizes the cast in the blacks.

5   Look at the Parade scope.

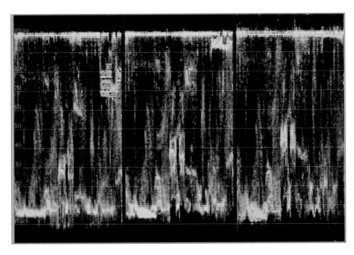

You should notice two things. First, the bottom of the blue graph now approximately matches the level of the red and green graphs. Second, the whites are still out of whack. Work remains to be done.

6   Click the Whites Select Auto-balance Color button to the left of the Whites color balance control.

Now you want to click a region in the image that's supposed to be white. That seems easy enough, because there's plenty of white in the image.

7   In the Canvas, click the side of the white building.

Nothing happened! How can this be? The Parade scope clearly shows a blue cast in the whites. This situation illustrates an important rule you need to remember when you use the Whites Select Auto-balance Color button.

8   Press Control-Z to turn on luma range checking in the Canvas (or choose View > Range Check > Excess Luma).

Now you can clearly see that the area you tried to select is overexposed. When digital video is overexposed, the result is that all values over the maximum digital limit are clipped, and the resulting parts of the image are pure white. These areas will not have the color cast you're trying to correct because they're artificially white. Extreme whites that are likely to be overexposed—such as lens flares, glints, or hot highlights—are not good candidates for the Whites Auto-Balance eyedropper.

You need to pick a new area of the picture. The shirt of the man standing next to the clown seems like a good choice. It's not overexposed, and it clearly looks like it has the blue cast you're trying to eliminate.

9   Press Control-Z to turn off luma range-checking in the Canvas.

10   Click the Whites reset button to the right of the Whites color balance control.

11   Click the Whites Select Auto-balance Color button, and then click the man's shirt.

Immediately, you should see another unexpected problem.

Instead of correcting all of the whites in the image, it turns them sepia. If you look at the Parade scope, the balance has been horribly skewed. Apparently the shirt is supposed to have a slightly higher blue level. You need to find something else that is supposed to be white.

12 Click the Whites reset button next to the Whites color balance control.

Next, try the phone logo on the side of the phone kiosk.

TIP Zoom in on the Canvas to make it easier to click smaller regions of white in an image. Press Z to select the Zoom tool, and click the phone logo twice. To return to the normal zoom level, press Shift-Z, and press A to select the Arrow tool.

13 Click the Whites Select Auto-balance Color button, and then click the whitest group of pixels within the phone.

The result is a compromise. The building has become warmer, but this may be due to the quality of light at that time of day, or the fact that the paint on the building is a warmer shade of white. (In either case, a quick chat with the director of photography should clear that up.)

The important thing is that the faces, which seemed anemic before, are now looking a little healthier, which is confirmed by the graph in the Vectorscope. Unfortunately, in this example, there is no absolute benchmark for the accuracy of this correction, and it becomes a matter of preference and experience.

As you can see, the effectiveness of the Auto-Balance eyedroppers is highly dependent on selecting the right pixels in the image. This process may involve some detective work on your part.

Sampling from the Mids

When correcting color casts, you typically need to adjust only two color balance controls to balance the image. Why? Because the Whites color balance control primarily affects the top 75 percent of the image. (The influence of this control falls off at this point, fading out around 10 percent luma.) Everything from dark gray shades of color up to white is affected.

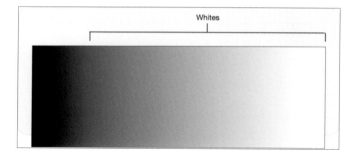

You probably noticed, however, that there are three eyedroppers, and so far you've ignored the one for mids.

In general, you should begin to color balance a scene by working in the whites or the mids to make the scene natural and realistic. Then, depending on the scene, additional adjustments may or may not be necessary.

If there's nothing white in the frame, your next best bet is to sample something that's as close to 50 percent gray as possible using the Mids Auto-Balance eyedropper. The mids typically make up a large percentage of an image, and the Mids color balance control has influence over the colors falling between 10 percent and 90 percent luma, with the maximum area of influence being the center 75 percent.

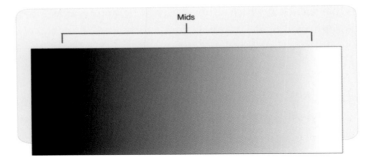

If the entire image is lit with light of the same color temperature, you may get away with balancing just the mids. The advantage of doing the primary color balancing with the mids is that you can avoid overly tinting the bright whites or deep blacks, if these regions are relatively free from color casts. This is, of course, highly dependent on the distribution of color throughout the three luma zones of the image. Every image is different and requires a unique approach.

Manipulating Color Directly in the Blacks, Mids, and Whites

As you've seen, the Final Cut Pro color correction filters let you separately manipulate the colors in the blacks, midtones, and whites zones of an image.

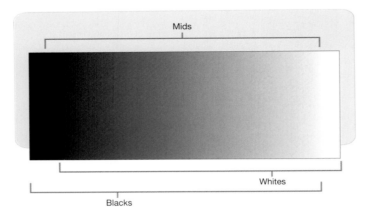

Any control that targets the blacks will affect only colors found in the shadows of the image, from full black up into the mid-gray tones.

Any control that targets the whites will affect only colors found in the highlights, from the mid-gray tones up to white.

Any control that targets the mids affects all the colors found in the midrange of the image, which constitutes the largest percentage of the viewing area.

These three zones have a great deal of overlap. For example, the controls that affect the mids extend their influence into the blacks and whites, but the effect tapers off before reaching the extreme blacks and whites, in order to preserve the ultimate black and white points you want to define.

Learning Each Color Wheel's Zone of Influence

Before moving to a practical example of color balancing, let's do one last grayscale exercise. (It's the last one, we promise!) This time you'll explore the amount of overlap exerted by each color control.

1   In the Browser, open the Exercise 03 - Blacks, Mids, Whites bin.

2   Double-click the *Blacks, Mids, Whites* sequence.

3   Double-click the **Gradient** clip in the sequence to open it into the Viewer, and then click the Color Corrector 3-way tab at the top of the Viewer. (A Color Corrector 3-way filter has already been applied.)

The clip you'll be working on first is another linear gradient generator, this time with the black on the left and the white on the right. It's an ideal way to see the effect each color control has on varying areas of image tonality, stretching from absolute black to absolute white.

4   Click the Blacks color balance control, and drag the balance control indicator in any direction to tint the blacks within the image. It's not necessary to drag all the way to the edge; just drag until the blacks are well tinted.

As you can see, the Blacks color balance control actually influences color well into the mids. It's important to see, however, that this influence tapers off gently toward the end, so that by 80 percent luma the control is barely having an effect, and this control has absolutely no effect on the upper 10 percent of whites.

5   Click the Blacks reset button.

6   Drag the Mids balance control indicator in any direction.

Predictably, you can see that the mids area of influence is strongest in the center region of luma, tapering off at the blacks and whites, leaving them unaffected.

7   Click the Mids reset button.

8   Drag the Whites balance control indicator in any direction.

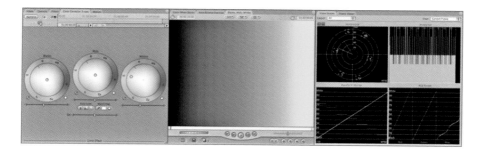

The effect of the whites adjustment is pretty much the inverse of the blacks, such that the lower 10 percent of the luma range remains unaffected.

9   Take a minute to play around with all of the color balance controls at once, and observe how the colors mix together.

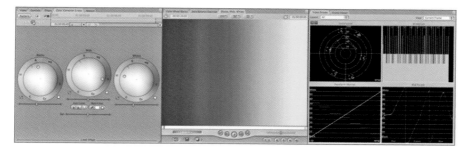

You can see that the blacks and whites both have a profound effect on the mids, yet a strong mids adjustment still manages to create a unique tint at the center of the gradient. Furthermore, you should also observe that the extreme blacks and whites remain unaffected by changes to either of the opposing controls.

You should now have a complete understanding of how the three color balance controls allow you to influence the color balance in each of the three zones of tonality. It's time for you to put this knowledge to a real-world test.

Color Balancing Zones of Lightness in an Image

Now you're going to use everything you've learned to color correct a shot manually, without using any automatic controls. In the process, you'll see that, with practice (and the help of the video scopes), it's often easier and faster to manually address color casts and other issues within an image.

1   Open the *Color Balancing Zones* sequence.

2   Double-click the **Phone_Call_CU.mov** clip in the sequence to open it in the Viewer. At the top of the Viewer, click the Color Corrector 3-way tab. (A Color Corrector 3-way filter has already been applied.)

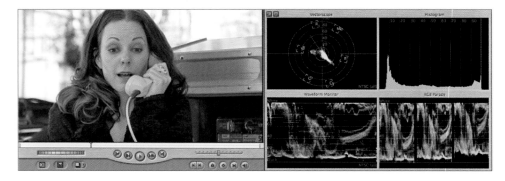

Ordinarily, you would first adjust the contrast with the Blacks, Whites, and Mids sliders. In this case, you're lucky: The shot has exactly the contrast the client wants, so you can skip this step.

3   Look at the Parade scope.

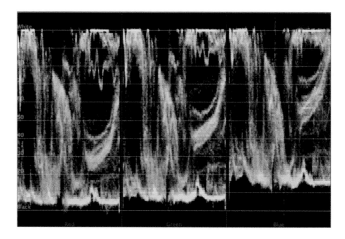

The Parade scope reveals that the blacks have abnormally high blue levels, so this is the first thing you'll need to address.

4   Look at the Vectorscope.

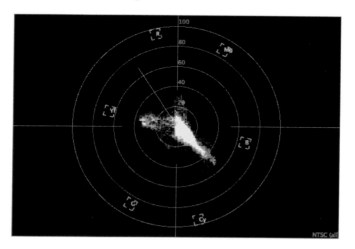

The scope reveals an offset into the blues. This provides you with a valuable clue about how to resolve the color cast issue.

5   Look at the Blacks color balance control, and find the direction of the complementary color that's opposite the strongest channel in the Vectorscope.

This tells you the direction in which you want to drag the Blacks balance control indicator to neutralize the color cast.

6   Drag the balance control indicator in the direction of the complementary color—in this case, somewhere between yellow and red.

Keep dragging, with one eye on your image, another eye on the Vectorscope (to keep track of the overall shift in hue), and a third eye on the bottoms of the three graphs in the Parade scope to make sure they become relatively balanced.

Don't worry if you don't drag the control very far. In real-world images, you'll typically find that very small changes in the color balance controls have a very big impact.

TIP At first, you may not notice any movement while dragging a balance control indicator. By default, the balance control indicators in the color correction filters move in very small increments, which is appropriate for most corrections. If necessary, you can Command-drag to make adjustments in larger increments.

When you're happy with the quality of the blacks, it's time to work on the whites.

7   Because the color cast in the whites is also in the blues, also move the balance control indicator toward a point between yellow and red.

This time, as you drag, keep your eye on the woman's skin color. Because of the large degree of overlap between the whites and mids, this is an opportunity to warm up some of the highlights on her face.

As you make this adjustment, you'll run into the same problem you saw earlier, when the building you thought was white began to turn sepia. It can be helpful to spot something else in the picture that is being affected by the whites color cast. This image has few whites, but there are some highlights on the ring on her finger that can serve as a rough guide.

Again, don't be surprised if you find yourself making a small adjustment to avoid severely tinting the background. In color correction, a little goes a long way. In any event, keep your change minimal, because there's one more step you can take.

8   In the Video Scopes tab, choose Vectorscope from the Layout pop-up menu.

For the last step in this procedure, you're going to boost the red channel in the mids to make the woman pop out a little more from the background. As you do this, keep a close eye on the Vectorscope, so you can keep track of how closely her adjusted skin tones come to the Flesh Tone line.

9   Drag the Mids balance control indicator in the direction of the complementary color—in this case, somewhere between yellow and red.

This will be your most subtle adjustment of all. You want to drag the balance control indicator out far enough to add more color to her face and some luster to her hair, but you don't want to move it out so far that the image turns brown.

NOTE ▶ If at any point you feel that you're doing more harm than good, don't get frustrated. It's easy for your eyes to get tired after looking at the same color shifts for a long time. Just click the Mids reset button and start over.

As you drag the balance control indicator, keep your eye on the Vectorscope. You'll see the portion of the graph that corresponds to her flesh tones near the Flesh Tone line, but they don't have to lie directly on the line. Indeed, if they did, she might look a little sallow. In this case, having the traces of the Vectorscope fall just above the Flesh Tone line seems to produce the most pleasing results, but this is a matter of interpretation.

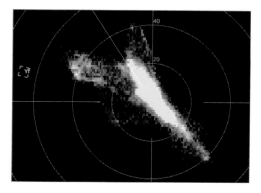

With this last adjustment, you're finished!

10 To see the before and after for this exercise (which is quite dramatic), select and deselect the Enable Filter checkbox beside the "eye" icon at the top of the Color Corrector tab.

In this lesson, you've learned how to perform the most common color correction task there is—identifying color casts in images and adjusting them. You've learned some of the most common ways of spotting problems in your images by using the video scopes, and you've learned precise methods of adjusting the different regions of an image, based on the luma zone that a particular set of colors happens to fall into.

The **Color.fcp** project file contains a sequence called *Color Balancing Zones—Completed* that contains a finished version of this lesson. You can compare your own work to the color corrections in that version.

Lesson Review

1. What is primary color correction?

2. What is a color cast?

3. Which color channels does the Mids color balance control affect?

4. What happens when you mix a color with its complementary color?

5. If the traces in the Vectorscope extend all the way out to the 80 percent ring, what does that mean?

6. If the bottoms of the three graphs in the Parade scope are all around 0 percent, but they aren't lining up, which color balance control should you adjust to correct the apparent color cast?

7. Which two Select Auto-balance Color controls should you use first?

8. Do the areas affected by the color balance controls overlap?

Answers

1. The first adjustment of the contrast and color balance of the overall image.

2. An unwanted color that appears to tint the image.

3. Trick question. Each color balance control affects all color channels together.

4. They neutralize each other.

5. The image is very highly saturated.

6. The Blacks color balance control.

7. The Blacks and Whites.

8. Yes.

3

Lesson Files Lesson Files > Lesson 03 > SceneContinuity.fcp

Media Bar Scene

Time This lesson takes approximately 120 minutes to complete.

Goals Use comparison to aid in color matching

Color grade a scene from beginning to end

Learn a workflow for color matching

Use Frame Viewer, Copy Filter controls, and playhead sync during color correction

Lesson 3
Scene Continuity

Color grading in Final Cut Pro is fast, flexible, and easy. In the coming lessons you'll be working in Color, but there are some advantages to doing at least some of your grading work in Final Cut Pro. For example, you can make incremental changes to your clips while you're still editing. Since the color corrections are applied as filters, the corrections stick with the clips even if you completely reedit the sequence.

Although you don't necessarily need to have your edit completely locked before sending it to Color, that's the typical workflow (as you'll learn in Lesson 4). Furthermore, if you do eventually send your sequence to Color, grading you did in Final Cut Pro's Color Corrector 3-way will automatically be sent along with the clips.

For these reasons it's worthwhile to learn the whole spectrum of color grading tools available in Final Cut Pro. In this lesson you'll correct a whole scene in Final Cut Pro, utilizing a variety of features, tips, and tricks designed to speed the process and streamline your workflow. You'll begin, as always, by correcting a single shot using the methods covered in the previous lessons. Then, to create a sense of visual consistency among each coverage shot, you'll use the same tools, with some new techniques, to match the look of the initially corrected shot to every clip in the scene.

Achieving Visual Harmony

In a dramatic program, most scenes portray an event that takes place at a single time, in a single place. As such, the general intensity and color of the lighting should be consistent from shot to shot.

This is often at odds with the logistics of filmmaking, where the light may be quite different from one angle of coverage to another. It's especially true for projects shot outdoors using available light. If the scene took several hours to shoot, the quality of light in Actor 1's close-up may be very different from the quality of light filmed two hours later in Actor 2's reverse close-up.

When the lighting is different in two consecutive shots, the cut between those shots becomes noticeable. The audience may not understand why, but they'll notice a difference, and this will defeat the editor's goal of achieving seamless continuity. Any discontinuity in the look of consecutive images can be jarring and may take the viewer out of the moment as surely as a poorly timed edit.

Visual harmony is important for many types of programs. Reality TV, documentaries, and interview shows all aim to integrate footage shot in different lighting conditions into a coherent whole. Although there may be no real need to fool anyone into thinking that the shots happened at the same time and place, any unjustified change in lighting or color from one shot to the next can distract viewers from the flow of the program and the point you're trying to make.

Regardless of the lighting variances or the color of the source media, the color correction tools you use to make corrections to a single clip can also balance the colors of multiple clips in a scene. In this way, you can impose a seamless continuity of lighting and color that may be lacking in the original edit, so that every angle appears to be in exactly the same time and place, and all of the clips fit together.

Getting Started

1   Open Lesson Files > Lesson 03 > **SceneContinuity.fcp**.

    If your workspace isn't already set up to include the video scopes in the Tool Bench window, set this up now.

2   Choose Window > Arrange > Color Correction to arrange your layout to accommodate the Video Scopes tab.

Comparing Two Clips

It may sound obvious, but before you can correct one clip to match another, you must be able to compare both images in such a way as to quickly and accurately identify their differences. Before getting started with color correcting a scene, you'll spend a little time familiarizing yourself with clip comparison techniques in Final Cut Pro.

Toggling Between Images in the Canvas

The process of comparing two images is deceptively simple. It's always essential to judge the quality of an image using a calibrated broadcast-quality monitor, and not your computer's display, but it's even more critical when you start balancing the color of an entire scene.

For this reason, the most reliable and accurate method for comparing two images is also the simplest solution: flipping back and forth between two clips while watching the images change on your broadcast monitor.

The Show Edit commands allow you to temporarily jump to other edit points in the Timeline and then return to the frame at the initial position of the playhead:

▶ Show Previous Edit (Control–Up Arrow) toggles the last frame of the clip located immediately to the left in the Timeline.

▶ Show 2nd Prior Edit (Shift–Control–Up Arrow) toggles to the last frame of the second clip to the left in the Timeline.

▶ Show Next Edit (Control–Down Arrow) toggles to the first frame of the clip immediately to the right.

▶ Show 2nd Next Edit (Shift–Control–Down Arrow) toggles to the first frame of the second clip to the right.

▶ Show In Point (Control–Left Arrow) toggles the display of an In point only if you have defined an In point in the Timeline or Canvas.

▶ Show Out Point (Control–Right Arrow) toggles the display of an Out point only if you have defined an Out point in the Timeline or Canvas.

In this exercise, you'll practice using these keyboard shortcuts to compare shots in an edited sequence.

1   If you have an external broadcast monitor connected to your computer, make sure that it's set up properly, and that External Video is set to All Frames.

2   With the *Scene 1* sequence open, move the playhead to the third clip of the sequence, **Side Wide Angle (02).**

Its image appears simultaneously in the Canvas and in the broadcast monitor.

3   Hold down Control–Up Arrow.

The playhead immediately jumps to the last frame of the previous clip, showing you how the last image from the previous clip will segue into the current clip.

NOTE ▶ If the Show Edit keyboard commands don't respond, move the playhead off the first frame of the clip and repeat the command.

4   Release the keys you've been holding.

The playhead goes back to its initial position.

5   Press Control–Up Arrow a few times, and notice how you can flip back and forth between your images, instantly getting a sense of the differences between color and brightness.

When you quickly jump back and forth between images, your eyes don't have time to adjust to each image, which makes it easier to spot variations.

As you flip between images, glance at the video scopes, and notice how they update with the image. You can use the Show Edit commands to compare images numerically, as well as visually, by flipping between their graphs on the scopes. This is an important technique that you'll be using often.

6   Hold down Shift–Control–Up Arrow.

This time, the playhead jumps to the last frame of the second clip to the left. When correcting a scene with many angles of coverage, pressing Control–Up Arrow and Shift–Control–Up Arrow lets you quickly compare many different clips to get a sense of the colors throughout the scene.

7   Release the keys you've been holding, and press Control–Down Arrow and then Shift–Control–Down Arrow, to jump to the clips to the right of the current playhead position.

These commands are very useful when you're balancing shots that appear next to one another in a sequence. But if you want to balance clips that appear in entirely different parts of your program, you'll need to use the Show In Point and Show Out Point commands.

8   Set an In point at the current playhead position.

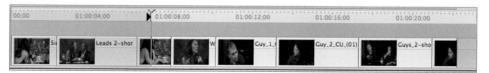

9   Park the playhead anywhere on the last clip in the sequence.

10   Hold down Control–Left Arrow.

The playhead jumps to the In point. This shortcut is useful for comparing two clips that are separated from one another in a sequence. It's also good for comparing the current frame with a specific frame in an adjacent clip, and not just In or Out points.

Making Side-by-Side Comparisons with the Frame Viewer

Another useful tool for comparing two images is the split-screen function found in the Final Cut Pro Frame Viewer.

As you have learned, the Frame Viewer lets you display other edit points relative to the current position of the playhead. The Frame Viewer also lets you compare two images *within the same frame* using a split-screen mode.

1 Move the playhead to the first clip in the sequence.

2 In the Tool Bench window, click the Frame Viewer tab.

By default, the Frame Viewer is set to a vertical split-screen mode, showing the current frame with filters on the left side of the frame, and the current frame without filters on the right. No filters are applied to the current clip, so there's no visible split in the image.

Like the View options in the video scopes, the Frame Viewer is flexible enough to compare a range of images in split-screen mode. The two pop-up menus underneath the image frame itself let you assign images to each part of the split-screen mode.

3 From the pop-up menu at the lower right of the Frame Viewer (next to the blue square), choose Next Edit.

The left side of the Frame Viewer screen now displays the current frame, and the right side displays the first frame of the next clip to the right. As you saw in the menu, there are numerous options for comparing clips in your sequence, most of which correspond to the Show Edit commands you used previously.

If you look carefully at the corners that define the left half of the split screen, you'll see four square, color-coded handles. Each control and menu in the Frame Viewer is color-coded green or blue. These colors correspond to each of the two pop-up menus at the bottom of the Frame Viewer. The pop-up menus define which clips in the Timeline appear in each half of the frame, and they relate to the timecode values (at the top of the Frame Viewer) that show you which frames are being viewed.

In the current split-screen view, you can see that there is a color discontinuity between the two shots, but it may be difficult to make an "apples to apples" comparison because there is no single visual element shared by both images. Fortunately, you can customize the split between the two images.

4   At the bottom of the Frame Viewer window, click the H-Split button.

Now, instead of the vertical split screen, there is a horizontal split screen.

If you're ever confused about which clip is in which part of the screen, you can rely upon the color-coded handles that appear within the frame. In the current horizontal split, the four green corner handles in the bottom half of the screen correspond to the green icon next to the lower-left pop-up menu that's set to Current Frame. The blue half-handles, then, correspond to the icon next to the lower-right pop-up menu set to the Next Edit relative to the current frame.

At this point, you can compare the woman's shoulder in one shot to her arm in another, but it's still difficult to make an accurate comparison.

5 Click the Swap button.

The images are reversed on either side of the split, but it's still difficult to compare the lighting on her arm in each picture.

TIP You can also swap the two sides of a split screen by clicking the H-Split or V-Split buttons repeatedly, as long as you haven't customized the split rectangle.

6 Move the pointer to the lower-left edge of the split screen. When the pointer turns into a Resize pointer, drag the left edge to the right until you can see the woman's arm in each clip.

The Frame Viewer split screen is incredibly flexible because the split between the images is defined by a user-customizable rectangle. You can independently drag each of the four corner handles and each side of the split around the frame, so you can selectively compare any two areas of an image, regardless of their positions. Having made the adjustment, you can now compare the woman's arm in each clip, and the difference between the two images is obvious.

There are several ways you can manipulate the split between two images.

7 Drag up the lower-right corner handle of the split screen so that the split area is a small square.

8 Move the pointer into the center of the split, and when the pointer becomes a hand, drag the split around in the frame.

By moving the split rectangle, you can easily compare different parts of both images.

9 Click the V-Split button to reset the Frame Viewer to a vertical split screen.

10 In the Timeline, move the playhead to the second clip.

The clips displayed in the Frame Viewer always correlate to the current playhead position. As you move the playhead around in your sequence, the Frame Viewer updates to display the appropriate images.

As you move around the sequence, however, you should notice one crucial thing: The only image that is displayed on your external broadcast monitor is *the current frame at the position of the playhead*.

The best time to use the Frame Viewer is after you make the first few corrections, flipping between clips and viewing the external monitor. Later, if you're having difficulty determining the difference between an uncorrected clip and another clip that has been corrected relative to the broadcast monitor, the split screen might give you more clues (particularly if flipping between both pictures and examining the video scope graphs isn't revealing enough).

Split screen is also a good way to view your results as you begin learning how to correct a second shot to match a first, but you should always, always flip between both images on your calibrated broadcast monitor to finish the job.

Setting Up for Scene-by-Scene Color Correction

Several interface options make it easier to color correct a scene. In this section, you'll set up Final Cut Pro to take advantage of these options. Bear in mind that these settings are a matter of personal preference—what's good for one colorist may not work for another.

Be aware that some Final Cut Pro features that have nothing directly to do with color correction can still provide numerous benefits to the colorist.

Setting Playhead Sync to Open

As you've seen, all color correction in Final Cut Pro is done with filters, and the color correction filters have custom controls in the Color Corrector 3-way tab of the Viewer. Opening another color-corrected sequence clip into the Viewer automatically reveals its Color Corrector parameters within the same tab, as long as the Color Corrector 3-way tab is already open.

You can use this behavior to automate opening clips into the Viewer by using the Open setting in the Playhead Sync pop-up menu in the Viewer or Canvas. As its name implies, the Open playhead sync setting automatically opens into the Viewer any clip that becomes visible in the Canvas.

If all of your clips have color correction filters applied, simply moving the playhead to another clip automatically opens its color correction controls into the Viewer. This saves you a few mouse clicks, and it ensures that you are always adjusting the color correction controls of the clip you're looking at.

> **NOTE** ▶ Although this is a useful way to work, you are advised to leave playhead sync set to Off while doing the exercises in this lesson, unless otherwise instructed.

1 Open the *Scene 1 - Finished* sequence.

2 In the Timeline, double-click the first clip to open it into the Viewer.

All of the clips in this sequence have been color corrected, so they all have Color Corrector 3-way filters applied.

3 In the Viewer, click the Color Corrector 3-way tab to display the first clip's color correction controls.

4 From the Playhead Sync pop-up menu in the Canvas, choose Open.

5 Drag the playhead through the Timeline from left to right, pausing briefly at each clip.

As you scrub from clip to clip, you'll see how the Viewer window automatically displays the same image as the Canvas.

6 Move the playhead to the third clip in the sequence.

The Open playhead sync mode works even with the Show Edit commands.

7 Select the Timeline, press Control–Up Arrow, and then press Control–Down Arrow.

Notice how the Color Corrector controls update every time the playhead moves. It might take a moment or two, but the Viewer always updates.

Although this style of working is convenient, there are many times you'll want to disable the behavior. For example, you must turn playhead sync off if you want to keep open the Color Corrector 3-way tab from one clip in order to scrub over to another section of the Timeline and drag that filter onto another clip, or when you're using the Match Hue controls.

If you routinely use the Open playhead sync mode, periodically check that Open is selected in the Playhead Sync pop-up menu, because it's fairly easy to accidentally deselect this mode.

Also note that Final Cut Pro always opens the clip on the highest track that has Auto Select enabled. If you have clips on multiple tracks, Option-click the Auto Select control to select just the track that you want to color correct.

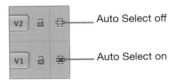

Auto Select off

Auto Select on

Choosing Timeline Options

There are several Timeline options you can set that make it easier to navigate and manage filters in a sequence. In this exercise, you'll set up the Timeline to take advantage of these options.

1   Open the *Scene 1* sequence in the Browser.

2   In the Browser, Control-click the *Scene 1* sequence and choose Settings from the shortcut menu.

3 In the Sequence Settings dialog, click the Timeline Options tab.

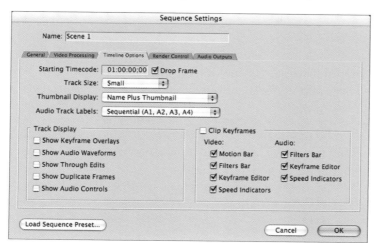

4 If it's not already selected, from the Thumbnail Display pop-up menu, choose Name Plus Thumbnail.

Because you're not changing the edit points while you color correct a sequence, you don't have to worry too much about the computing overhead of redrawing the thumbnail images. In any event, thumbnails are incredibly useful for quickly spotting which clips come from the same angle of coverage, which facilitates copying filters among similar clips.

5 Select the Clip Keyframes checkbox, and deselect everything within the Clip Keyframes section except for the Video: Filters Bar option.

The Filters Bar option adds green stripes (filter bars) underneath every clip that has a filter applied, which enables you to determine, at a glance, which clips have color correction filters applied. This is great for keeping track of which clips have been color corrected, and which ones you have yet to work on.

Left, filter applied; right, no filter applied

6   Click OK to close the Sequence Settings dialog.

7   Move the pointer to the top of track V1 in the Timeline.

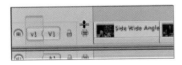

8   When the pointer turns into the Resize pointer, drag up the top of the track to make it taller.

As useful as the Timeline's clip thumbnails are, they don't do you any good if you can't see them.

If you're working on a sequence with a lot of video tracks, you might consider dragging down the border between the video and audio tracks, obscuring the audio tracks to make room for more video tracks.

TIP ▶ It's pretty typical for colorists to begin work on a program after the picture has been locked, so accidentally moving a clip, even a few frames, when you meant to just double-click it is a bad thing. If you lock all of the audio tracks, but not the video tracks, of a sequence you're correcting, and keep Linked Selection turned on, you can minimize your risk of inadvertently nudging clips around.

Color Correcting a Complete Scene

Now that you've set up your window layout, learned how to compare images, and customized your Timeline, you can start working on an actual scene.

Choosing a Reference Shot

The first thing you need to do is determine which clip to use as the starting point for color correcting the scene. In general, you want to choose a reference shot that contains most of the characters that appear in that scene. If your scene features two characters, look for a 2-shot that clearly shows both actors. If it's a group scene, find the widest shot that's representative, with as many people as possible clearly visible, which makes it easier to balance the skin tones in each individual's close-up with the skin tone in the corrected reference clip.

In any event, it's important to work on a reference clip that is an average shot from that scene, because after you've made your corrections and stylistic adjustments to that clip, you'll be comparing every other clip in the scene to that reference. If you pick a shot that's anomalous in any way (such as the only shot in which someone's in a spotlight, or standing in a shadow), you run the risk of incorrectly balancing all the other clips in that scene.

> **TIP** It's always a good idea to communicate with the director and cinematographer to determine if they have an opinion about which shot most represents the intended look of the scene.

1   If it's not already open, double-click the *Scene 1* sequence, and choose Window > Arrange > Color Correction to reset the window layout.

2   Scrub through the first four clips in the Timeline, and see if you can pick the best one to use as a reference shot.

The fourth clip is the easiest to rule out. As a close-up, it shows the least amount of background, and it excludes all the other actors in the shot.

The first and third clips (both from the same angle of coverage), appear to fit the bill at first glance. They're wide shots, and they show every character in that scene. The problem is that the two most important characters (according to the director) are shown in profile, and we see only the back of the woman's head. On second thought, this is not an ideal starting point.

This leaves us with the second clip in the sequence, **Leads 2-shot**. It's the best shot of both lead actors, and it's wide enough to show a lot of the foreground, as well as the wall behind the actors. Correcting this shot will give you an excellent starting point for balancing this scene.

Developing the Scene's "Look"

One of the interesting things about being a colorist is that your job is one-third technician and two-thirds artist.

On the one hand, you have an obligation to provide a reasonably strong video signal, pleasingly visible detail, and minimal noise, and to keep your adjustments within the accepted broadcast limits.

On the other hand, you have an obligation to achieve your client's creative goals, to make shots darker or lighter, warmer or cooler, more saturated or less, depending on the aesthetic needs of the program. Assuming you have well-exposed footage, it's usually easy to strike a balance between both parts of the job.

Remember, as you correct this first shot, it's critical to view the output on a properly calibrated broadcast monitor.

> **TIP** This exercise provides only suggested changes. Feel free to veer off at any time and create your own look. To see the complete, color-corrected sequence, open Scene 1 - Finished from the Browser.

1   Locate the second clip in the sequence, the one you've chosen as the reference shot for the scene, and apply a Color Corrector 3-way filter.

If you turned on Clip Keyframes earlier, a green filter bar appears underneath the second clip to show you that a filter is applied.

2   Open the second clip into the Viewer, and click the Color Corrector 3-way tab.

3   Press Control-Z to turn on Range Check > Luma.

It's always a good idea to turn on range checking while you make adjustments, to give you an instant warning if you push anything too far.

4   Adjust the Blacks, Mids, and Whites sliders to set the black point of the graph in the Waveform Monitor at 0 percent and the white point for highlights at 100 percent. Watch the range-check icon at the top of the Viewer, as well as the Waveform Monitor, while you make this adjustment. Afterwards, lower the Mids slider just a few points to deepen the shadows.

NOTE ▶ If an image doesn't have any bright whites, or highlights, or any section that would plausibly go all the way up to 100 percent, it's neither necessary nor desirable to automatically boost the level of the brightest area in the image to 100 percent. In these cases, adjust the white point relative to how bright the lightest area in the picture would realistically be. This will keep the contrast from becoming artificially high. In other words, don't set someone's face to 100 percent white just because it happens to be the brightest element in a very dark picture.

5   Make any necessary adjustments to the Blacks and Whites color balance controls, using the Vectorscope and the Parade scope as your guide.

Neutralize the yellowish cast, and warm up the skin tones. To do that, add some cyan to the blacks to create true blacks, and add some blue to the whites to clean them up.

6 Add some red to the mids, to give some kick to the skin tones and create the impression of warmer lighting in the room.

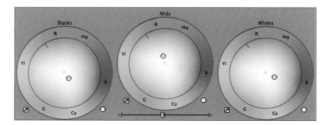

7 Press Control-Z to turn off Range Check > Luma.

Next, you'll correct the other clips in this sequence so they match the tone and color you've achieved in your reference shot.

Matching Contrast Between Two Shots

The two clips that are adjacent to the **Leads 2-shot** reference clip are from the same angle of coverage, **Side Wide Angle**. You'll begin balancing the rest of the scene to the corrected reference clip by working on the first **Side Wide Angle** clip. As always, the first step is to adjust the clip's contrast—in this case, to match that of the reference shot.

It's useful to note that the human eye is more sensitive to changes in brightness than in color, so you want to take particular care to make the contrast of all shots in a scene match as closely as possible.

1 Move the playhead to the beginning of the first clip in the sequence, **Side Wide Angle (01)**.

2   With the Timeline active, press Control–Down Arrow a few times, flipping between this clip and the previously corrected reference clip to its right. Examine the two clips for differences in contrast.

As you flip back and forth, make sure you check both the visual image and the graphs in the video scopes. When you're examining differences in contrast, the Waveform Monitor is a good guide.

In comparing the two waveform graphs, note that the black point in the uncorrected clip to the left is not as low as in the corrected clip.

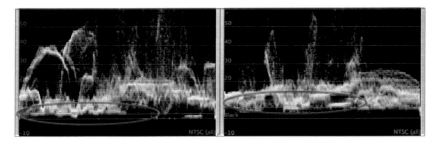

You should also notice that some of the distributions within the midtones are a little high, and the white point of the first clip's graph seems to match that in the second clip. In other words, the densest clump in the middle of the graph on the left (which is probably the cocktail bar surface) is about three percent higher than the densest clump in the graph on the right. This makes the **Side Wide Angle (01)** clip seem slightly brighter. This also tells you that you'll later be making an adjustment to the Mids slider.

There's a good way to measure these differences. Once you've spotted an identical feature in each graph, such as the cocktail bar, move the pointer within the Waveform Monitor, and an indicator appears. By dragging the indicator to line up with different features in the graph, you'll get a tooltip at the top of the Waveform Monitor that displays the digital percentage. The tooltip can help you determine how much correction you need to make.

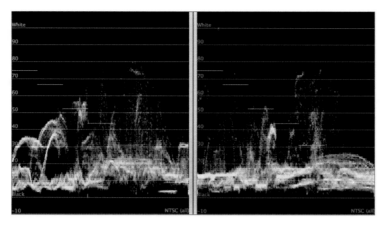

Side Wide Angle (01)   Leads 2-shot

In this example, the first clip to the left measures the top of this feature at about 21 percent; the reference clip at the right measures the same feature at about 18 percent—a 3 percent difference, but enough to be noticeable.

Learning which parts of the graph correspond to which areas of each shot takes practice. Remember that the Waveform Monitor scans the entire image from left to right, drawing a graph based on the brightness of each vertical slice of the picture. Bright parts of the picture, such as the woman's arm, cause upward curves in the midtones at the middle of the graph. Highlights, such as the candles, cause spikes into the whites at the top of the graph. Dark areas, like the man's jacket sleeve and the bar surface, will cluster near the bottom of the graph.

TIP Sometimes it's easier to see how the graph corresponds to the image when the clip is moving. To ensure that the scopes update while the sequence is playing, open the RT menu in the Timeline and choose Video Scopes Playback.

3   Add a Color Corrector 3-way filter to the **Side Wide Angle (01)** clip, and open it into the Viewer.

4   Adjust the Blacks slider so that the average distribution at the bottom of the Waveform Monitor graph for **Side Wide Angle (01)** approximately matches that of **Leads 2-shot**. This will be a very slight adjustment, so you may want to Command-drag the Blacks slider so it doesn't snap to the center position.

If necessary, make the Timeline active and press Command–Down Arrow a few times to flip back and forth, comparing your results before making further adjustments.

5   Drag the Mids slider a few points to the left, lowering the mids so that the overall level of brightness in both clips appears to be the same and the relative distributions start to line up in the middle of the Waveform Monitor graphs.

This will also be a slight adjustment—one that requires you to look at the image, in addition to watching the scopes.

It's important to realize that although the top and bottom of the waveforms are important, the distribution of values between them is even more important to the overall clip brightness. Even if the tops and the bottoms of the two graphs line up, the clips won't match if the inner distribution of values is significantly different.

6   To check the adjustment you've just made, make the Timeline active, and press Control–Down Arrow a few times, flipping between this clip and the reference clip, to make sure your correction matches. If it doesn't, keep making adjustments, checking the video scopes and flipping between images until you're satisfied that the shots match.

Matching Color Between Two Shots

Now that the contrast of the second clip has been set to match the reference shot, it's time to adjust the color.

1   In the Video Scopes window, from the Layout pop-up menu, choose Parade and make sure that View is set to Current Frame.

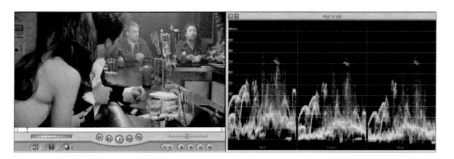

2   Make the Timeline active, and press Control–Down Arrow a few times, flipping between the **Side Wide Angle (01)** clip and the **Leads 2-shot** clip, comparing the images on the monitor and the graphs in the Parade scope.

The Parade scope shows you the balance of red, green, and blue in an image. When you're comparing two images, the Parade scope is a powerful tool for identifying exactly which color channels need balancing, and in which luma zones.

As you toggle back and forth, look at the bottom of each graph. You should notice that, compared to the reference clip, the blues are too low and the reds are too high. This tells you what kind of adjustment you need to make to the Blacks color balance control.

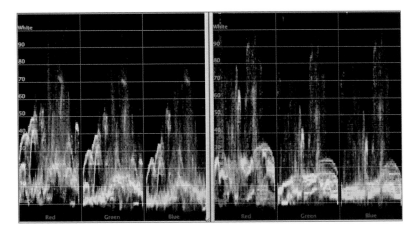

3   Drag the Blacks balance control indicator somewhere between the Cy (cyan) and B (blue) targets, until the bottoms of the red, green, and blue graphs match those of the reference clip.

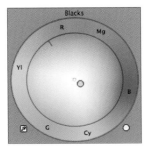

To check your work, make the Timeline active, and press Control–Down Arrow a few times to compare the images and the graphs. Keep making adjustments until you're satisfied. When you're finished, the bottoms of the graphs should approximately line up.

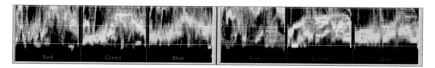

4   Toggle between the images again, this time examining the tops of the graphs.

You should see that the first clip has much more yellow in the highlights of the skin tones than the reference shot. The tops of graphs in the Parade scope reveal this as green and blue channels that are too strong (remember that red + green = yellow).

5   Drag the Whites balance control indicator toward the B (blue) target to neutralize the yellowish cast in the highlights, but not so far as to overcompensate and tint the highlights blue.

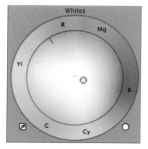

For this last adjustment, it's a bit difficult to accurately spot the tops of the red, green, and blue graphs, because there are so few values there. This would be a good time to increase the brightness of the traces.

6   In the upper-left corner of the Scopes window, click the Traces Brightness button.

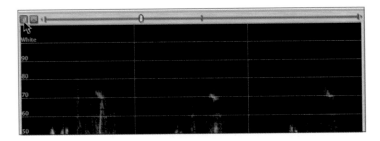

A slider appears next to the buttons.

7   Drag the slider to the right to increase the visibility of the video data.

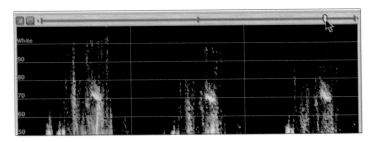

This makes it much easier to identify the color data in the brightest areas of the shot. When you're happy with the whites color balance setting, you may want to lower the brightness again to a more modest setting.

Now that the blacks are black, and the highlights are equally neutral to those in the reference image, it's time to adjust the mids to complete the match. For this last adjustment, you'll rely on the Vectorscope.

8   In the Video Scopes window, from the Layout pop-up menu, choose Vectorscope.

After you've matched the colors in the blacks and the whites, it often becomes difficult to see how the colors in the mids line up in the Parade scope. In these cases, the Vectorscope can give you a clearer picture of the differences between the overall color temperatures in two images.

9   Once again, make the Timeline active and press Control–Down Arrow a few times to compare the images and their graphs.

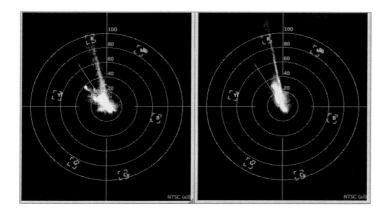

You should immediately see that the first clip doesn't have as much saturation toward the reds as the reference image. In particular, the cluster of values that fall just above the Flesh Tone line in the reference image's Vectorscope (to the right in the preceding figure) extends all the way up to about 33 percent, and the same cluster of values in the Vectorscope to the left is down around 18 percent—a large difference.

10 For **Side Wide Angle (01)**, drag up the Mids balance control indicator toward the Flesh Tone line until the cluster of values at the center of the Vectorscope matches those displayed by the reference clip. If necessary, make the Timeline active and flip back and forth, adjusting and comparing until you're satisfied you have a match.

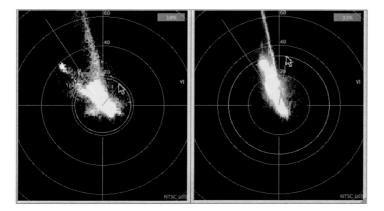

When you're finished, the shots should match just about perfectly. Play through both clips to make sure.

Copying Filters Forward to Other Clips from the Same Angle

Before you make any more manual adjustments to clips in this scene, it's time to ask yourself if there are any more clips featuring the same angles of coverage and with the same lighting. If so, you can copy the color correction filters from the corrected clips along with their settings, and apply them to other clips shot from the same angle.

It's very common for scenes to be constructed using repeated sequences of clips drawn from a few angles of coverage. For example, if there are three angles of coverage—shot A (a master shot of the room), shot B (a two-shot), and shot C (a close-up of actor 2)—the scene might be edited like this:

A–B–A–C

That's the situation in this scene. A quick look at the Timeline should reveal that the third clip is from the same angle as the first clip you corrected (**Side Wide Angle (02)**). So, you might as well copy the color correction filter forward to save yourself some work and guarantee consistency.

To facilitate this, each Color Corrector 3-way filter has a group of Copy Filter controls that let you copy the currently open filter and its settings and apply them to clips that follow it in the sequence.

The Copy Filter controls work similarly to the Show Edit commands. There is one control to copy the current filter forward to the next clip in the sequence, and a second control to copy it to the second clip forward. As in the hypothetical edited sequence (A–B–A–C), shots from the same angle rarely fall next to one another in narrative filmmaking, so these controls allow you to skip adjacent shots and apply the correction to the next instance of a shot from the same angle.

1   Make sure the color correction filter from the first clip in the sequence is open in the Viewer, and click the Copy to 2nd Clip Forward button.

If you turned on Clip Keyframes in the previous exercise, a green filter bar appears underneath the third clip to show you that the filter has indeed been applied.

Playing through the sequence will show that all three clips are properly balanced. The ease with which color correction filters can be propagated through a sequence brings up an interesting issue—if you make a change to any of the filters that are applied to these clips, you'll need to copy that change to any other clips that have an identical correction.

This is because after you've copied a filter to another clip, its settings are completely independent of the original filter. However, the Copy Forward commands have an additional function to help you in this situation. If you use those commands to copy a color correction filter to another clip that already has a color correction filter applied, the settings of the filter in the second clip are overwritten to match those in the current filter.

2   Make sure the color correction filter from the first clip is open in the Viewer, and drag the Sat (saturation) slider to the left to noticeably desaturate the image.

3   Play through the sequence to verify that the first and third clips don't match.

4   Move the playhead back to the first clip and open the Color Corrector filter into the Viewer.

5   Click the Copy to 2nd Clip Forward button.

6   Play through the first three clips again and verify that the third clip has changed to match the first.

7   Press Command-Z twice to undo this change.

You'll notice that there are also buttons for copying color correction filter settings *from* color correction filters that are applied to the first and second clips behind the current clip (in the Timeline). For more detailed information on using the Copy Filter controls, see the Final Cut Pro documentation.

Matching Color with the Match Hue Controls

So far, you've learned how to manually adjust contrast and color to match shots. When you develop a facility with the tools, this is often the fastest way to proceed, and they certainly afford you the greatest amount of control in any possible color correction.

However, the color correction filters have another feature to make your life a bit easier: The Match Hue controls, found in the middle of the Color Corrector 3-way filter's custom controls, underneath the Mids controls.

The Match Hue controls automate the process of balancing a color within one zone of luma to match a designated color in a different clip. It does nothing to adjust contrast; you must adjust that manually. However, it does provide a way to quickly and automatically adjust color balance controls to match a specific hue that you select, similar to the way Auto-Balance eyedroppers work in the color balance controls.

Match Hue works well with clips that are from the same location, matching the color of a subject in one clip to the color of the identical subject in another clip. In the scene you're currently balancing, for example, the woman appears in every shot that's been corrected, and the location and situation are identical, even though the lighting varies from shot to shot. This is an ideal situation in which to use the Match Hue controls.

You can use the Match Hue controls in other situations, but your success will be completely dependent on your ability to accurately select analogous colors in each shot. For example, it's a mistake to assume that you can match the skin tone of any two people with similar skin color. Subtle differences in hue, even by a few percentage points, may result in significant deviations in the end result. Still, even in less than ideal situations, the Match Hue controls may provide you with a starting point if you're unsure how to proceed.

1   Move the playhead to the fourth clip in the sequence, **Woman CU**.

2   Apply a Color Corrector 3-way filter to the **Woman CU** clip, open it into the Viewer, and click the Color Corrector 3-way tab to view its controls.

This clip has a yellow/red cast similar to that found in other clips in this scene, but a closer examination reveals that it's different enough not to benefit from automatic application of any of the filters from the clips you've already color corrected. Because it's the same actor as in the reference shot, however, and because the clip is an insert shot (a close-up taken from the same angle as the wider two-shot), this is a perfect candidate for using Match Hue.

Before you do anything else, you need to adjust the contrast of this clip to match the reference clip. Otherwise, the Match Hue controls won't work as you expect.

3   Press Control–Shift–Up Arrow a few times to flip between the reference shot and the current shot, comparing the Waveform Monitor graphs.

4   Adjust the Blacks, Whites, and Mids sliders until the contrast ratio is identical, and the overall brightness in the midtones matches.

The adjustments will be fairly subtle, and you may see the value of relying on a comparison of the Waveform Monitor graphs. The yellow cast becomes a bit more pronounced when you brighten the image. You might find that making this adjustment visually would boost the brightness too high, because the color cast gives the illusion that the image is darker than it really is. The Waveform Monitor, however, provides a more objective reference.

With the contrast matched, you can use the Match Hue controls.

5   Click the Select Auto-balance Color button (the eyedropper).

A tooltip appears with the only instruction you'll ever need, an exhortation to choose a color to which you want to match the current clip—but neglecting to mention that it should be from a second reference clip.

It's important to understand that the Match Hue controls only make an adjustment to one of the three color balance controls, in an attempt to match a hue you select in a second reference image. The saturation and luma of the selection are ignored. You can indirectly control which color balance control is adjusted—the Blacks, Mids, or Whites—by the area of the reference image you choose with the eyedropper.

The first thing you need to do is to identify a frame in the reference image containing clear highlights, midtones, and shadows in the subject you want to match.

6   Move the playhead back to the already-corrected **Leads 2-shot** clip that you've been using as the reference image, and scrub through the clip until you find a frame of the woman in profile, with a clear highlight visible on her forehead. (The first frame of the image is good.)

7   Because the entire image needs to be matched to the reference clip, and the location is identical, begin by clicking a highlight in the woman's forehead with the eyedropper.

Immediately, two things happen. First, the Match Color indicator is populated with the hue you just selected.

Second, the Whites Select Auto-balance Color button turned green.

NOTE ▶ If the Whites Select Auto-balance Color button didn't turn green, and the Mids or Blacks Select Auto-balance Color button turned green instead, you didn't successfully pick a highlight. In the Match Hue controls, click the Select Auto-balance Color button again and try clicking the highlight in the reference image again.

At this point, the Match Hue controls are set up for you to make the match.

8   In the Color Corrector 3-way tab of the Viewer, click the now-highlighted Whites Select Auto-balance Color button.

9   Move the playhead back to the **Woman CU** clip, and scrub forward until you find a similar frame with the woman in profile that shows a clear highlight on her forehead matching the highlight you picked in the reference shot. (There's a suitable frame midway through the clip.)

10 Click the highlight with the eyedropper.

Immediately, the Whites color balance control is adjusted, and the highlights are rebalanced.

The success you have with the Match Hue controls is completely dependent upon which pixels you click with the eyedropper. If the result is significantly off, you probably mismatched a value in the whites with a value in the mids, or vice versa. For this reason, the Match Hue controls may sometimes appear to be more idiosyncratic than they really are. The bottom line is that you have to be very careful when choosing reference and match colors. If necessary, zoom in to the Canvas to better see which pixels you're selecting.

Next, you're going to match the hue of the blacks.

11 Reset the Match Hue controls by clicking the Reset Match Color button.

12 In the Match Hue controls, click the Select Auto-balance Color button (the eyedropper), move the playhead back to the first frame of the reference clip, and click the shadow of her cheek.

If you chose the right part of the image, the Blacks Select Auto-balance Color button turns green.

13 Move the playhead back to the clip you've been correcting, scrub back to the frame range showing the woman in profile, and then click the green Blacks Select Auto-balance Color button in the Color Corrector 3-way tab in the Viewer.

14 Click a shadow in her cheek that's similar to the first shadow you picked.

Again, you'll know you picked well if the image assumes a closer match. If it doesn't, you can click the Blacks reset button and repeat steps 11 through 14, picking different areas of the image.

It still seems that there's a bit of a yellow cast to her face. The even distribution of the cast would indicate that it's time to use the Match Hue controls on the mids.

15 Reset the Match Hue controls, and then click the Select Auto-balance Color button (the eyedropper). Move the playhead back to the first frame of the reference clip, and click a midtone color somewhere between the highlight and shadow.

If you've chosen well, the Mids Select Auto-balance Color button should turn green.

16 Return the playhead to the clip you've been correcting, scrub back to the frame range showing the woman in profile, and then click the green Mids Select Auto-balance Color button in the Color Corrector 3-way tab in the Viewer. Click a midtone on her forehead similar to the midtone you picked on the reference image.

Assuming you chose good colors, the Mids color balance control is adjusted, and the image should now be a good match to the reference image.

As you can see, the Match Hue controls pack a lot of functionality into a minimal interface. To use Match Hue well, you need to have a solid understanding of how the colors of an image fall into the blacks, mids, and whites. The same criteria you would use to decide whether to adjust the Blacks, Mids, or Whites color balance controls manually also apply to the use of the Match Hue controls. In fact, you can elect to use Match Hue for only one or two of the color balance controls, adjusting the others manually.

There's one other thing you should know. Once the Match Color indicator and Blacks, Mids, or Whites Select Auto-balance Color buttons are set, these controls are available from every color correction filter in your sequence. This allows you to make the same adjustment in several different clips. To return to using the Select Auto-balance Color buttons for making regular blacks, mids, and whites balances, you must click the Reset Match Color button.

Choosing and Balancing a Second Group of Images with Different Contrast

The second half of this scene focuses on two people on the other side of the room. Because it's in the same scene, you'll want to match the color in these clips to the color in the clips you've just corrected. The lighting in the **Guys_2-shot** seems to closely match the lighting in the insert close-up shots that accompany it. If you focus on matching **Guys_2-shot** to the original reference shot for this scene, there's a chance you might also be able to apply that single correction to the insert shots, saving yourself more time and effort.

In any event, it's always good to start with a shot that has as many of the people in the scene as possible. Because the skin tones of people in any scene will vary slightly, finding the ideal look for the wide shot will provide you with a reference for each close-up insert shot.

1   In the Timeline, move the playhead to the first frame of the **Leads 2-shot** clip you've been using as a reference shot, and set an In point in preparation for flipping between this clip and the next one you'll be correcting.

2   Move the playhead to the **Guys_2-shot**, and scrub through to find a representative image.

3   Add a Color Corrector 3-way filter to the **Guys_2-shot**. Open that clip into the Viewer, and click the Color Corrector 3-way tab.

4   Press Control–Left Arrow a few times to flip between the reference clip and the current clip, getting a sense of the contrast corrections you'll need to make.

In this clip, the black level matches the reference clip, and the mids and whites also seem to be in the ballpark, but there's a noticeable difference in brightness between the two images. The **Guys_2-shot** appears darker on average than the reference. A closer examination of the bottoms of the scopes reveals that the dense cluster of values representing the shadows in the current clip is much narrower than the same cluster of values in the graph of the reference clip.

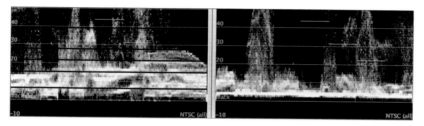

The shadows are being compressed without being crushed. This means that the shadows are so dark that you can't make out any detail, but there is detail there if you want to extract it. You can do this with a particular combination of settings.

NOTE ▶ It's also worth noticing that the highlights are considerably shinier in this shot than in the reference clip. This will be addressed by the same correction.

5   Drag the Mids slider to the right, stretching up the blacks so that the detail in the shadows approximately matches the reference image, while leaving the blacks pegged to the bottom.

Don't worry if this temporarily makes the highlights too bright; you'll address them in a second step. For now, it's important to pull some detail out of the shadows.

6   Drag the Whites slider to the left, compressing the whites and bringing down the top of the waveform graph to match the highlights in the reference clip.

The end result of this somewhat unconventional correction is that you've brought some detail out of the shadows, and minimized the shine on the actors' faces, by selectively reducing the contrast in the clip—while boosting the overall lightness.

7   Select and deselect the Enable Filter checkbox a few times to see a before-and-after comparison.

8   Use whatever techniques you prefer to match the color balance in the blacks, whites, and mids in the `Guys_2-shot` clip to the reference clip.

You can do this manually by dragging the color balance control indicators, or you can try to use the Match Hue controls, even though there is no clearly analogous character in this shot. As you work, see if you can determine which of the two men has the pinker skin tone.

When you're finished, the resulting adjustments in the color balance controls should look something like this:

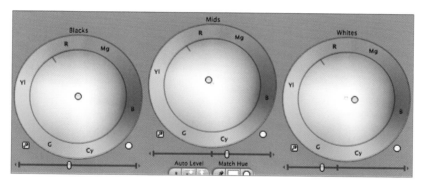

Dragging Filters onto Other Shots

In the preceding section, you corrected the two-shot so that you could apply the same correction to the two identically lit close-ups. One of the nice things about insert shots is that they're often lit with the same lighting setup. (Often, but not always, so don't count on it.)

If the lighting matches, your job is easy. If not, it's no big deal—you can still try using the first shot's settings as a starting point.

1   Make sure the color correction filter applied to the `Guys_2-shot` is open in the Viewer, and deselect the Enable Filter checkbox.

2   Press Control–Up Arrow and Control–Shift–Up Arrow a few times to compare the uncorrected waveforms of all three clips.

In this case, you've gotten lucky. The black point, white point, and mids distributions in the Waveform Monitor, and the color balance in the Parade scope, seem to match for all three shots.

This means you can copy the correction you've made to the **Guys_2-shot** clip to the other close-up shots. However, the distribution of clips is a little too awkward to use the Copy Filter controls, and besides, you want to apply this filter and its settings to three clips all at once. This is a good time to drag a filter from one clip to copy it to a selected group of other clips.

3   In the Viewer, select the Enable checkbox to turn the filter back on.

4   Click the **Guy_1_CU** clip, and then Command-click the next two instances of the **Guy_2_CU** clips.

5   With these clips selected in the Timeline, click the Drag Filter button, and drag the filter onto one of the selected clips in the Timeline.

6   When the clips highlight, release the mouse button to apply the filter to all three selected clips.

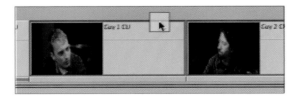

You're finished!

Lesson Review

1. What are your principal goals when color correcting a scene?
2. What do you want to look for when choosing a reference shot to begin correcting?
3. When matching two shots, what's the first thing you do?
4. What are the Copy Filter controls for?
5. What is the Parade scope best at showing?
6. What are the Show Edit commands for?
7. What kind of clips can you usually use the same color correction filter settings for?

Answers

1. To maintain consistency in shots that appear in the same scene, that occur at the same time, and in the same location.
2. A shot that's representative of the scene, perhaps a wide angle that shows the actors and the environment, and ideally a clip that has most of the actors within that scene onscreen at one time.
3. Match their contrast.
4. They copy a filter and its settings forward to other clips in the sequence.
5. Color balance in the blacks and whites.
6. Flipping back and forth between clips to compare them.
7. Clips with identical lighting, from the same angle of coverage.

4

Lesson Files	Color Book Files > Lesson Files > Lesson 04 > IntroToColor.fcp
Time	This lesson takes approximately 90 minutes to complete.
Goals	Send a sequence from Final Cut Pro to Color
	Navigate projects in the Color Timeline
	Tour the rooms of the Color interface
	Explore Color's task-based workflow
	Set preferences for your sequence
	Experiment with simple color adjustments

Lesson **4**

Introduction to Color

So far you've been working exclusively in Final Cut Pro, and it should be apparent that you can do a tremendous amount of color grading without ever leaving that program. However, Apple Color provides a whole new level of professional-quality grading tools that greatly increase the type and amount of changes you can make to your clips.

The myriad advantages of working in Color will become clear as you work through the remainder of the lessons in this book, but beware: Color looks and operates somewhat differently from the other programs in Final Cut Studio, and there is a moderately steep learning curve that you must traverse before you'll be comfortable using it.

But don't fear! This lesson will introduce you to this powerful program and will guide you through the most common workflow. You'll begin in Final Cut Pro, send your sequence to Color, tour the Color interface, familiarize yourself with Color's intuitive task-based workflow, set preferences for your sequence, and experiment with some simple adjustments while you get to know the most important tabs, or *rooms*, in the Color interface. Finally, you'll send your finished work back to Final Cut Pro, returning you to that familiar interface where you can choose how you want to output your completed project.

Setting Up Your Computer

First of all, ensure that your system meets the minimum hardware requirements for using Color effectively. To display images properly, Color requires at least the standard graphics card that is included in any Mac Pro, 24-inch iMac, 2.5 GHz or faster Power Mac G5 Quad, or 17-inch MacBook Pro. The graphics card must have at least 256 MB of VRAM for 32-bit rendering, and 512 MB of VRAM to work with RED or DPX files.

Also, to show the entire Color interface, your primary display must be set to a minimum resolution of 1680 x 1050 pixels. A lower resolution compromises the interface, shrinking interface text to an illegible size. For best results, you should use two monitors. When launching Color with two monitors, the software will automatically enable Dual Display Mode.

Additionally, to access Color's full functionality, you'll need a three-button mouse. This includes the Mighty Mouse that is provided with the desktop computers listed above, or any three-button, Macintosh-compatible mouse. To configure a three-button mouse, go to your computer's System Preferences, and in the Keyboard & Mouse pane set the left button to Primary Button, the right button to Secondary Button, and the middle button to Button 3.

Setting Up a Project

Before you start color correcting, you'll send a sequence of three clips from Final Cut Pro to Color. This is a common, real-world workflow that you're likely to use for all of your sequences.

1   In the Finder, navigate to Color Book Files > Lesson Files > Lesson 04.

2   Double-click **IntroToColor.fcp** to open the project in Final Cut Pro.

    The Leverage sequence should be open in the Canvas and Timeline.

3   Examine the clips in the sequence.

The sequence has already been partially graded using the Final Cut Pro Color Corrector 3-Way filter. There is a timecode generator filter applied to one of the clips, and a transition effect on one edit.

4   Double-click the first clip to open it into the Viewer.

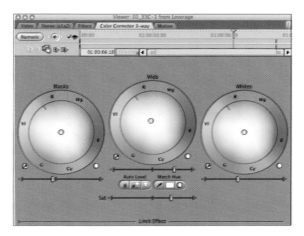

5 Click the Color Corrector 3-way tab to bring it forward.

6 Click the Visible checkbox on and off to see the effect of the filter.

The contrast has been significantly increased to give the shot much more tonal range.

NOTE ▶ Be sure to leave the filter turned on. These settings will be retained when the sequence is sent to Color.

7 Double-click the second clip in the sequence and click the Color Corrector 3-way filter in the Viewer.

8 Deselect the Visible checkbox to turn off the filter.

By turning off the visibility of the filter, its settings will be ignored when the sequence is sent to Color.

NOTE ▶ There are additional limitations to how the Color Corrector 3-way filter is translated into Color. If there is more than one filter applied in Final Cut Pro, only the last enabled filter will be applied, and any filter with Limit Effect settings applied will be ignored.

9 Play through the remainder of the sequence.

The rest of the clips all have various issues that you'll address in Color. The third shot has a color cast, the fourth shot is partially overexposed, and so on.

NOTE ▶ There is more to preparing a project for color grading than this simple example covers. For more information, you can search for "preparing your sequence to go to Color" in the Color Help menu.

10 Choose File > Send to > Color.

NOTE ▶ If the Send to > Color command is dimmed, verify that either the Canvas or Timeline window is active.

The Send To Color dialog appears.

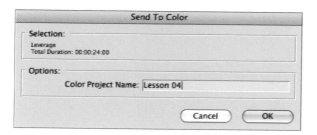

11 In the Color Project Name field, type *Lesson 04*, and click OK.

Color will open automatically, and an identical sequence will appear in the Color Timeline.

The Color project is created and saved in your Documents > Color Documents folder with a *.colorproj* extension.

NOTE ▸ That default location can be changed in the User Prefs tab of the Setup room.

TIP ▸ Alternatively, you could launch Color, create a new project, and import your clips, but sending to Color directly from Final Cut Pro maintains your editing decisions, and processes only the edited portions of the clips in your sequence. Additionally, many settings from Final Cut Pro's Motion tab and Color Correction 3-way filter will be translated directly to Color.

Final Cut Pro and Color communicate with each other through a language called *XML*. When you send your sequence from Final Cut Pro to Color, the software uses XML to track information about all of the video, audio, and effects editing you did in your Final Cut Pro sequence. Color reads this XML to re-create your sequence in the Color Timeline. If you have any audio clips, effects (except the Color Corrector 3-way filter), Motion projects or templates, or generators in your Final Cut Pro sequence, Color will temporarily ignore them or they'll appear as offline files in the Color Timeline. But because all of those elements are still described in XML, they will reappear when you return your rendered clips to Final Cut Pro.

TIP In Color 1.5, you can now import and grade still images and freeze frames sent from Final Cut Pro; just be sure any freeze frames are on track V1.

This communication between Final Cut Pro and Color saves you the time and trouble of having to import individual clips into Color before you can begin your color grading. Also, because the edited version of your footage is sent to Color, media management becomes easier because Color is working only with your used media.

Understanding the Eight Rooms: Color's Task-Based Workflow

The Color interface is divided into two windows: the Viewer and the Composer. In the Viewer window, you see your video image and the various scopes. In the Composer window, you'll find the Timeline, as well as all the color-correction controls, which are divided into eight tabs called *rooms*. Each room performs a different function in the color grading workflow, and they're arranged from left to right in the order in which you'll typically apply corrections. Additional tabs appear at the bottom of some rooms and access additional tools and controls. These tabs are also arranged in the order in which you would typically use them.

Viewer Window   Tabs of each of the eight rooms   Composer Window

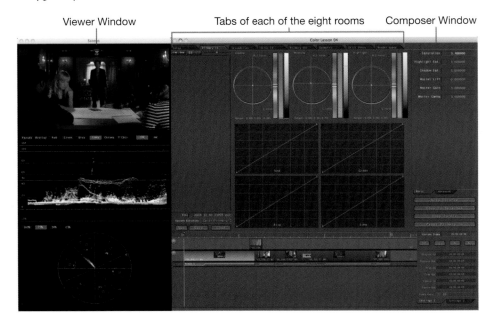

Setup Room

In the Setup room, you customize user preferences and project settings, such as interface colors, Auto Save, and Broadcast Safe specifications. The Setup room also contains areas in which you can view a sequential list or graphical display of all your shots, group shots together that will require the same corrections, and save entire grades for future use.

Primary In Room

In the Primary In room, you begin your color corrections, making adjustments that affect the entire image, such as contrast and color balancing.

Secondaries Room

In the Secondaries room, you apply color corrections to specific portions of the image, rather than to the entire image. For example, if you'd like to enhance only the color of a sky or a person's face, you would perform that work in the Secondaries room.

Color FX Room

In the Color FX room, you combine and apply imaging filters to create styled looks using a node-based system. Effects that you build in the Color FX room can be saved and applied to future shots.

Primary Out Room

The Primary Out room is almost identical to the Primary In room except that the final corrections made here are applied after the changes that were made in all the other rooms. Final tweaks can best be made in the Primary Out room.

Geometry Room

In the Geometry room, you adjust the size and position of the frame, draw custom shapes for isolating secondary color corrections, and motion-track shapes to moving objects.

Still Store

In the Still Store, you can save freeze frames of shots and use a split-screen display to compare them with other shots in the Timeline.

Render Queue

In the Render Queue, you choose which shots you want to render before returning the sequence to Final Cut Pro.

Navigating Your Sequence

Before you can utilize the powerful grading tools in Color, you have to understand which clips will be affected as you adjust Color's controls. Color's Timeline is visible no matter which room is active, and it provides an overview of your entire project. When you use the Send To Color command from Final Cut Pro, your entire Final Cut Pro Timeline is replicated in Color, including multiple layers, speed effects, and transitions with handles (although Color does not display or render transition effects).

Navigating Clip to Clip

The Color Timeline navigation is similar, but not identical, to the Timeline navigation in Final Cut Pro. Navigation buttons are located to the right of Color's main Timeline display.

1   Press Home to move the playhead to the beginning of the sequence.

2   Click the Next Clip button (or press the Down Arrow key) to jump from clip to clip.

3   Click the Previous Clip button (or press the Up Arrow key) to move backward one clip at a time.

4   Press the Left and Right arrows to step through individual frames of the current clip.

    TIP You can also drag the playhead in the ruler area to move to a new frame or to scrub through your clips.

    It's very important to understand that the Timeline playhead position determines which clip is affected by changes you make in any of the color correction rooms.

Moving from clip to clip will update the controls in the rooms to show the settings that are currently active for that clip. Active clips are displayed in a lighter color than the other clips.

NOTE ▶ Although you can select a clip in the Timeline, doing so will not activate it for grading.

5   Position the playhead over the first clip, **01_33C-1**.

Playing Clips

It is absolutely critical to preview your clips often during color grading work. Remember, you're working on moving images; while you make adjustments that might appear perfect on a single frame, other sections of the same clip may require different adjustments.

Color has two playback modes. In the default mode, playback loops around the current clip; in the alternate mode, playback moves from clip to clip across an entire sequence or a marked area (as it does in Final Cut Pro). You can verify which mode you're in by checking the positions of the In and Out points in the Timeline ruler.

The In and Out points indicate which area of the Timeline will be looped when you begin playback.

Although Play Forward and Play Backward buttons are present in the Timeline navigation area, it's far more intuitive to use the familiar keyboard shortcuts: spacebar, J, K, and L.

NOTE ▶ The J, K, and L shortcut keys work only when the Timeline is active.

1   Press L (or the spacebar) to start playback.

The clip plays and loops until you press K or press the spacebar a second time.

2   Choose Timeline > Toggle Playback Mode (or press Shift-Command-M).

The In and Out points move to encompass the entire sequence.

3   Press L or the spacebar again.

Now the sequence plays across multiple clips.

TIP ▶ You can set a custom playback range by placing manual In and Out points in the Color Timeline by pressing I and O.

Locking and Hiding Tracks

Color's Timeline includes a wide variety of editing tools, such as Ripple, Roll, Slip, Add Edit, and others that you probably use in Final Cut Pro. However, editing in Color will undermine your ability to round-trip between Color and Final Cut Pro.

Because of this, when a Color project is created using the Send to > Color command in Final Cut Pro (as previously described), Color automatically locks the Timeline tracks to prevent any accidental changes.

You can tell if a track is locked by the presence of a lock icon in the upper-left corner of the track. You won't be able to make any editorial changes to the clips on that track unless you unlock it.

Tracks can be locked or unlocked by right-clicking (or Control-clicking) the track and, from the shortcut menu, choosing Lock Track or Unlock Track.

Attempting to unlock a track triggers a warning about Final Cut Pro interoperability.

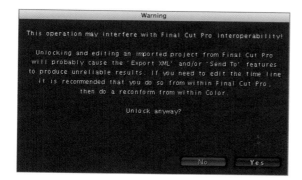

Also found in that shortcut menu is the Hide Track command. Hiding a track disables clips on that track from appearing in the Viewer or in the grading rooms. Applying this command is similar to clicking the Enable button in the Final Cut Pro Timeline track header area.

> **TIP** You can use this command to hide the clips on V2 or a higher track that are obscuring a clip on a lower track.

1 Right-click the bottom track in the Timeline.

2 From the shortcut menu, choose Hide Track.

The track is hidden and the Viewer displays black. Color correction cannot be applied to clips on a hidden track.

3   Right-click the track again, and from the shortcut menu, choose Show Track.

NOTE ▶ Hidden tracks can still be rendered, and when the sequence is returned to Final Cut Pro, tracks hidden in Color will not be hidden in Final Cut Pro.

Zooming In and Out

Although editing clips in the Color Timeline is a rare occurrence, it's common to zoom in and out to better see the boundaries of the clips you're grading.

1   Choose Timeline > Zoom In or press Command-+ (plus).

The Timeline zooms in.

2   Choose Timeline > Zoom Out or press Command-– (minus).

The Timeline zooms back out.

TIP ▶ Pressing Shift-Z zooms the Timeline to fit, just as in Final Cut Pro.

This is a familiar and easy way to zoom in and out on the Timeline. Color provides another way to zoom, but it's hidden in a nontraditional place. If you right-click the Timeline ruler and drag, Color enables a zooming function.

3   Right-click the ruler area of the Timeline and don't release the mouse button.

4   With the right mouse button still held down, drag right to zoom in and drag left to zoom out.

TIP ▶ If you're working with a multi-touch trackpad, you can use a pinch open gesture to zoom in and pinch close to zoom out. You can also scroll through the Timeline using a two-finger swipe gesture.

Resizing Tracks

In addition to zooming in and out on the temporal scale, you may also want to enlarge your Timeline tracks to see the thumbnails more clearly, or reduce the tracks to view more of them simultaneously.

Color tracks can be resized in a manner similar to the way track sizes are adjusted in Final Cut Pro.

1   Click the black line beneath the clip icons in the Timeline.

NOTE ▶ Don't click the bar beneath the grade tabs; this expands the area showing the grades and corrections applied to the clips.

2   Drag the line up or down to enlarge or shrink all Timeline tracks.

TIP ▶ Shift-drag to enlarge or shrink individual tracks.

Managing Grades in the Timeline

Below the tracks containing the video clips, the Timeline includes an additional area to display what grade is currently applied to the active clip. This is called the grade track.

1   Drag the line below the grade area to expand it and reveal the additional details present on the first clip.

The pink bar indicates that there are primary color correction settings applied to that clip. This is referring to the corrections made in Final Cut Pro and automatically imported into Color.

For more information on organizing and managing grades, see Lesson 8.

> **NOTE** ▶ The image above includes grades and correction settings that will not appear in your project file.

Exploring the Setup Room

In the Setup room, you'll set all of your project preferences. It's critical to choose project preferences early in the process to ensure that you'll see and render your shots properly.

The Shots Tab

1   At the top of the Composer window, click the Setup tab.

    The Setup room has its own set of tabs at the bottom, with which you can make additional modifications. The tabs are arranged left to right in the order in which you typically will use them.

2   At the bottom of the Setup room, click the Shots tab.

    The window displays a sequential list of all shots in the Timeline. Clicking a shot in the list also selects the clip in the Timeline.

The Grades Tab

1   At the bottom of the Setup room, click the Grades tab.

    Here is where you save favorite *grades* and quickly apply them to other shots in the Timeline. A grade contains settings from all of the other Color rooms. Room-specific settings also can be saved (within each room) and are called *corrections* rather than *grades*.

The Project Settings Tab

1   Click the Project Settings tab.

> **NOTE** ▶ On smaller screens, this tab's name may be abbreviated as Prjct Settings.)

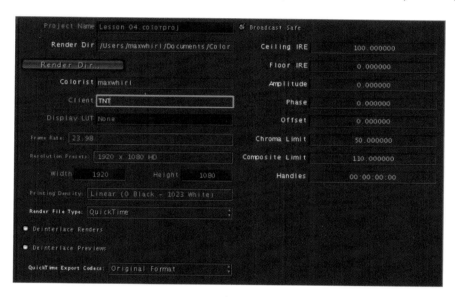

Here, you customize settings specific to the current project. Many of the settings deal with the technical specifications of video clips, but other fields are available to enter the names of the colorist and the client.

2   In the Colorist field, type your name; then press the Tab key to move to the Client field. Type *TNT* and press the Enter key.

The Broadcast Safe checkbox (in the top right of the Project Settings tab) is selected by default. This checkbox instructs Color to automatically ensure that your corrections don't exceed the signal specification standards of broadcast television.

Although this is helpful, it simply clips values that exceed the legal limit, which is not the most desirable way to limit the signal. For more specific control over your broadcast-safe settings, you typically use the Primary Out room, described later in this lesson.

The Messages Tab

1   Click the Messages tab.

The Messages tab displays warnings and errors to help you troubleshoot technical problems you may encounter while working with Color. Yellow messages are warnings and red messages are errors.

NOTE ▶ You should not see any warnings in your Messages tab.

The User Preferences Tab

1   Click the User Prefs tab.

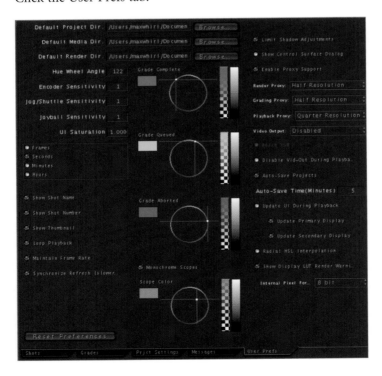

Here you customize application settings, such as interface preferences, and choose your media and project directories. The default Scope Color is orange. The grayscale gradient strip on the right controls the Scope Color's brightness. You may find that increasing the brightness improves the scopes' readability.

2   Drag the contrast slider up toward white.

The scopes in the Viewer window change from orange to white.

3   Deselect the Monochrome Scopes checkbox to turn it off.

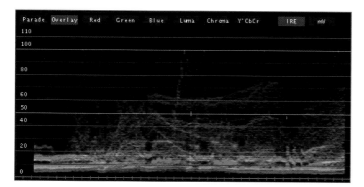

The scopes change to display colored traces in the Overlay, Parade, and Vectorscope. All other scopes turn white.

Applying Basic Grades

The Primary In room is where color correction begins. Here, you make adjustments that change the appearance of the entire image, such as fixing poor contrast and neutralizing unwanted color casts.

1   Click the Timeline ruler directly above the first clip.

Changes made in any room affect the clip currently under the playhead in the Timeline.

2   At the top of the Composer window, click the Primary In tab (or press Command-2).

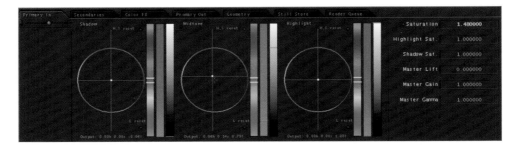

At the top half of the room are three controls that affect the hue and saturation of the shadows, midtones, and highlights of your current clip. These are called *color balance controls*.

These controls are effectively the same as the controls in Final Cut Pro's Color Corrector 3-way tab. The three gradient strips to the right of each wheel are sliders: The first two sliders are alternative controls for hue and saturation, and the third slider, called the Contrast slider, adjusts contrast.

The Contrast slider is equivalent to the slider beneath the wheels in Final Cut Pro.

Because in Final Cut Pro, this clip had a Color Corrector 3-way filter enabled, the settings in this room are automatically adjusted to match those filter settings as closely as possible.

3   To familiarize yourself with this interface, move your pointer over the Shadow color balance control, and drag the white dot (handle) in the center of the color balance control toward the edges of the wheel.

TIP▸ You can actually drag anywhere in the color balance control to move the white center point.

Notice how the darker areas of the image change color in the Viewer window.

4   Move your pointer over the rainbow gradient to the right of the Shadow color balance control.

This is the Shadow Hue slider. Notice the two cyan horizontal lines in this slider. These indicate the current shadow color. To the right of the Hue slider is the Saturation slider.

5   Drag the Saturation slider up and down.

Notice how the color you added to the shadows becomes more or less intense. As you drag, also notice how the color balance control's handle moves farther from and closer to the center of the balance control. This slider controls the amount of color that the balance control is adding to the image.

6   Drag the Hue slider up and down.

Notice how the color of the image changes. As you drag, also notice how the color balance control's handle moves in a circular way. Using the Hue slider is an alternative way to adjust one aspect of the color balance control handle position.

The rightmost slider, which looks like a grayscale gradient strip, is the Shadow contrast slider, which controls the black level of the image.

NOTE ▶ The cyan line at the bottom of the Shadow contrast slider moves up and down as you drag but it will remain pinned at the bottom even as you lower the slider's value below its starting value. Watch the image changing in the Viewer and the Waveform Monitor to see the effect of changing this slider.

There is one more important part of a color balance control: the reset buttons.

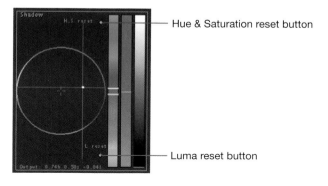

Hue & Saturation reset button

Luma reset button

The Hue and Saturation values (which form the coordinates for the handle in the wheel) are reset by clicking the cyan dot at the top right of the wheel. The contrast (or *luma*) value is reset by clicking the cyan dot to the bottom right of the wheel.

7   Click the Hue & Saturation reset button to reset the color balance control to its default settings.

> **NOTE** ▶ The Shadow contrast slider was adjusted in Final Cut Pro, so unless you made changes, you may not want to reset it now.

The Primary In room contains many other controls that you'll explore in more detail in the next few lessons. These controls allow you to manipulate your image in diverse ways, from the curves beneath the color balance controls, to the list of parameters in the upper right of the window, starting with Saturation.

▶ **RGB vs. YUV**

As an application, Color operates in a different color space from Final Cut Pro. If you're used to Final Cut Pro, you're used to a YUV (actually $Y\check{}C_bC_r$) color space in which contrast values are stored in a channel that is separate from color values. In a $Y\check{}C_bC_r$ space, adjusting the contrast has absolutely no effect on the color. In RGB, changing the contrast will change the color values, and vice versa. Similarly, in Color, the red, green, and blue channels are truly discrete, so (with rare exceptions) changing red values will have no actual influence on the other channels. (There may be a perceived change, but that's a different issue.)

In Final Cut Pro, stretching contrast (spreading out the white and black levels) tends to result in a perceived decrease in saturation (although saturation is mathematically unaffected). In Color, stretching contrast tends to increase saturation. This is sometimes a good thing, because it adds color richness at the same time that it increases the contrast, but you want to be aware of this in case the added saturation is not intended.

On this first clip, the Saturation value is displayed in yellow, indicating that it's set to a non-default value. In this case, that setting came from an adjustment to the Saturation slider in the Final Cut Pro filter.

8   Click the cyan dot to the left of the Saturation control.

The parameter is reset to its default value and the excess saturation is removed from the shot.

As you grade, you'll frequently want to compare your work with the original image.

9   Choose Grade > Disable Grading (or press Control-G).

All color correction adjustments are disabled. A message appears in the Timeline to warn you that grading is turned off.

Original   Graded

10   Press Control-G again to enable the grade and see the improvement that simple white and black level adjustments can make.

Viewing Your Images

Before we continue, it's important to learn a little more about the Scopes window. The Scopes window displays your current clip, as well as Color's video scopes. The video scopes measure various components of your video signal. A video signal consists of two parts: *luma* and *chroma*. You can monitor those parts discretely or in useful limited combinations using different scopes.

You can configure your window layout to view multiple scopes simultaneously. There are four scopes to choose from: the Waveform Monitor, the Vectorscope, the Histogram, and the 3D Color Space Scope. Each of these scopes provides vital information that might not be entirely apparent by looking at only the video image. Additionally, each scope contains options to limit or expand what information is displayed (such as displaying red, green, and blue channels separately, or viewing the scopes in different color spaces).

In single-display mode, the Viewer window shows the video on top and has two scope areas below.

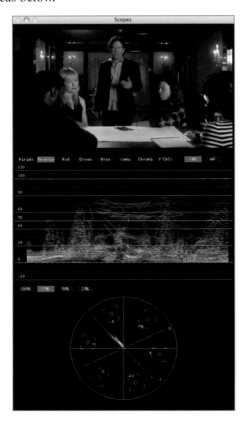

In dual-display mode, the Scopes window occupies an entire display and is divided into quadrants.

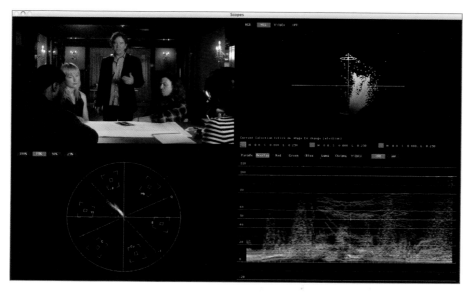

1 In the Scopes window, double-click the video image.

The video expands to fill the entire window.

2 Double-click again to return the video image to the small size.

You can also right-click the video to switch between full screen and quarter screen from the shortcut menu that appears.

Using the Waveform Monitor

The Waveform Monitor in Color works exactly like the same control in Final Cut Pro. It measures only the luma, or the brightness and contrast, of a video image. To comply with broadcast standards, the scope's reading, or graphs (sometimes called *traces)* should generally lie between 0 and 100 IRE (or 0 – 700 mV) on the Waveform Monitor.

TIP ▶ To switch the scale of the Waveform Monitor between IRE and mV, click the labels at the upper-right corner of the scope.

1 In the Timeline, click the ruler above the second clip (the one on track 2).

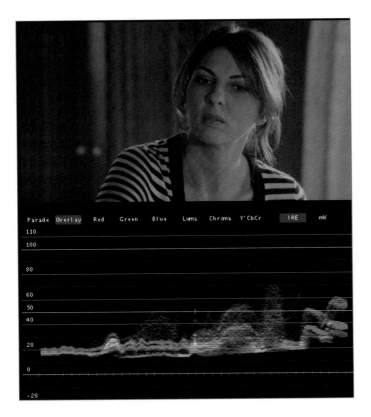

The Primary In room updates to show the settings for this clip. Even though this clip also had a Color Corrector 3-way filter applied in Final Cut Pro, you disabled the filter, so the settings here are all at their defaults.

As you learned in Lesson 1, the Waveform Monitor illustrates that this shot has a narrow tonal range with no true blacks and no bright highlights. Changes made to the contrast sliders (Shadow, Midtone, or Highlight) will be clearly visible in the Waveform Monitor.

In Color, this scope can display a wide range of different views depending on the label selected above the scope.

2   Click the Parade label.

The scope changes to a Parade display, showing the red, green, and blue channels separately.

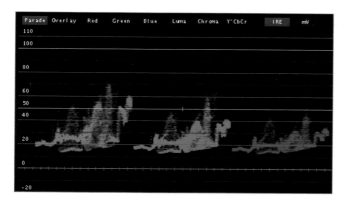

3 Click the Overlay label.

The scope shows the red, green, and blue channels but superimposes them on the same graph.

4 Click the Luma label.

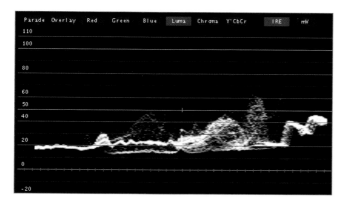

This screen shows just the luma values and is most similar to the default Waveform Monitor scope in Final Cut Pro.

5 Drag the Shadow, Highlight, and Midtone contrast sliders and observe the impact they make on the Waveform Monitor.

The Shadow contrast slider primarily affects the darkest areas at the bottom of the trace, the Highlight contrast slider primarily affects the brightest areas at the top of the trace, and the Midtone contrast slider adjusts the entire image.

Using the Vectorscope

Just like in Final Cut Pro, the Vectorscope in Color measures the chrominance, or hue and saturation, of a video image. The Vectorscope's overlay includes labels for the primary and secondary colors of light: red, magenta, blue, cyan, green, and yellow. When the graphs in the Vectorscope extend toward one of these labels, it indicates the presence of that color in the image. The saturation of that color is represented by the distance that the graph extends from the scope's center.

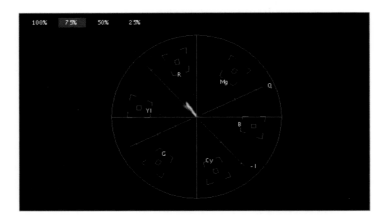

1   Drag the handle (white dot) in the Midtone color balance control to various positions.

As you drag, watch how the Vectorscope's graph moves toward the different color labels, indicating that you're adding that color to the image.

2   Click the Hue & Saturation reset button for the Midtone color balance control to cancel this adjustment.

Because many images contain only modest amounts of saturation, you may need to zoom into the Vectorscope to better see where the trace is located.

3   Click the 50% label above the Vectorscope to zoom in on the view.

   TIP ▶   If you're using a multi-touch trackpad, you can also pinch open to zoom in on the Vectorscope or pinch close to zoom out.

4   Click the 75% label to reset the scope to the default view.

▶ Trust Your Scopes

Our eyes are easily tricked and easily fatigued. You may think that an image seems overly dark or skewed toward a certain color, but that perception is often just in comparison to another shot, or in comparison to the way the shot looked before you began adjusting it.

The reason Color provides so many scopes and so many ways to view them is to give you something to trust in addition to your own eyes. Although it may take you additional time to grow comfortable reading the scopes, they offer an objective view of the exact mathematical values of the pixels in your image. No matter how accurate your grading reference monitor or computer display is, scopes will always be an essential tool in balancing shots, especially after a long day. Put your trust in them, though ultimately, there is no mechanical substitute for your own eyes.

Color includes two other scopes to aid you in your work, the Histogram and the 3D Color Space Scope. These scopes will be described in later lessons.

Using Auto Balance

Although Final Cut Pro provides a variety of tools to simplify the grading process, Color generally requires you to make all of your adjustments manually. There is one "magic button" you can sometimes use to automatically stretch the tonal range of a low-contrast image.

1   In the middle right side of the Primary In room, click the Auto Balance button.

Original   Graded

The image is adjusted so the darkest pixels are set to black and the brightest pixels are set to white. In Color, this is done on a channel-by-channel basis and any adjustments you made to the contrast sliders are automatically reset.

You'll learn more about using the Auto Balance control (and when it's not such a good idea) in Lesson 5.

Copying from One Clip to Another

Just like Final Cut Pro, Color contains many tools specifically designed to speed your work when grading scenes that use multiple similar shots. The simplest example of this is taking the adjustments you make on one clip and applying them to another.

In this project, the first and fifth shots are nearly identical, and so they will probably use the same settings.

1   Double-click the first clip to select it.

2   Choose Grade > Copy Grade > Mem-bank 1.

3   Click the fifth clip to select it.

4   Choose Grade > Paste Grade > Mem-bank 1.

    The grade is copied from the first clip to the fifth clip.

NOTE ▶ Any previously applied settings will be replaced.

5   Play the fifth clip to ensure that the new settings don't need any further adjustments.

Color allows you to store five different grades in memory while you're working. Lesson 8 covers this feature in more detail, as well as the myriad other tools used for managing grades in complex projects.

Performing Secondary Corrections

In the Secondaries room, you perform color adjustments on isolated portions of an image rather than on an entire image. You can limit the adjustments using vignettes (masks), keys, curves, and combinations of all three.

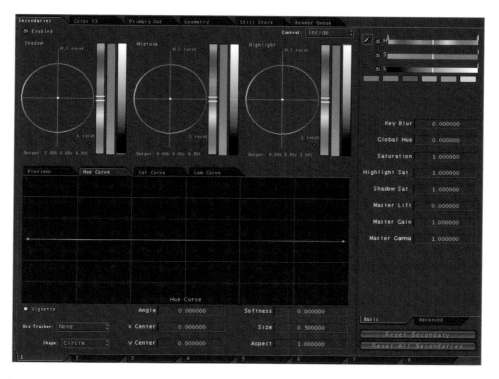

In this example, you'll create a simple vignette and limit a color adjustment to that masked area.

1   In the Timeline, position the playhead over the last clip in the sequence (**07-33D-1(A)**).

NOTE ► If you click a clip instead of moving the playhead, the clip will be selected, but corrections will still be applied to the clip under the playhead. Make sure the playhead is parked over the last clip.

If you examine the shot, you'll notice that the dark-skinned man on the left of the frame is very hard to see, so you'll create a vignette around that part of the image and brighten it without modifying the rest of the shot.

2   At the top of the Composer window, click the Secondaries tab.

The Secondaries room has color balance controls similar to the Primary In room, but the difference is that their effect will be limited to the portion of the image selected using the other controls in this room. In later lessons you'll learn how to utilize all the different controls in the room, but for now, you'll just learn the ones necessary to perform this effect.

3   Select the Enabled checkbox at the top of the window to turn on the Secondary correction.

4   Select the Vignette checkbox beneath the preview area in the middle of the window.

Several things happen. A yellow boundary appears in the Preview area displaying the shape and position of the vignette. Changes you make in the color balance controls at the top of the window will affect only the area inside the shape.

Also, the Viewer updates to show the image in black and white except for the area inside the vignette. This is called Desaturated Preview mode, and it's used to help you precisely position the shape.

> **TIP** ▶ You can't drag the shape in the Viewer; you must do it in the preview area in the center of the Secondaries room.

5   Click anywhere in the circle shape and drag it to the left edge until it encloses the man but not much more.

6   Drag the handles on the bounding box of the circle to stretch it vertically so it better matches the shape of the man's face.

7   To give the vignette a soft edge, position your pointer over the Softness parameter and middle-click, dragging upward to increase the setting to approximately 0.10.

TIP ► You can also middle-click and drag in the preview area to add softness to the shape.

The shape now has an inner and an outer circle to show the range of softness.

8   Drag the vignette so the outer edge aligns with the edge of the man's face.

On the right side of the preview area, three Matte Preview Mode buttons determine what is displayed in the Viewer window.

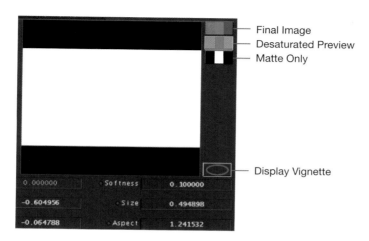

By default, the Desaturated Preview button is enabled.

9   Click the bottom button, Matte Only, to display your selected pixels as white in the Viewer.

10   Click the top button, Final Image, to see the final result of your correction.

     Because you haven't made any changes yet, the image in the Viewer looks just like the original.

11   Click the Display Vignette button to turn off display of the vignette in the Viewer.

     Now you're ready to make adjustments to the man's face using the color balance controls.

12   Drag the Highlight contrast slider upward to add illumination to the man's face.

     The change is limited to the area inside the vignette.

13   Select and deselect the Enabled checkbox at the top of the Secondaries room to see the results of the effect.

Original

Graded

The Secondaries room offers a multitude of additional controls, both for controlling the selection, and for modifying that selection to create different effects. Color allows for eight different secondaries on any single clip.

Employing Color FX

In the Color FX room, you stylize shots using filters and effect presets. This room contains three panels. On the left is the Node List, which contains a wide variety of filters and preset effects. The open area in the middle of the Color FX room is the Node View, where you can string together filters to create complex and unique effects. The right section contains two tabs: Parameters, where you adjust selected filters, and Color FX Bin, which stores preset collections of nodes.

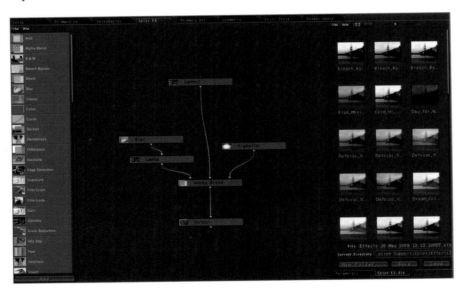

NOTE ▶ By default, your project will not have any nodes or presets showing.

1   If it's not already active, in the Timeline, double-click the last clip in the sequence (**07-33D-1(A)**).

2   At the top of the Composer window, click the Color FX tab.

3   In the Node List, double-click the Duotone node.

By default, the Duotone node tints your image sepia. In the Parameters tab, there are Light Color and Dark Color controls, employing the familiar color balance control interface.

4   Experiment by adjusting these controls, and observe how your image is affected in the Viewer.

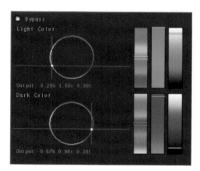 

5   At the top of the Parameters tab, click the Bypass button to disable the node's effect.

6   Click the Color FX Bin tab.

In this bin, you can find a variety of effects presets to perform common effects, such as bleach bypass, day for night, and myriad dream looks.

7   Double-click Bleach_Bypass_Adjustable (the first one in the list).

The preset automatically applies a tree of nodes to create the overall effect.

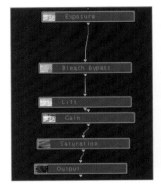 

NOTE ► Applying a new preset replaces the existing nodes in the Node View.

8 Double-click Blue_Movie_Look, and notice that a different tree of nodes is applied.

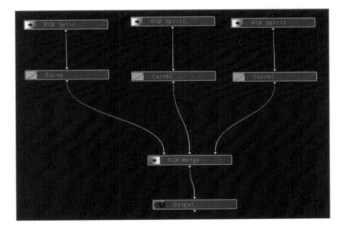

9 In the Node View, drag to select all the nodes in the tree, and press Delete to remove them.

Applying Final Touches

The fifth tab activates the Primary Out room. The controls there are nearly identical to those of the Primary In room; however, the effects are applied after the effects in the other rooms are applied. For example, if you wanted to apply several secondary corrections to parts of your image and then make a single global change to the results, you would make that global change in the Primary Out room.

One of the most common uses for the Primary Out room is to make adjustments that address possible violations of broadcast signal requirements. Although the Broadcast Safe setting in the Project Settings tab of the Setup room clips any signals that exceed the legal limit, for the best results you'll want to rein in such excesses gradually to eliminate possible artifacts or strange color shifts generated by the automatic clipping.

Because changes you make in the Primary In, Secondaries, and Color FX rooms can combine and affect each other, limiting and correcting for broadcast requirements is best done after those other adjustments have been completed. The Primary Out room is the last image processing stop prior to rendering, making it the ideal room for such work.

1   Position the playhead over the fourth shot (the third shot on track 1).

Lamp is being clipped at 100 IRE

If you examine the Waveform Monitor, you'll see that the bright lamp is being clipped, removing all detail from that bright spot. The clipping occurs because the Broadcast Safe checkbox is selected in the Project Settings tab.

2   Press Command-0 to switch to the Project Settings tab.

3   Click the Broadcast Safe checkbox in the upper right to deselect it.

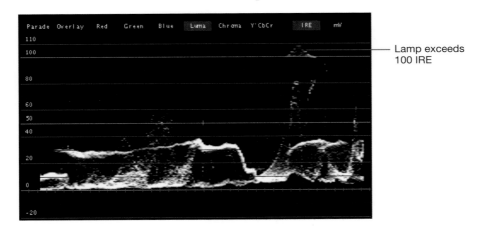

Lamp exceeds 100 IRE

Notice that now the Waveform Monitor shows the lamp area exceeding the legal limit.

4   Click the Primary Out tab to open that room.

The Primary Out room looks nearly identical to the Primary In room.

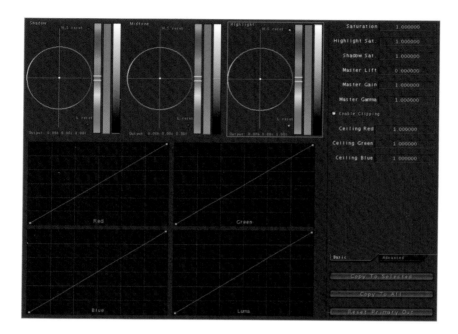

5 Drag the Highlight contrast slider down until the Waveform Monitor shows the lamplight safely below 100.

> **TIP** ▶ You may also adjust the Midtone and Shadow contrast sliders slightly to keep the overall luma the same; just be sure to keep the brightest spots under 100.

This allows the subtle shading within the lamp to remain visible so that the bulb in the center is brighter than the edges, while still ensuring that the whole image is broadcast safe.

NOTE ▶ Depending on your monitor type and configuration, you may not see a visible change in the Viewer window. Trust the Waveform Monitor as an indicator of the relative white values in the image.

Panning and Scanning

In the Geometry room, an image can be resized and repositioned for a pan and scan effect. Also, custom shapes can be drawn here to isolate areas in the image prior to performing secondary corrections in the Secondaries room.

1   At the top of the Composer window, click the Geometry tab.

The bounding box around the image in the large preview area indicates the visible area of the frame. Inside that box, there are two additional boxes to indicate action-safe and title-safe boundaries. By changing the bounding box size and position, you can scale the image, and create pan and scan effects.

2   Drag any of the corners of the bounding box to adjust the size of the frame.

3   Drag inside the bounding box to adjust the position of the frame.

4   Drag the edges of the bounding box to adjust rotation.

The Viewer shows the image following your adjustments. In this example the shot has been resized from an MCU to a CU; also the bright lamp has been cropped out of the frame.

The Pan&Scan tab on the right displays the settings numerically, allowing you to enter specific values.

The Geometry room is also where you create custom shapes for limiting corrections in the Secondaries room, and where you control trackers so Color can move masks and corrections along with an object as it moves within the frame. These features will be covered in extensive detail in later lessons.

Utilizing Still Stores

In the Still Store room, you can compare different frames in the Timeline. For example, you may want to perform a before-and-after comparison between an original unmodified shot and its color-corrected version. Or, if the same object appears in two different shots, you may want to compare them to maintain shot-to-shot consistency.

1   At the top of the Composer window, click the Still Store tab.

    For this introduction to the Still Store, you'll correct the color cast on shot 3 by comparing it to clip 1.

    First you must park the playhead on the frame you wish to compare to.

2   Position the playhead near the end of the first clip, where the standing man is close to the table.

3   Choose Still Store > Store (or press Control-I).

The frame is saved as a freeze frame, and a thumbnail appears in the Still Store room.

4   Click the Still Store tab at the top of the Composer window, or press Command-7.

5   At the top of the Still Store, drag the Icon Size slider to adjust the size of the thumbnail.

6   If the stored image does not appear in the viewer, press Control-U to activate the Still Store.

7   Move the playhead to the third clip (the second clip on track 1).

The right side of the viewer updates to show the new frame, while the left side shows the stored still. You can see the actor's face clearly in both frames.

It's very obvious that the colors don't match, but it may be less obvious how to fix them. First you must identify the nature of the color cast. This is most easily identified in the Vectorscope.

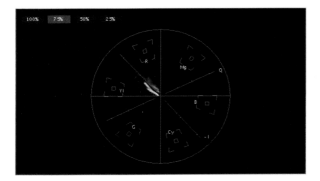

You can see two distinct bars, which show the color values for each half of the screen.

8   Press Control-U to turn off the still store.

Now, only the one (left) trace remains visible, and you can see that it's shifted toward yellow.

9   Press Control-U again to turn the still store back on.

Your goal is to move the trace from the yellow clip on top of the trace representing the wide shot, so that they have the same tone.

10 Press Command-2 to open the Primary In room.

11 Drag the handle in the Midtone color balance control away from yellow (from the left to the right) until the traces converge and the Viewer shows that the skin tones are an approximate match.

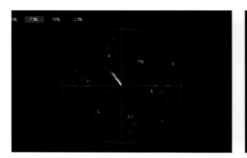 

TIP Do not make the mistake of dragging the Midtone color balance handle toward red or magenta. Even though the wide shot appears to have more red and magenta than the close-up, the Vectorscope shows you that the close-up has a range of colors, but that they're all skewed uniformly toward yellow. When fixing a cast, think in terms of removing the color you don't want rather than adding the color you do want.

In the Still Store, you can control the position and direction of the split.

12 Click the Still Store tab.

13 Experiment with the settings in the right side of the window to modify the way that the split screen is drawn.

TIP ▶ You can also control the shape and position of the split screen by manually adjusting the Transition and Angle settings.

14 Deselect the Display Loaded Still checkbox (or press Control-U) to disable the split-screen effect in the Viewer.

Introducing the Render Queue Room

In the Render Queue room, you decide which shots you want to render before returning your sequence to Final Cut Pro.

1 At the top of the Composer window, click the Render Queue tab.

2 At the bottom of the Render Queue room, click the Add All button.

Each shot is added to the queue.

3 Click the Start Render button.

As Color renders, it creates new media files on your disk with your rendered corrections. These files are saved in the format and to the destination that you specify in the Project Settings tab of the Setup Room.

4 Once rendering is complete, choose File > Send to > Final Cut Pro.

Final Cut Pro comes to the foreground, and a new sequence is created with the additional label *"from Color."*

5   Double-click this sequence to open it.

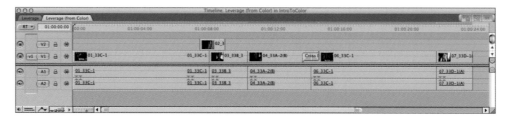

The sequence looks identical to the original. Even though the clips retain their original names, they now point to the new files created in Color.

6   Right-click the first clip in the sequence and choose Reveal in Finder.

Color always names files by the order in which they appear in the sequence. In Lesson 13, you'll learn more about how to manage Color's output files as well as how to make additional changes in Color and have them propagate back to Final Cut Pro.

7   Switch back to Final Cut Pro.

In the new sequence, the color correction filter that was applied to the first two clips is no longer applied, but the timecode filter on the fifth clip is still there.

8   Double-click the fourth clip and click the Motion tab.

You applied changes to the Pan and Scan settings for this clip in Color. Rather than rendering those modifications into the file, Color rendered the file at its original size, and the scale settings were applied in Final Cut Pro.

Your show is ready to output to tape, to Compressor, or the output method of your choice. The round trip between Final Cut Pro and Color is complete.

Lesson Review

1. In which room are project-specific settings configured?

2. How can you move a sequence from Final Cut Pro to Color?

3. To apply a correction to an isolated portion of an image, which room should be used?

4. What is the difference between the Primary In and Primary Out rooms?

5. What is the difference between a node and a Color FX preset?

6. In which room do you create pan and scan effects?

7. What are the purposes of the three vertical strips located next to the color balance controls?

8. True or false: When making an adjustment to the Highlight contrast slider, the darkest areas of the image are somewhat affected.

9. True or false: The Still Store is where freeze-frame effects are made.

10. How do you choose which clip is affected by the color correction rooms?

Answers

1. The Setup room.

2. In Final Cut Pro, choose File > Send to > Color.

3. The Secondaries room.

4. The Primary Out room applies its corrections after the other effects have already been applied.

5. A node is an individual effect module. A Color FX preset is a collection of nodes, prearranged to create a certain effect.

6. In the Geometry room.

7. The three strips are sliders for changing the hue, saturation, and contrast.

8. True.

9. False.

10. In the Timeline, double-click the clip, or position the playhead over that clip.

5

Lesson Files   Color Book Files > Lesson Files > Lesson 05 > Primary_Grading.colorproj

Time   This lesson takes approximately 75 minutes to complete.

Goals   Familiarize yourself with the Primary rooms

Auto-balance clips, and learn when not to use auto-balancing

Adjust lift, gain, and gamma using contrast sliders

Correct color shifts using color balance controls

Use curves to remove color casts

Set complex curve settings to control contrast

Combine controls to create complex effects

Primary Grading

When most people think of color correction, they think of a few common tasks: fixing incorrect white balance or removing an unwanted color cast, matching skin tones in two separate shots, or controlling contrast levels. Although these represent only a sampling of color grading tasks, all of them fall into the category of *primary* color correction. Color can perform all these tasks (and quite a few more) in one of its Primary rooms.

Primary color correction means making changes that affect the entire image—which covers the vast majority of color grading work. Color's Primary rooms (Primary In and Primary Out) contain a variety of controls and tools that facilitate primary corrections with both precision and flexibility.

In this lesson we'll repeat some of the exercises you performed in Lessons 1 and 2, but with different footage, and using Color instead of Final Cut Pro. Of course, every shot is unique and requires a unique approach. Because Color has many different ways to perform similar operations, you'll learn how and when to employ the different tools for performing these common grading tasks.

Exploring the Primary Room

The Primary room has four main sections.

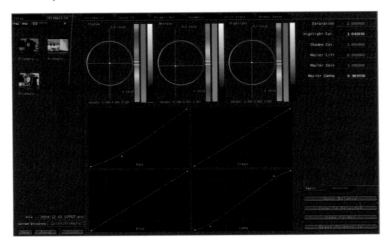

The bin on the left contains saved primary corrections, giving you quick access to settings that you may wish to reuse.

> **NOTE** ▶ Your project may not have any saved primary corrections yet, so your screen may look different from the image above.

In the upper-middle section are the three familiar color balance controls , where you can adjust the shadows, midtones, or highlights of your clip independently. These wheels may be the most versatile and commonly used controls in the entire program. They allow you to modify the color balance and contrast for each range of luma in the image. You've already used these controls in Lesson 4, and used the very similar controls in the Final Cut Pro Color Corrector 3-way filter in the earlier lessons.

Below the color balance controls are curve controls for the red, green, and blue luma channels, along with an overall luma channel curve control.

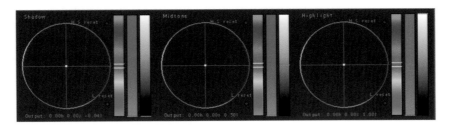

These controls offer multiple ways to affect the overall color of your video based on individual color channels rather than the luma ranges governed by the color balance controls. The Luma curve control lets you make detailed and complex adjustments to the contrast of the image.

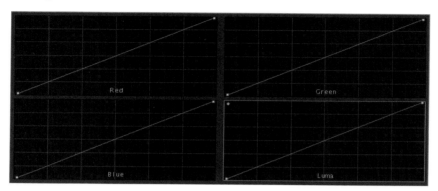

Although Final Cut Pro's Color Corrector offers a single saturation slider, Color provides more precise and flexible tools for manipulating image saturation.

On the right side of the Primary Room are the Basic and Advanced tabs. The Basic tab includes Saturation controls for the midtones, highlights, and shadows.

The lower three controls are similar to the contrast sliders in the color balance control section. While the Shadow contrast slider raises the black point while pinning the white point in place, the Master Lift parameter raises the levels of the entire image, effectively "lifting"

the waveform in the Luma scope. (This works the way the Shadow contrast slider works when Limit Shadow Adjustments is disabled in the User Prefs tab in the Setup room.) Master Gain affects the contrast of the highlights (leaving the black point alone), and Master Gamma affects the contrast of the midtones. Although the contrast sliders provide visual feedback, these controls offer the ability to enter a specific numerical value.

The Advanced tab allows you to independently control the lift, gain, and gamma of the red, green, and blue channels. The Printer Point controls here simulate the effect of exposing different colored lights to film in traditional color timing.

As you can see, there is quite a bit of overlap in the different controls in the Primary room, and it's easy to offset the effect of one control by manipulating another. Although this may seem confusing, the overlap is actually the key to mastering the art of grading. By applying a strong effect with one control, and then mitigating some of the effect with another, you can perform delicate and subtle effects, finessing your images with amazing precision.

Using the Auto Balance Control

Because it's common to begin correcting an image by adjusting its white and black points, Color provides a one-button solution intended to simplify the process. In fact, Color's *auto balance* evaluates the red, green, and blue channels independently, discretely setting the brightest and darkest points of each channel. Often this results in a simple dramatic improvement to your shot as you saw in Lesson 4.

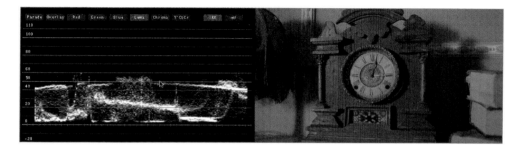

1   Open Lesson Files > Lesson 05 > **Primary_Grading.colorproj**.

2   If your media does not appear in the Timeline, the media is offline. Choose File > Reconnect Media and navigate to Lesson Files > Lesson 05 > Media. Click Choose.

3   Make sure the first clip (**SHOT02_CLOCK**) is active and click the Auto Balance button (located below the tabs at the bottom of the Saturation panel).

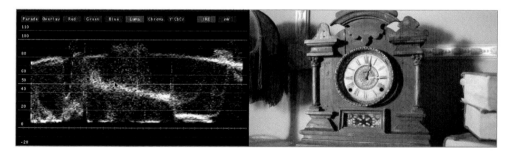

Voilà! The contrast is automatically stretched so the darkest pixel in the frame is set to pure black and the whitest pixel is set to pure white. The image looks almost like a film of grime has been wiped off the screen.

At first glance, Auto Balance may appear to be an amazing fix-it tool that you'll automatically want to apply to all your clips, but there's a catch—several of them, actually.

First, the Auto Balance feature looks only at the current frame. Although that frame may look great, other parts of the shot may still need fixing, or may have been negatively affected by that adjustment.

Additionally, if an image has black letterbox margins, as many video clips do, the Auto Balance will see the true black in the margin and won't change the black level in the image, even if it desperately needs it.

4   With the Timeline active, press the Down Arrow key to advance to the second clip in the sequence (Letterbox).

The image is somewhat washed out. The Waveform Monitor shows that the contrast can be stretched in both directions (the darkest blacks are up at 20 IRE, and the brightest highlights are at around 92-93 IRE), but if you look closely, you'll see the solid line at exactly 0% indicating the letterbox.

5   In the Primary In room, click the Auto Balance button.

The letterbox fools the Auto Balance control, and the blacks are not adjusted at all. The image still looks washed out, although the white levels now have been boosted to exactly 100%.

Auto Balance can make the same mistake for the white levels. If there's a one-pixel highlight in someone's eye or a burned-in timecode appears in the clip, Auto Balance will leave the white level unchanged.

6   To correct the black levels manually, drag the Shadow Contrast Slider down until the darkest traces (on the right side of the Waveform Monitor) reach 0 IRE.

Furthermore, although auto-balancing may be a quick fix, it's no replacement for manually customizing your contrast. Even the clock shot arguably looked better before the auto balance was applied and stripped it of the pale orange cast that gave the shot its unique period look.

Plus, even though Auto Balance does perform a quick-and-easy contrast adjustment—which may be an improvement in many shots—you didn't send your project to Color for quick-and-easy fixes. You came for fine control over every aspect of your images. For that reason, professional colorists rarely use the Auto Balance control.

Resetting Auto Balance

You may have noticed that when you click the Auto Balance button, none of the controls visible in the Primary In room moved to effect the color change. (Actually, if you have any settings applied in the Primary In room when you activate Auto Balance, they'll all be reset to their defaults.) The controls that are modified when you use Auto Balance are hidden in the Advanced tab.

Red Lift	-0.002956
Green Lift	-0.002956
Blue Lift	-0.002956
Red Gain	1.043452
Green Gain	1.090861
Blue Gain	1.074653
Red Gamma	1.000000
Green Gamma	1.000000
Blue Gamma	1.000000
Printer Points Calibration	7.800000
Printer Points Red	25
Printer Points Green	25
Printer Points Blue	25

To remove the effect of the Auto Balance, you need to reset each of the number sliders by clicking the cyan dot beside each control.

TIP You can identify when a number slider has been moved from its default setting because the numbers are shown in yellow. At the default, they appear white.

Rather than making six clicks, you can remove the Auto Balance effect by clicking Reset Primary In (below the Auto Balance button). This restores all controls in the Primary In room to their default settings.

This also resets the Shadow Contrast slider adjustment made in step 5.

Grading with the Color Balance Controls

The color balance controls allow you to independently manipulate the shadows, midtones, and highlights (called *tonal ranges*) of an image. However, each range has significant overlap (as indicated in the following diagram). Because of this overlap, changing a setting in one range will affect the others, but to a varying extent.

Red: Shadow control influence, Blue: Highlight control influence,
Green: Midtone control influence

Furthermore, the controls corresponding to each range of tonality can adjust both the color balance and contrast for that range.

Using the Contrast Sliders

Because you always begin by adjusting contrast, first you'll explore the contrast controls in each of the ranges.

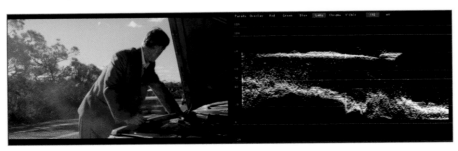

1   With the Timeline active, press the Down Arrow key to advance to the third shot in the sequence (**RHRN_SHOT01_EXTCAR**) to make it the active clip.

2   Drag the Shadow contrast slider up and down.

Your pointer disappears when you drag, but the darkest areas of the image get darker or brighter. You can also see a cyan line in the slider move up when you drag above the default value.

▶ **Limit Shadow Adjustments**

The Shadow contrast slider has a different effect when you change the Limit Shadow Adjustments setting in the User Prefs tab of the Setup room.

1   Choose Color > Preferences (or press Command-comma).

The Setup room is brought to the front with the User Prefs tab active.

2   In the upper-right corner of the window, deselect Limit Shadow Adjustments.

3   Press Command-2 to switch back to the Primary In room.

4   Raise the Shadow contrast slider, and observe the Waveform Monitor.

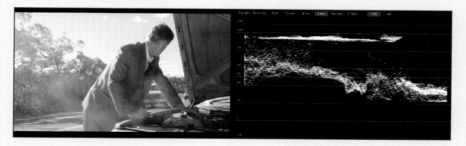

Now, the entire luma component moves uniformly up or down as you drag.

5   Press Command-1 to switch back to the Setup room.

Continues on next page

▶ **Limit Shadow Adjustments** *(continued)*

6   Click the Limit Shadow Adjustments checkbox to reselect it.

7   Switch back to the Primary In room and move the Shadow contrast slider again.

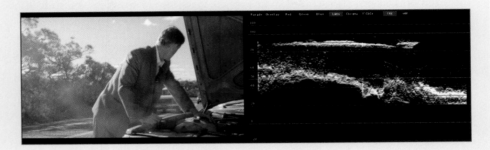

In this setting, dragging the Shadow contrast slider weights the effect toward the shadows.

NOTE ▶ Changing the Limit Shadow Adjustments setting affects all corrections in the project. Corrections made using the Shadow Contrast slider on any clips in the project will suddenly produce different results.

When the Limit Shadow Adjustment setting is turned off, this effect is called *lift* because it uniformly lifts the overall luma of the image. The other contrast sliders have nifty names too: The Midtone contrast slider adjusts the image's *gamma*, and the Highlight contrast slider adjusts the image's *gain*.

By manipulating an image's lift, gamma, and gain, you can exert precise control over the tonality of your image and correct a variety of exposure problems, as well as create many different *looks* to support or emphasize the content of the scene.

8   Click the Reset Primary In button in the lower-right corner of the room to remove any miscellaneous changes you may have made.

Correcting Contrast in a Shot

Proper contrast settings require that the darkest areas of the image be set at true black, and the brightest areas at true white. This is what the Auto Balance setting does, but now you'll do it manually.

1   Lower the Shadow contrast slider until the lowest traces on the Waveform Monitor (representing the darkest part of the man's head and the dark shadows in the car's engine compartment) just reach the 0% line.

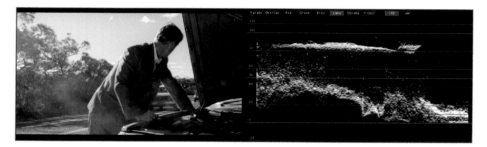

2   Raise the Highlight contrast slider until the highest traces in the Waveform Monitor (representing the clouds and the highlights on the man's back) reach 100%.

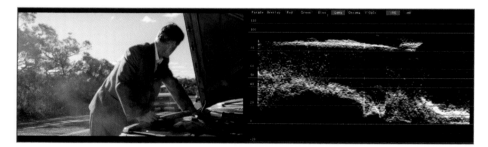

You've manually done what the Auto Balance control does, but this is just the beginning. The blacks are true black and the whites are true white, but the distribution of grays can be adjusted in myriad ways.

3   Lower the Midtone contrast slider slightly.

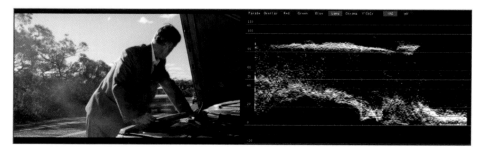

This appears to darken the image, giving it a richer look, but doesn't lower the white point, so overall exposure still appears correct.

To reinforce this look, you can *crush* the blacks further, reducing the detail in the darkest shadows, while still leaving the highlights unaffected.

4   Lower the Shadow contrast slider a bit more, until the details disappear in the trees at the lower left.

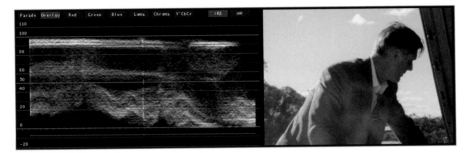

The image now has a good range of contrast levels (the contrast *ratio*), with enough richness in the darks to give it a dramatic, high-contrast look.

▶ **Compare and Contrast**

Contrast plays a huge role in the way a viewer interprets a scene. First of all, our eyes are vastly more sensitive to subtle changes in contrast than to nuances of hue or saturation. There's a fairly obvious evolutionary explanation for that, as hunting (and being hunted) requires recognizing prey (or predators) amidst complex backgrounds such as forests or meadows. In fact, at night, the cones in our eyes (which detect color) become mostly ineffective, and the rods (which detect luma) take over.

We "like" high-contrast images because they make it easier for our eyes to make sense of what they're looking at. When there are a lot of subtle gradations of gray it's hard to see the distinctions, so our brains literally have to work harder to interpret what we're seeing. This translates into our emotions too; it's far easier to decide between two extreme choices than between a number of subtly different options.

You can use this bit of physio-psychology to affect your audience in a deliberate way. If you've got a high-stakes scene where the difference between the character's

▶ **Compare and Contrast** *(continued)*

actions means life or death, choosing a high-contrast look will serve to amplify or reinforce the content of the scene. Similarly, if your story or scene is about the subtleties of a complex situation, you might opt for a lower-contrast look to put your viewers in the same emotional state as the protagonist you want them to identify with. Of course, you can also invert these effects to create deliberate dissonance and confound convention.

Adjusting Color

When the overall contrast is set to your liking, you can begin modifying the color values. The color balance controls allow you to set the hue and saturation values independently by using the sliders, or you can adjust them at the same time by dragging the handle in the center of the balance control.

Although contrast values are most easily viewed in the Waveform Monitor (especially when it's set to monochrome), color values can be viewed in the Vectorscope, or in the Waveform Monitor when it's set to Parade or Overlay (and the scopes are not set to monochrome scopes in the User Prefs tab of the Setup room).

1   In the Waveform Monitor, click the Parade button.

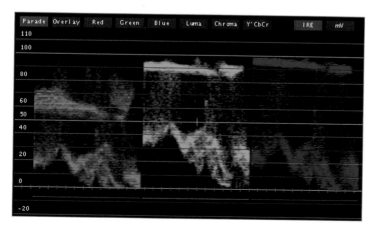

The three color channels' relative chroma values are displayed side by side.

2   In the Waveform Monitor, click the Overlay button.

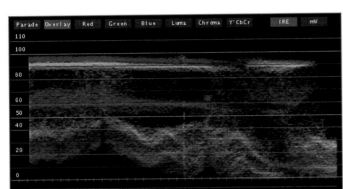

The three waveforms are all superimposed over the same graph.

In the Viewer, you can see that this image has a blue-green hue to it. This is reinforced in the Waveform Monitor; the peak of the red channel is much lower than the blue and green levels. This makes sense, as the main colors in the shot are the blue sky, the green trees, and the greenish suit the man is wearing.

The Vectorscope also gives you important information about the distribution of colors in the shot. Although the large concentration of traces near the cyan target makes sense, given the abundance of sky in the shot, you might also notice that the entire bulk of traces is shifted off-center toward the cyan and green targets.

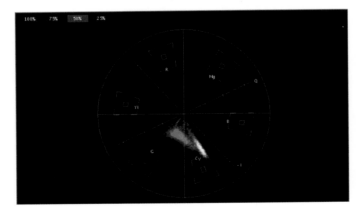

This is a great clue as to how to fix the image.

3   In the Midtone color balance control, click the handle (the white dot) and drag
it around.

> **TIP** ▶ You can actually drag anywhere in the balance control to move the white
> center point.

As you drag farther from the center point, you add more saturation and the angle
you drag toward determines the hue you assign. Adjusting the color balance controls
adds a color *influence* to your image. All of the color values in the range you adjust
are moved toward that color. This is different from tinting an image when a uniform
color cast is added to the image.

4   Drag the handle away from the green/cyan targets (toward red/magenta) while watching the Vectorscope, and keep dragging until the scope traces are more centered.

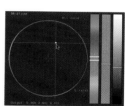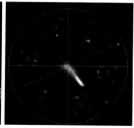

As you make this adjustment, you'll see that the whole image begins to improve and
look more naturalistic, throughout the duration of the shot.

Original

Corrected

Rather than going further with this one clip, move on to the next clip, which provides
similar challenges that you'll solve in a different way.

5 Click anywhere in the Timeline to make it active, and then press the Down Arrow key to move to the next clip.

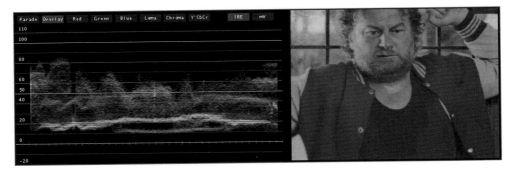

This clip has a cool overall look, which is appropriate for the intense dramatic nature of the scene, so you wouldn't necessarily want to eliminate that. But the skin tones are a bit too pallid and could use a little warming. Additionally, the contrast is very limited, and should be stretched to give the image more depth and intensity.

6 Starting with the contrast, lower the Shadow contrast until the lowest red traces reach 0% in the Waveform Monitor.

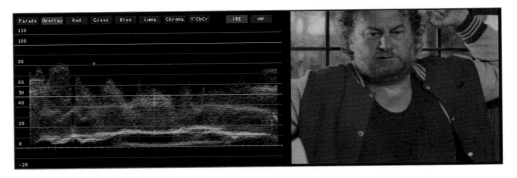

This corrects the black level just like you did with the previous clip.

7 Next, raise the Highlight contrast until the range at the upper left just begins to touch 100% in the Waveform Monitor.

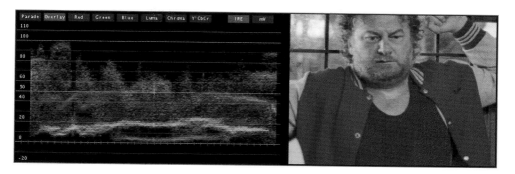

As always, fixing the contrast immediately provides a significant improvement to the image. Next you want to warm up the skin tones by adding red-orange to them, but without affecting the rest of the image.

You can do this very quickly right in the Primary In room. The skin tones are mostly in the highlights and midtones of the image, so you can begin by modifying those ranges.

8 Drag the Midtone color balance control handle slightly toward red/orange (to about 11 o'clock).

9 Drag the Highlight color balance control handle slightly in the same direction.

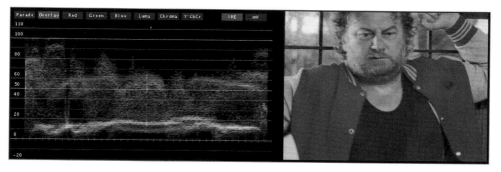

This succeeds in warming up the skin tone, but it also warmed the rest of the image.

One of the secrets of effective color correction is to combine controls to create complex effects. Here, you can use the Shadow color balance control to moderate the effect of the other two ranges.

10 Drag the Shadow color balance control in the opposite direction (to around 5 o'clock) until the darker areas of the image return to their original cool tones.

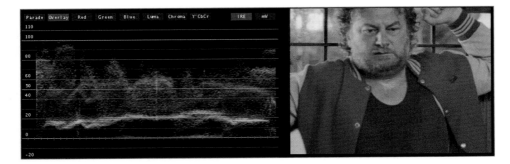

When done right, color correction should be subtle. Small movements can have significant impact, so it's always best to make tiny adjustments until you've achieved the desired result.

It's also nice to recall how far you've come, as you make those many small changes.

11 Press Control-G to toggle between the original uncorrected image and its corrected version.

12 Continue making adjustments to the three color balance controls until you're satisfied with the image.

Remember to play the clip occasionally to see how the settings you change affect the whole clip. Later in this clip, the person throwing the money steps into the frame briefly. You may want to stop on one of those frames to ensure that you're happy with the skin tones of that person as well.

Resetting the Primary Parameters

As you're working in the Primary In room, you may find that you've gone too far down one path and you want to start over again. You already know about the reset buttons in the corner of each of the controls, but another control can reset the entire Primary In room.

1 Click the Reset Primary In button, located in the lower-right corner of the Primary In room.

This restores all the controls in the room to their default values.

2 Before you continue to the next exercise, press Command-Z to Undo the reset, or, for more practice, take a few minutes and re-grade the clip.

Grading with Curves

Working with the color balance controls is a powerful, flexible, and effective way to grade shots, but it's not the only way. The RGBL curve editors offer a different approach to correcting your clips.

Rather than dividing the image into ranges of brightness, the curves isolate the red, green, blue, and luma channels independently. These controls are ideal for making corrections across the entire contrast range, but along an isolated color. For example, you would use these controls to apply a quick and easy white balance correction to a video clip, or to remove an unwanted color cast.

In the real world, you'll use both the color balance controls and the curves in concert, tweaking a variety of settings in both places to achieve the overall look you desire.

Manipulating curves effectively takes some practice and, as with the color balance controls, small curve adjustments can cause big changes in the image.

1   With the Timeline active, press the Down Arrow key or click the Timeline ruler area to move the focus to the next clip.

Although this clip could benefit from some contrast adjustment, its bigger problem is a slight cyan cast that you'll work to eliminate. To familiarize yourself with the curve editors, you'll correct the cyan cast prior to expanding the contrast, even though in the real world this would not be a typical workflow.

First of all, you must figure out which curve will affect cyan, which means thinking about the color wheel. A quick glance at the Vectorscope (or any of the color balance controls in the Color interface) reveals that cyan and red share the same axis, making them *complementary* colors. So, adjusting the red curve should add or remove cyan from the image.

2   Click in the midpoint of the red curve to create a handle and drag slightly toward the upper-left corner of the graph, adding red, and thereby removing cyan.

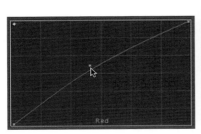

This reduces the amount of cyan in the image and, because you clicked in the center of the curve, it mostly affects the midtones.

3   Drag the handle you created in step 2 down toward the lower left, so that you're moving only the lower portion of the curve.

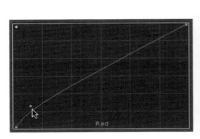

This limits the cyan reduction to the image shadows. You can see this in the Viewer in the way that the color is pulled out of the suit and the dark background, while the skin tones and white color of the shirt still have a cyan cast.

4   Drag the point to the top of the graph.

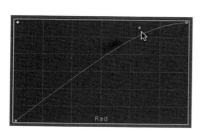 

Now the cyan is removed only from the highlights. The shirt and skin tones become more neutral, but the suit and background still have the color cast.

You can also observe how the curves change the image by examining the scopes.

5   Drag the graph handle around as you watch the Waveform Monitor and Vectorscope.

With the Waveform Monitor set to parade or overlay mode, it's very clear that only the red channel is affected.

6   Observe how dragging the point near the top of the curve graph limits the effect on the red highlights (the red traces near the top of the Waveform Monitor) and dragging near the bottom limits the effect on the shadows.

7   Keep dragging the handle around, while you watch the Vectorscope.

The red curve moves the entire image along the axis between red and cyan.

8   Drag the blue or green curves and observe the way the traces in the Vectorscope are limited to those other axes.

9   Click the reset button in the upper-left corner of all three curves.

Controlling Contrast with Curves

In addition to controlling individual colors, you can use a curve editor to modify the luma channel, which controls the overall image contrast.

Changing the Luma curve yields results similar to modifying the contrast sliders in the color balance controls, but the curve editor lets you make extremely specific contrast adjustments in user-selectable ranges of image tonality.

1   To better monitor the changes you'll be making, click the Luma button at the top of the Waveform Monitor to view just that channel.

2   Click to add a handle in the Luma curve, and drag it toward the bottom of the graph.

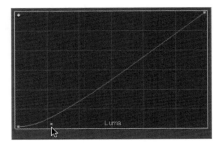

Observe the Waveform Monitor to see how the shadows are moved closer to the 0% bar.

3   Click near the top of the Luma curve to add another handle and, this time, drag it to the left to increase the values near the top.

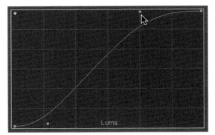

Observe the Waveform Monitor, dragging until the traces are near the 100% bar.

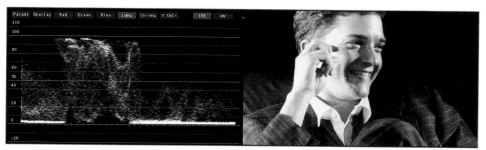

NOTE ► Dragging the handle outside the graph deletes the point altogether.

Now that you've set the black and white points, you can still make additional changes to the main slope of the curve.

4 Click the middle of the Luma curve and drag a tiny amount toward the upper-left corner until you see some detail emerge in the seat behind the actor.

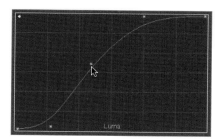

These changes affect the tonality of the image just as the contrast sliders in the color balance controls do, but the curve editor has an advantage because you can add as many points as required, instead of the three overlapping settings.

The overall shape of the Luma curve controls the distribution of gray values across the range of the image, known as the *gamma* of the image. Different recording media, such as film, digital cinema cameras, and video cameras each have different gamma settings that can be simulated using this curve.

Understanding Additional Controls

The Basic and Advanced tabs at the right of the Primary In window offer several ways to perform the same tasks you performed using the curves and color balance controls.

As you've probably begun to realize, the Primary In room provides many ways to apply the same types of effects. Some colorists may gravitate toward the balance controls or the curves, and old-school film color timers might be more comfortable using the printer point controls in the Advanced tab. There is no right or wrong way to employ these different tools.

One distinguishing element of the controls in the Basic and Advanced tabs is that they allow precise numerical entry, so you can quickly make relative adjustments—lowering a value by a set amount, or exactly matching the values across multiple clips.

Although you can always type a number directly into these fields, Color also allows you to treat these controls as virtual sliders. When your pointer is positioned over any of these fields, rolling your mouse scroll wheel will raise or lower the values. Alternatively, you can middle-click and drag the slider left or right to set the value lower or higher.

1   With the Timeline active, press the Down Arrow key to move to the next clip (**10_OLDPLANES**).

    This shot needs some contrast adjustment, as well as some minor color work. First is to set the black and white points.

2   In the Basic tab of the Primary In room, middle-click the Master Lift value and drag left. Watch the Waveform Monitor, and darken the image until the shadows are just approaching 0%.

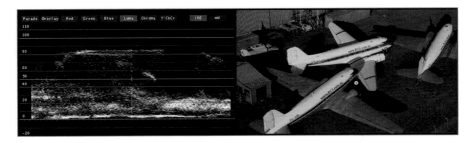

This sets the approximate black point.

3   Middle-click the Master Gain control and drag right until the Waveform Monitor
    shows the white levels nearing 100%.

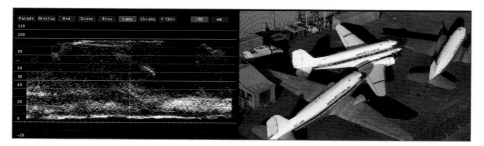

This sets the white point, but the image can still use some color adjustments. The
airplanes appear very yellow, making them look dirty and old. Rather than use the
curves or color balance controls to offset the yellow, you can use the saturation sliders
to remove all color from the brightest highlights in the image.

4   Middle-click the Highlight Sat. control and drag left to remove saturation from the
    highlights. Watch the image in the Viewer and stop dragging when the planes appear
    clean and white (at approximately .25).

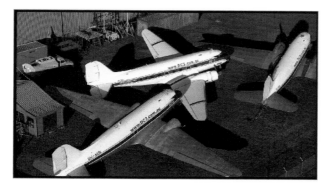

The Shadow Sat. slider also can be used to quickly remove a color cast from the shadows of an image, giving the blacks a more *inky* look. The 3D Color Space Scope can
be a great aid in performing this sort of correction.

5   If the 3D Color Space Scope isn't already showing, right-click (or Control-click) the
    Vectorscope and choose 3D Color Space to enable that scope.

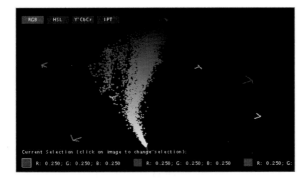

The 3D Color Space Scope is like a Vectorscope extruded into three dimensions along the axis of luma; so in addition to the six color targets, there are also targets for black and white, indicating the contrast of the image. To make it even easier to read, the traces are colored (even when the monochrome scopes setting is enabled).

TIP You can also view this scope in different color spaces by clicking the buttons above the graph.

6 Drag around in the scope to rotate it until the black is on the top and the red is on the left (as illustrated in the figure above).

In this image, you can see that a fair number of red traces are present in the shadow area of the scope and they're far from the center axis. This indicates that the shadows have some saturated red color.

7 Middle-click the Shadow Sat. control and drag to the left to decrease saturation in the shadows. Watch the 3D Color Space Scope as you drag.

8 The red traces near the black point draw close to the middle axis, and in the Viewer, you can observe the shadows become more monochromatic.

The Primary In room is incredibly versatile and you'll undoubtedly find yourself employing the controls in many situations. Because each of the controls (color balance controls, curves, number sliders, and so on) affects the picture differently, you can exercise your artistry by combining and overlapping them in unique and unexpected ways.

Lesson Review

1. True or false: The Primary rooms are only for changing primary colors.
2. How do the sliders to the right of the color balance controls affect the color balance control itself?
3. Identify three situations in which auto balance is likely to produce undesirable results.
4. How do you remove the effect of the Auto Balance command?
5. Do colorists typically correct color or contrast first?
6. Can curves contain multiple control points?
7. How are the curve editors different from the color balance controls?
8. How do you change the value of the numerical fields in the Basic tab?

Answers

1. False. Primary corrections affect the entire image.
2. The Hue slider controls the angle, the Saturation slider controls the distance from the center, and the Contrast slider has no visible effect on the balance control, but affects the black and white levels for that brightness range.
3. Letterboxed clips, BITC (burned-in timecode) clips, and clips in which the content changes significantly across the duration of the clip.
4. Click the Reset Primary In button.
5. Contrast is usually corrected first.
6. Yes.
7. Curves affect color channels and color balance controls affect brightness ranges.
8. Type a number in, or position the mouse pointer over the field and rotate the mouse scroll wheel, or middle-click the field and drag left or right.

6

Lesson Files   Color Book Files > Lesson Files > Lesson 06 > Secondaries.colorproj

Time   This lesson takes approximately 75 minutes to complete.

Goals   Master the concept of secondary corrections

Isolate specific colors for corrections using the eyedropper and HSL qualifiers

Mask discrete sections of an image using simple shapes called vignettes

Control the inside and outside of a vignette independently

Use curves to limit corrections to a specific hue

Lesson 6

Basic Secondary Grading

Although adjustments made in the Primary rooms affect the entire image, often you want to modify a portion of the frame discretely. For example, you may want to adjust an actor's skin tones; or if you're working with an image shot outdoors, you may need to make color adjustments to the sky. Perhaps you want to add some saturation to the blues while removing some from the reds. Furthermore, you may want to employ masks to limit corrections to a certain shape or object within the frame. Any changes that affect a limited section of the shot are considered *secondary* corrections, and so are done in the Secondaries room of Color.

Whereas primary corrections are typically used to correct exposure and color balance problems, or to match the overall appearance of your shots, secondaries are where you can define a unique *look* for your shots, and where you can do the detailed finessing that colorists relish.

Because secondaries modify limited portions of the frame, it's common to employ many of them in the same shot.

For example, in the image above, the sky, bushes, human skin, and sand each have individual corrections applied to them. Color's Secondaries room has eight tabs that make it possible to perform eight different corrections simultaneously. When you take into account the ability to control the inside and outside of the selected areas this allows for 16 independent secondary controls. So you'll never run out of secondaries.

Three Types of Secondaries

There are three different types of secondary corrections performed in the Secondaries room: *key-based* corrections, *vignette-based* corrections, and *curve-based* corrections.

Key-Based

Key-based corrections are controlled by selecting a range of color using the HSL qualifiers—Hue, Saturation, and Lightness sliders—in the upper-right corner of the Secondaries room.

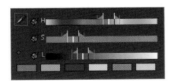

TIP ▶ You can also use the eyedropper or color swatches to select the desired color.

This is called *key-based secondary correction*, because it works the same way as traditional bluescreen or greenscreen color keying. These sorts of secondaries are perfect for working on sections that fall in a specific range of color and lightness, such as skies, skin tones, and other color-based selections, regardless of whether they appear contiguously within the image.

NOTE ▶ Key-based corrections work the same way as the Limit Effect controls in Final Cut Pro's Color Corrector 3-way.

Once you've identified the color you want to modify, any changes you make in the color balance controls will apply only to that selected color.

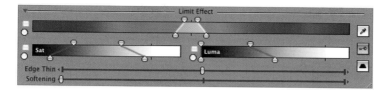

Vignette-Based

You employ vignette-based secondaries when the area of the frame you want to limit is not based on a color, but rather on a shape. You may want to use a simple circle or rectangle, or you may draw a custom shape in the Geometry room. Such shapes can encompass a range of colors.

Once a mask has been created, changes made in the color balance controls will affect only the area within (or outside of) that isolated region.

> **TIP** Masks and keys can be combined in the same secondary to create a selection based on a combination of color and shape.

Curve-Based

Another way to apply an effect to a limited section of your image is to use the secondary hue, saturation, and luma curves in the center of the Secondaries room.

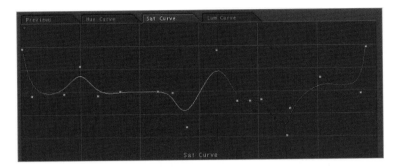

Although these curves resemble the curves in the Primary rooms, and can be manipulated in a similar way, the secondary curves work very differently.

The spectrum displayed on the length of the curves allows you to make hue, saturation, and luma adjustments to a limited range of that spectrum.

Performing Key-Based Secondaries

One common type of secondary correction involves identifying a specific color and applying a correction to just that color wherever it appears in the frame.

1   Open Lesson Files > Lesson 06 > **Secondaries.colorproj.**

2   If your media does not appear in the Timeline, the media is offline. Choose File > Reconnect Media and navigate to Lesson Files > Lesson 06 > Media. Click Choose.

    Your Timeline playhead should be parked on the first clip, the overhead shot of the stadium. This clip has already had some primary color correction applied to stretch out the contrast, but the green grass field looks dark and ugly. This is a perfect example of a situation where a secondary correction can bring some life back to a part of an image.

3   Click the Secondaries tab.

4   Select the Enabled checkbox at the top of the window.

NOTE ▶ Setting this checkbox is required to activate the controls in the Secondaries room, but it's so small and out of the way that it's easily forgotten. Clicking the eyedropper activates this automatically, but it's a good practice to turn it on manually whenever you're beginning a secondary correction. It's often useful to turn these on and off to quickly show directors or producers the subtle changes that have been made.

5   Click the eyedropper in the upper-right section of the Secondaries room.

A red crosshair appears in the Viewer. Your next click will establish the color that you'll isolate for the secondary effect. But before you click, you can increase the range of colors to be keyed by dragging across the colors in the image.

6   Drag the red crosshair across the football field.

The color of the field is selected, and now any changes you make to the color balance controls will be limited to that selection.

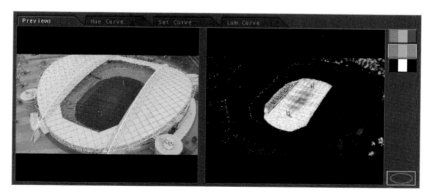

In the Previews tab in the center of the Secondaries room, the key is displayed as a white selection in a field of black. The Matte Preview Mode buttons to the right of the matte view control the display in the Viewer.

By default, the middle button (gray-green-gray), which displays the selection in color, is active, and the rest of the image is in grayscale.

7 Click the black-white-black button to set the Viewer to display the mask only.

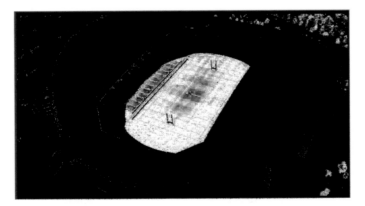

This provides a larger and more detailed view of the masked area in the Viewer.

Depending on exactly how you dragged to select the green field, other unwanted areas of the image may also have been selected. In the image above, you can see some white areas in the lower-left and upper-right corners of the image. These areas will be affected by any corrections you make, which is undesirable in this case.

Although it's not essential to get a "perfect" key in order to make a great secondary, you can tidy up the key using the HSL sliders beneath the eyedropper. The goal is to make the area you want to select appear white, while the area you don't want should be black. Areas that appear in gray will be semi-transparent.

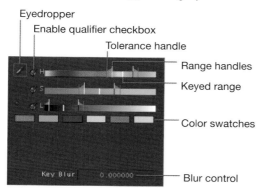

The areas between the handles indicate the hue, saturation level, and brightness level to be keyed.

You can drag the area between the handles to select a new range. Dragging a handle allows you to shrink or expand the selected range symmetrically, and Shift-dragging moves one handle without affecting the other. The outside edge of each handle defines its tolerance, allowing you to taper off the effect gradually.

8 Shift-click the left range handle of the Hue slider and drag it to the right until the white specks outside of the stadium disappear, but stop before the grassy area itself begins to disappear.

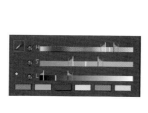

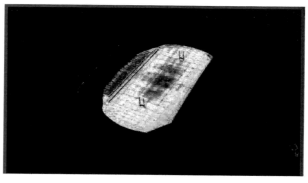

9 Drag the Lightness range handles closer together until they're nearly touching, and then drag the tolerance handles and soften the selection.

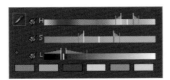

NOTE ▶ Depending on the specific selection you made in step 5, you may need to make slightly different adjustments to create the optimal key.

10 Middle-click the Key Blur number slider and drag to the right to about .75. If you don't have a three-button mouse (even though the software requires it), type in *.75*.

NOTE ▶ Remember, keying for color correction is very different from pulling a key for compositing. By softening the key, you ensure that the effects you make will blend better into the surrounding image. If you over-soften, you'll notice a halo around the selected area.

TIP ▶ In general, you can expect to use a blur of around 1 to 2 for HD or high-resolution film scanned images. For lower resolutions or very grainy footage, you may need to use a setting of 2 to 4. Note that the maximum value is 8.

Now that you've effectively isolated the field, you're ready to enhance its color.

11 Click the Final Image display button (red-green-blue) to the right of the matte in the Previews tab.

This sets your Viewer to display the final corrected output.

12 Drag the Shadow contrast slider up slightly.

13 Drag the Midtone color balance control handle toward yellow-green (about 8 o'clock) until the field takes on a nice, healthy, fresh-grass look.

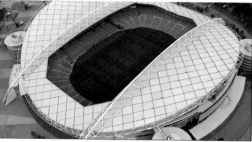

As you make these adjustments, you can see the green traces begin to separate from the center blob in the Vectorscope. While the area in your selection grows greener, notice that the rest of the image remains unaffected.

This sort of keyed secondary is highly effective on skin tones, skies, or any other element that can be isolated by its color values.

Original

Corrected

Keying with HSL Qualifiers

In some cases, the eyedropper is not the best way to select the range of color you want to isolate. For example, you may want to select an area of your image based only on its brightness, or only the saturation level.

This can also aid in keying highly compressed footage, such as HDV. Such footage discards far more color (chroma) data than it does luma, so if you want to key based on a color, you're likely to get jagged edges. But if you key based only on the lightness, you can achieve a much smoother edge.

As stated earlier, keying for secondary color correction rarely requires such a perfect smooth edge, but there are still cases where you may want to key using the Hue, Saturation, and Lightness qualifiers independently.

1 In the Timeline, press the Down Arrow key to move to the next shot (**Leverage03**).

This is an extremely challenging shot. The DP deliberately underexposed so there would be some detail to work with in the window, but that meant letting the subject of the shot go dangerously dark.

To address this, you can use a luma-only key to isolate the dark areas, and then brighten those areas without blowing out the window too badly.

2 In the Secondaries room, select the Enable checkbox.

3 Shift-drag the right range handle of the Lightness slider to asymmetrically limit the lightness range until the matte in the preview area clearly defines only the darkest portion of the image.

4   Shift-drag the tolerance handle to soften the right side of the qualifier until just before you see any white creep back into the black area in the preview.

You can see the selected area in the preview area in the middle of the window. You can view the matte in the Viewer window to get a more precise look.

5   Click the Matte Only button on the right side of the preview area.

The Viewer displays the keyed area.

6   Middle-click the Key Blur setting and drag to soften the overall key slightly. Approximately 1.0–1.2 is appropriate for this footage.

This softens the edge of the matte slightly.

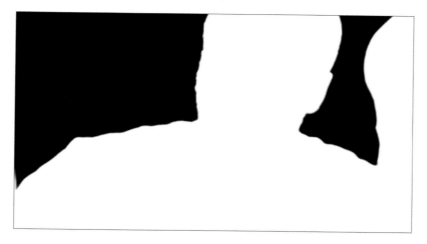

NOTE ▶ The preview area does not display matte softness. It's only visible in the Viewer window.

Now that the matte has been selected, you can work on fixing the exposure issues.

7   Click the Final Image button.

8   Drag the Highlight contrast slider up to lighten the brightest range of the selected area. Drag until the luma output reaches approximately 1.5.

The foreground of the image is brightened but the window is unaffected.

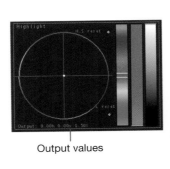

Output values

9 Drag the Shadow contrast slider down, to bring the darkest areas back toward black.

This is an improvement, but there is plenty of detail in the man's jacket that can be brought out by lifting the midtones.

10 Drag the Midtone contrast slider up until the luma output reads approximately 1.0.

This adds yet more detail to the foreground, but raises the darkest areas above black again.

11 Drag the Shadow contrast slider down again until the lowest traces in the Waveform Monitor are resting on the bottom line.

12 Click the Enable checkbox at the top of the Secondaries room off and back on to see the results of your work.

Although the window still appears a bit blown out (due to the blooming effect around the edges of the actors' heads), the foreground is now clearly light enough to read the man's expressions, and a shot that might have appeared unusable has been resurrected.

Original   Corrected

Performing Vignette-Based Secondaries

Although keying is great for some footage, often a simple shape will do. When you want to add a gradient of color to enhance a sky or add a pool of light (or shadow) to an image to provide depth, Color's vignettes allow you to limit a correction to the area inside or outside a designated shape.

Just as with keying, you begin working with vignettes by isolating an area of the screen, and then make changes to the color balance controls to perform corrections on the isolated area. Also, just as with keying, the goal is usually not to achieve a level of fine precision, but rather to perform subtle enhancements.

1   With the Timeline active, press the Down Arrow key to move to the next clip (**03_HARBORTRACK**).

This is a dull shot of Sydney Harbour with flat exposure. However, with a bit of secondary correction, you can turn it into a masterpiece.

2   Click the Secondaries tab, if it's not already active, to bring that room to the front.

3   Select the Enable checkbox to turn on the secondary.

Color's vignettes are controlled by the settings beneath the Previews tab or graphically in the Previews tab.

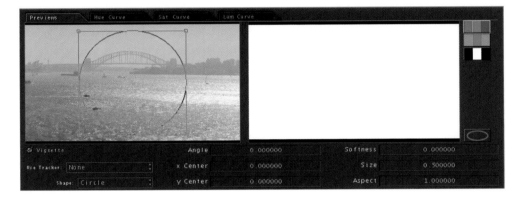

4   Click the Vignette button to enable the vignette effect.

A circle appears in the preview area.

For this example, you'll begin by adding some color to the sky using a rectangular vignette.

5   Click the Shape pop-up menu and choose Square.

The shape in the preview area turns into a square.

You can manipulate the shape directly in the preview area.

6   Click any corner of the square and drag it outward to enlarge the shape until it becomes a rectangle the size of the sky.

TIP Pressing Shift as you scale the shape will constrain the proportions.

7   Click anywhere in the middle of the shape to move it up so that it covers the sky.

8   Middle-click anywhere in the preview area and drag to soften its edges.

The softness is represented by inner and outer boxes around the shape that indicate the falloff range of the softness. The farther away from the original shape, the softer the edge of the effect will be.

NOTE ▶ Softness plays an important role when you need to disguise a mask. With moving shots, it's vital to not make masked corrections obvious to the viewer initially.

TIP ▶ You can continue manipulating the shape at this point, but be careful to drag the corners of the actual shape, not the boxes representing the softness.

9   Position the shape so that the bottom softness edge lines up with the horizon line.

Now that the shape is positioned, you can begin to make color adjustments.

10 Drag the Midtone color balance control toward blue.

The sky color gets deeper and richer.

NOTE ▶ You won't see the effect in the preview area. To see the results of your adjustments, watch the Viewer window.

11 Toggle Control-G on and off to see a quick before and after of the change you made.

Controlling Both Sides of the Selection

Defining a shape doesn't mean your corrections must be limited to the area within it. For every secondary correction, you actually have two sets of settings: inside and outside. Both are active all the time.

Often, making changes within a selection will compel you to make corresponding changes outside it. For example, adding a lighting effect generally requires lightening the inside area and darkening the area around it. Similarly, in the harbor shot, once you create a grade for the sky, you can quickly and easily set a grade for the water using the same mask.

1   Set the Control pop-up menu (above the Highlight color balance control) to Outside.

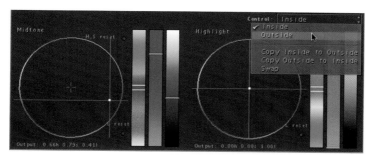

The blue color you added to the sky remains, but now any changes you make will be applied to the area outside the mask.

TIP ▶ The Inside and Outside control is available regardless of whether the secondary was created with a vignette or with a key.

2   Drag the Midtone color balance control toward the green/cyan (around 6 o'clock).

3   Drag the Highlight color balance control toward blue (around 4–5 o'clock).

This adds a nice tropical color to the water.

Once you've defined the basic looks for both inside and outside, you may find you want to make additional adjustments to the vignette shape or position.

4   Rotate the vignette slightly by middle-clicking and dragging the Angle control until it reads approximately -1.0000.

> **TIP** ► Press Option while dragging to speed up the drag adjustments, or press Control while dragging to slow down the adjustments.

5   In the preview area, drag the vignette up or down to finesse the location of the transition from sky to water.

6   If necessary, middle-click and drag the Softness control to adjust the softness of the mask edge and continue to adjust the color balance controls until you're satisfied with the results.

7   Press Control-G to toggle the grade on and off to see how far you've come.

With this one simple mask and a couple of quick adjustments, you've transformed this drab shot into something much more pleasing.

Original

Graded

Secondary Curves

The Secondaries room also contains a set of curves to enable hue, saturation, and luma adjustments based on specific hue values in your source image. For example, this allows you to boost the saturation of red while simultaneously removing it from green. You might use these curves to alter the hue of a single color range, turning all the blue areas to green without affecting any other colors.

These curves are popular controls among colorists partly because they're just fun to use.

1   In the Timeline, press the down arrow to activate the last clip (**01_JAIL**).

2   In the Secondaries room, select the Enable checkbox.

3   Click the Sat Curve tab.

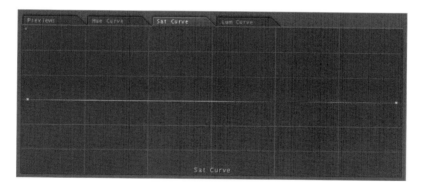

You manipulate these curves the same way as you do the ones in the Primary In room—by clicking to add control points (handles) and dragging the handles to new positions to perform the effect. The Sat curve controls the image's saturation; dragging up adds saturation and dragging down removes it.

The spectrum displayed on the curve indicates which parts of the curve affect which colors. Dragging the red section of the curve will limit the change to that color. You can control the amount of falloff by adding additional adjacent points.

In this example, you'll begin by removing saturation from the yellow-green wall and floor.

TIP ▶ Often it's practical to add several points to the line before adjusting any of them.

4   Add four points to the curve, two around yellow and two around cyan.

5   Drag the two inner points down until the wall becomes desaturated.

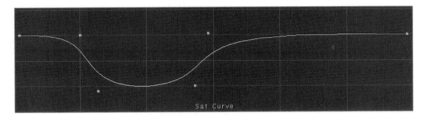

You may want to adjust the adjacent handles to increase or decrease the angle of the falloff.

Now you can add saturation to the orange jumpsuit using the same control.

6   Add two new points, one directly on orange, and one to the right of it, to limit
the effect.

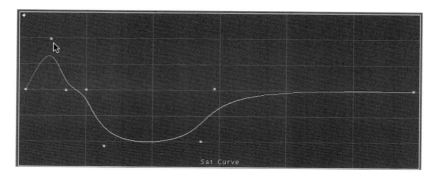

7   Drag the orange point upward to increase the saturation of that color.

This image doesn't have much that falls between the two areas you've changed, but if
you want to level off the area between the two sections, you can adjust the adjacent
points or add a new point.

8   Add another point directly on yellow and adjust it to create a flat area between the
boosted orange and the attenuated green.

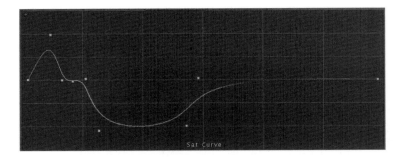

9   Press Control-G to toggle the grade on and off to see the results of your work.

TIP ▸ The curves wrap around, so adjusting the red on one side of the graph will affect the other side of the curve.

Changing Hue with the Secondary Hue Curve

Similar to changing saturation using the secondary Sat curve, the Hue curve allows you to change the color of a limited portion of the spectrum.

1   Click the reset button in the upper-left corner of the Sat Curve tab.

2   Click the Hue Curve tab.

3   Add three points to the curve in the red-orange area. (The built-in point on the left edge serves as your fourth point.)

Don't worry about making the points' positions precise.

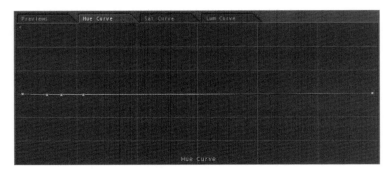

4   Drag the second point up to turn the orange elements in the shot purple.

> **NOTE ▶** You may have to move your point left or right to ensure that it affects the orange jumpsuit.

5   Drag the third point left or right until the entire jumpsuit is affected by the hue shift.

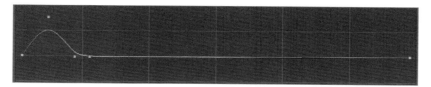

At this stage, you could continue making adjustments to change the hues of other colors within the shot.

These curves are easy to use and allow you to make quick, simple adjustments to various aspects of the shot based on hue. They aren't ideal for every situation, but they can be very effective with shots that have clearly contrasting ranges of color.

The third curve, the Lum curve, works exactly the same as the Hue and Sat curves and makes it just as easy to adjust the image. However, it's very easy to tear apart your image by making even modest adjustments with any of these curves, so many colorists choose to make such changes using the controls in the Primary In room or using the keying tools in the Secondaries room.

> **TIP** ▶ The curves are not limited by key- or vignette-based selections. They will always affect the entire image (limited only by the specific points on the curve).

Secondary corrections are incredibly versatile and powerful. Now that you've gotten the hang of how to use the various controls in this room, the next lesson will teach you how to combine them for even more varied and unique effects.

Lesson Review

1. What is a secondary correction?
2. What are the three main secondary controls?
3. What are the three matte preview modes and where are they selected?
4. How is a key color most often selected?
5. How is the falloff range set in the HSL qualifiers?
6. How is a vignette shape enabled?
7. Where is the vignette shape modified?
8. How do you soften the edge of a vignette?
9. True or false: Changing the Control pop-up menu from Inside to Outside resets your Inside settings.
10. Why are the Hue, Sat, and Lum curves considered secondary corrections?
11. True or false: The Sat curve allows you to change an image's saturation based on hue.
12. On what parameter does the Hue curve base its changes?

Answers

1. A correction that is limited to an isolated portion of the image.
2. Key-based, vignette (mask)-based, and curve-based.
3. Final Image, Desaturated Preview, and Matte Only; choose one of the three colored buttons at the right of the Previews tab.
4. Click the eyedropper and click or drag across a color in the Viewer window.
5. Drag just outside the qualifier handles to soften the selection.
6. Select the Vignette checkbox below the preview area on the Previews tab.

7. Change the vignette shape in the preview area.

8. Drag the shape with the middle mouse button in the preview area, or adjust the Softness slider in the Vignette controls section.

9. False. You can have both Inside and Outside settings simultaneously.

10. Because they affect only one portion of the image at a time.

11. True.

12. Hue.

7

Lesson Files Color Book Files > Lesson Files > Lesson 07 > AdvancedSecs.colorproj

Time This lesson takes approximately 75 minutes to complete.

Goals Apply multiple secondaries to create complex corrections

Further master key-based, vignette-based, and curve-based secondaries

Combine a key and a vignette in one secondary

Combine two keys in a single shot

Create custom-shaped masks

Adjust softness and other parameters of user shapes

Combine multiple vignettes in a single shot

Apply curve-based corrections to shots with existing secondaries

Lesson 7
Advanced Secondary Grading

Once you've mastered the various tools in the Secondaries room, you can begin to combine them to create an even greater range of effects and corrections. In fact, if you have a shot that requires secondary work, it's very likely you'll want to do more than one secondary. Major feature film colorists employ many secondaries on every single shot; they'll finesse skin tones (often independently for each character), tweak skies, and use other aspects of color and tone to control the audience's point of focus at every moment. There's no reason you can't put the same effort into your own work—and depending on your clients, you may be required to!

Secondaries can be combined in any way imaginable: You can employ multiple keys to treat distinct colors differently; isolate a specific region based on color, and further limit that region based on a vignette; incorporate multiple vignettes; and so on, all the while using the curves to further manipulate specific hues.

Additionally, the vignettes you've used so far have been limited to simple shapes, but using Color you can create custom shapes with a tremendous amount of flexibility—allowing you to isolate even challenging or complex regions. In this lesson, you'll learn how.

Using Multiple Secondaries

All this combining of effects can be done in multiple ways. Within the Secondaries room, you can employ curves, keys, and vignettes simultaneously. A range of color selected with a key can be further limited by enabling the vignette controls. The settings of the color balance controls will be applied to the combined selection (both inside and outside). The curves work simultaneously, ignoring the selection defined by the key and vignette settings, but limited by the points you set on the curve.

Furthermore, the Secondaries room contains eight tabs along the bottom, each one containing the full set of secondaries controls. This means you effectively have eight different Secondaries rooms for each clip, each one capable of all the complex effects described above. Plus each room has both an inside and an outside setting (for affecting the area within the key or vignette as well as the area outside of it).

Combining a Key and a Vignette

One very practical way to combine secondaries is to select a region of color using a key, and then limit that selection using a vignette. This is common in shots where the color you want to isolate appears in several objects within the frame. For example, you might use this technique to correct different characters' faces independently.

Pulling the Key

In this exercise, you'll use a vignette to correct the tone of a character's face while not affecting the similarly colored brick wall.

1   Open Lesson Files > Lesson 07 > **AdvancedSecs.colorproj**.

    The first clip in the project is a shot of a man peeking out from behind a green door.

2   If your media does not appear in the Timeline, the media is offline. Choose File > Reconnect Media and navigate to Lesson Files > Lesson 07 > Media. Click Choose.

The man is not visible in the initial frame, so first you must find a frame that shows the man's face.

3   Press the spacebar or L to play the clip until the door is open and the face is exposed. (This happens around frame 8:05, as displayed in the Current Frame field to the right of the Timeline ruler.)

4   Click the Secondaries tab (or press Command-3) to open the Secondaries room.

5   Click the Preview tab in the center of the window if it isn't already showing.

6   Click the Desaturated Preview button (gray-green-gray).

7   Click the eyedropper, and in the Viewer, drag the red crosshairs across the man's forehead and cheek until the entire face appears in color.

Although the face is easily selected, you'll notice that the brick wall contains many of the exact same colors, so that gets selected automatically as well.

For now, you don't need to worry about the brick wall, but you will need to adjust the key to exclude the area under the man's chin and further finesse the selection.

8 Shift-click the left range handle of the Lightness qualifier control and drag to the right until the area beneath the man's chin turns mostly black in the preview area.

TIP If you begin to remove the shadowed portion of the man's face, increase the tolerance handles (the outer lines) in the Lightness qualifier control to split the difference.

9 Drag the Saturation qualifier range handles slightly closer together to remove some additional white from that area.

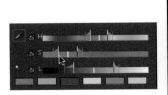

10 Middle-click the Key Blur number slider and drag to the right to increase the blur to about .75.

> **TIP** For color correction purposes, it's not essential to pull a perfect key.

Adding the Vignette

Now that you've got the face pretty well isolated, it's time to take care of that brick wall that has been accidentally included.

1 Click the Vignette button in the vignette area beneath the preview area.

2 Set the Shape pop-up to Square.

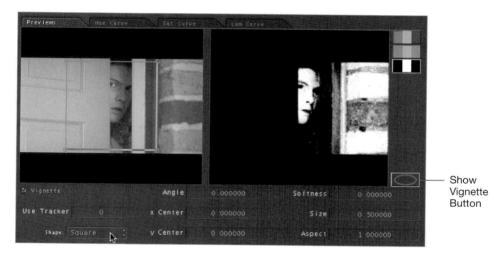

Show Vignette Button

3 In the preview area, use the mask handles to position the mask around the entire open doorway area.

> **TIP** You can display the vignette shape in the Viewer using the Show Vignette button in the bottom right of the Previews tab.

While in desaturated preview mode, the Viewer shows the combined selection of the key and the vignette. Remember that the vignette always *intersects with* the key selection. There is no way to add or subtract a vignette selection from a key selection.

4 Click the Final image button (red-green-blue).

The Viewer displays the shot in full color. Now you're ready to make your adjustment.

5   Drag the Midtone color balance control and watch the Vectorscope.

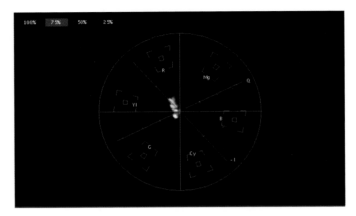

You can clearly identify the small blob of traces moving around that represent the skin tones of the face. (The rest of the traces don't move at all.)

6   Click the 50% button in the Vectorscope to zoom in slightly on the traces in the scope.

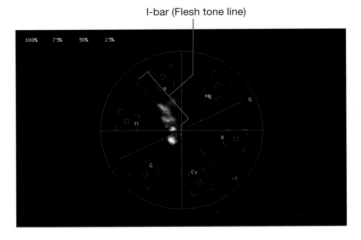

The upper-left bar of the diagonal yellow crosshairs in the Vectorscope (called the I-bar) indicates the color of natural-looking human flesh tones. Regardless of race or skin color, all human skin naturally fits close to this particular hue, and variations of skin darkness appear as a variety of saturation (the distance from the center of the scope).

As you drag your Midtone color balance control, you can easily move the color of the face so it sits right on that line, correcting the slightly red hue in the source footage.

7 Drag the Midtone color balance control, watching the Vectorscope, until the traces representing the face sit squarely on the flesh tone line.

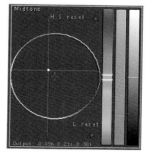

8 Drag away from the center (increasing saturation) until the traces just peek out from behind the other traces on the line.

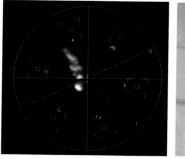 

This corrects the slight red tint present in the source footage, giving a healthy and natural look to the shot.

Using Multiple Keys

Although correcting the skin tones of the actor's face improves the shot somewhat, now that you're in here making secondary corrections, you'll likely start looking around for other things to improve.

One thing that might come to mind is that the green door could do with some increased saturation. Although there are a number of ways to accomplish this, one option would be to do another key on the color of the door. Using a key relieves you of the need to keyframe or track the movement of the door as the shot progresses, as you would if you'd selected it with a vignette.

Because the key in secondary 1 is already working to isolate the face, you need to open a new secondary.

1 Click the 2 tab at the bottom of the Secondaries room.

This opens a brand new Secondaries room, ready for new settings. The secondary corrections in room #1 will still affect the clip. The results of the two Secondaries rooms will be combined in the final shot.

2 Click the eyedropper and drag the red crosshairs across the door in the Viewer to select the door's color.

NOTE ▶ Because you left the Preview mode set to Final in Secondaries room #1, room #2 will default to that same setting.

3 Click the Desaturated Preview mode button to check your selection in the Viewer.

4 Clean up the matte by Shift-dragging the right range handle of the Hue qualifier to the right to expand the color selection. If necessary, adjust the other qualifiers until the door is well selected.

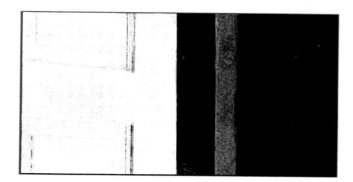

Don't worry too much about the doorjamb that's getting partially selected. It won't be affected very much by the change you plan to make, and in the worst case, you could always add a vignette to eliminate it from your selection just like the brick in the previous exercise.

5 Middle-click the Key Blur control and drag to the right to set the blur to about 1.

Now the door is selected and ready for correcting.

6 Click the Final Image button (red-green-blue) to display the full image in the Viewer.

The goal is to add some richness to the color, so you might be inclined to try boosting the Saturation slider in the Midtone color balance control.

7 Drag the Midtone Saturation slider.

Wait a minute! Rather than simply increasing the overall saturation, red is being added to the green door. This is not what you want.

8 Click the reset button for the Midtone color balance control.

9 Middle-click the Saturation parameter in the Basic tab beneath the keying controls and drag it to the right until it reaches about 1.5.

This control allows you to add saturation in a hue-neutral way. The other controls in this section work in a similar way.

10 Toggle Control-G to compare the graded image to the original.

Original   Graded

This illustrates how you can combine multiple keys (and multiple secondaries in general) to create more complex effects. If you wanted to continue working on this image, you could do another secondary (using either a key or vignette) to isolate the bricks and finesse them as well.

Remember that your overall goal is to control the viewer's point of focus. If the door and the brick were very well highlighted using contrast or saturation, they would pull attention away from the actor (who is presumably the most important aspect of the shot). However, if you did the opposite—highlighting the actor's face—you could compensate for any possible confusion that the shot's inherent composition might create.

Creating Custom Mask Shapes

By now, you've used vignettes in several examples but in each case you've used a very simple shape. The oval and rectangular masks accommodate an incredible range of situations; however, some shots require irregular and custom shapes. Color has a sophisticated tool for correcting such shots, using a combination of the Secondaries and Geometry rooms.

1   In the Timeline, press the Down Arrow key to move to the second shot in the Timeline (**Lakeside.move**).

This shot already has some primary correction applied, but the jacket of the man facing the camera needs to be adjusted to make it match the other shots in the film. It can't be keyed because the color is too similar to some colors in the sky, the water, and possibly even some of the skin tones.

A simple oval or rectangular mask also won't work, due to the irregular shape of the jacket. The best solution is to employ a custom user-defined shape.

2   Press Command-3 to bring the Secondaries room to the front (if it's not already there).

3   Click the #1 tab at the bottom to make sure you're working on secondary #1.

NOTE ▶ Color will always default to showing the same secondary tab as used in the previous shot.

4   Select the Enable checkbox, and then select the Vignette checkbox.

5   Set the Shape pop-up to User Shape.

The Geometry room is automatically opened, with the Shapes tab in front, and a new shape selected. The next click you make will begin to draw the shape.

6 Click to add points that roughly outline the shape of the jacket. Don't worry about being too precise. Use the figure below as a guide.

7 When your shape matches the picture above, click the Close Shape button.

The shape is automatically closed. Color uses *B-splines* to control the size and position of the shape. That means you manipulate points to construct a polygon around the curved shape.

8 Adjust the points to make the shape more accurately surround the jacket.

TIP To move the entire mask as an object, drag the small green box with an X in it, in the center of the shape.

In Color, you can't delete points from your path, and you can add points only by opening the shape and then adding more points to the end of the path.

9 Click Open Shape.

10 Add new points to make your shape exclude the black t-shirt.

11 Click Close Shape and make any necessary additional adjustments.

Most masks used for color correction benefit from edge softening to make the change in the affected area more subtle. Although in the Secondaries room preview area you can soften a shape by middle-clicking and dragging the shape itself, in the Geometry room you must use the Softness slider.

12 Position your pointer over the Softness parameter name and roll the mouse scroll wheel upward to increase the softness of the shape to about .25.

The softness is represented by two additional outlines, each with their own control points. This allows you to vary the amount of softness for different sections of the shape, as well as the inside versus the outside.

13 Move the outside green handles so the actor's face and neck are totally outside the range of the shape.

14 Select the Hide Shape Handles checkbox to see the rough outline of the shape more clearly.

15 When you're happy with your shape, click the Attach button at the top.

This assigns the shape to the currently active secondary vignette.

16 Press Command-3 or click the Secondaries tab to bring the Secondaries room forward.

When the vignette is assigned to User Shape, all the vignette controls are dimmed, so any adjustments must be made in the Geometry room.

17 Click the Final Image button (red-green-blue).

18 Make sure the Control pop-up (in the upper right) is set to Inside.

19 Drag both the Midtone and Highlight color balance controls toward yellow to make the jacket appear more beige.

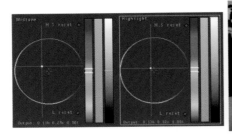 

20 In the Timeline, press the spacebar to play the clip.

Now that you can see the effect in action, you may want to return to the Geometry room and further adjust the shape.

21 Find the frame where the man's arm is at its rightmost point.

22 Press Command-6 or click the Geometry tab to make that room active.

23 Select shape untitled.0.

24 Click Hide Shape Handles to reactivate the handles.

25 Manipulate the shape and the softness handles while watching the Viewer to make sure the highlight on the man's right side is included in the matte (or whatever other adjustments your mask may need).

By dragging the yellow points, you move the entire shape; by moving the green points, you manipulate the softness boundary.

> **TIP** ▶ If you ever have a shape where the position of the handles causes the shape to contain an unwanted loop, the Reverse Normals checkbox will swap the points' positions to eliminate the overlapping area. But beware: The change affects only the Final Preview in the Viewer; the lines in the Geometry room will not actually update.

It's common to go back and forth between the Secondaries and the Geometry rooms frequently as you finesse the custom-shaped vignette effect. If your shape ever gets totally screwed up, you can always click the Detach button, begin drawing an entirely new shape, and then attach that one.

Engaging Multiple Vignettes

Vignettes are incredibly powerful, but often you need to combine several of them to adequately grade a shot. This is done using multiple Secondaries rooms, just like the earlier example involving multiple keys.

Although a number of vignettes can be applied to a single clip, Color does not allow you to subtract one mask shape from another (creating a doughnut hole) or otherwise combine multiple vignettes in complex ways, such as having two noncontiguous shapes treated as a single vignette. Each vignette allows you to change the settings within it, and if two masks overlap, applying the same settings to both would result in a double effect in the overlapping area.

In this exercise you'll add a lens vignette effect (a rounded edge darkening to the corners of the image) to the lakeside shot.

1   Press Command-3 to bring the Secondaries room forward.

2   Click the #2 tab to activate the second secondary.

The custom vignette on the jacket remains active, but a new Secondaries tab opens, ready for a new effect.

3   Select the Enable and Vignette checkboxes.

4   Set the Shape pop-up to Circle.

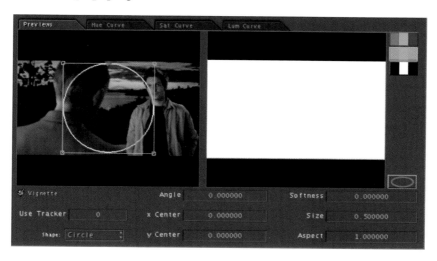

5 In the Previews tab, adjust the shape until the circle just exceeds the frame.

6 Middle-click and drag on the shape to soften its edge.

7 Set the Control pop-up to Outside.

8 Drag the Highlight contrast slider down until a subtle darkening is visible in the corners of the frame in the Viewer.

9   Adjust the size, position, and softness of the shape as necessary.

10   Press Control-G to toggle the grade off and on to see the overall effect you've applied (including the primary corrections that were done for you).

Incorporating Curve Effects

Don't forget that each Secondary tab can also include curve-based effects to modify the hue, saturation, and luma of your shots based on hue.

The secondary curves do not observe the settings in the key or vignette sections of the room. Curve effects are limited only by the control points you set to determine the hue you want to modify. However, because the secondaries are applied in numerical order, applying the curves in different Secondaries rooms may result in different effects based on the other secondaries you apply, including other curve effects.

For example, if you change the color of the sky in this shot from orange to magenta in secondary #2 and then reduce the saturation of magentas in secondary #3, the latter will affect the former.

> **NOTE ▶** It's important to note that curve effects are not keyframeable, so be careful when applying the effects to shots with dynamic contrast and color changes during a single take.

1   In secondary #2, click the Hue Curve tab.

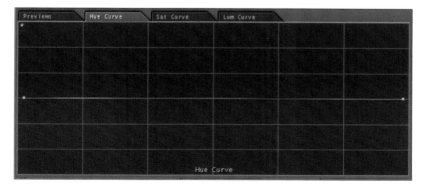

2   Add four points in the orange portion of the curve.

3 Raise the third point slightly to make the yellower tones more pink.

4 Lower the second point, making the redder tones more orange.

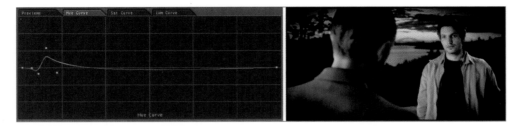

TIP ▶ Don't be afraid to add many points to the curve. The more points you add, the more precisely you can control the section of the curve being affected.

5 Click the #3 tab at the bottom of the Secondaries room.

6 Select the Enable checkbox to activate this secondary.

7 Click the Sat Curve tab.

8 Add points to boost the saturation of the orange colors and reduce the magenta.

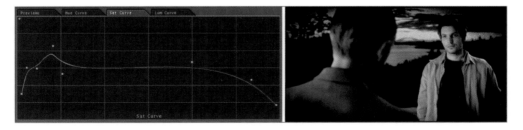

9 Press Control-G to turn off and on the entire grade and see the results of all your work.

TIP ▶ In some cases you could apply a similar effect by just using two curves in the same secondary. However, breaking them into separate secondaries this way allows you to turn them on and off independently using the Enable checkbox for each Secondaries room.

Original

Graded

The curve in secondary #3 affects the results of the secondaries that came before it. If you were to go back to secondary #1 and change the man's jacket to a pink or orange color, it, too, would be affected by the results of these curve adjustments.

Understanding how the different secondaries affect one another allows you to combine your effects in complex and interesting ways. For example, if you had made the man's jacket pink and wanted to boost the pink sky, but not the pink jacket, you would need to apply the jacket correction to a higher-numbered secondary.

Similarly, if you wanted a curve effect to be altered by a mask or key effect, you would need to apply it to a lower-numbered secondary.

Obviously these exercises only scratch the surface of what can be done by combining multiple secondaries in a single shot. Although applying many secondaries can increase render times, there is no reason not to employ them liberally to create fantastic and unique looks for all of your shots.

Lesson Review

1. True or false: Keys and vignettes can be combined in a single secondary operation.
2. How many secondaries can be applied to a single clip?
3. How do you control only one side of the HSL qualifiers?
4. Which control indicates proper flesh tone values?
5. How can you apply two key effects to a single clip?
6. Where can you adjust saturation in a color-neutral way?
7. How many points can a custom shape contain?
8. Can you add and delete points from a custom shape? If so, how and where?
9. Where can you control the softness of the inside of a shape independently from the outside softness?
10. How do you create a doughnut-hole effect where one mask punches out another?
11. Are secondaries applied in ascending or descending order?
12. Are the Hue, Sat, and Lum curves limited by key or vignette settings?

Answers

1. True.
2. There are eight Secondaries rooms for each clip, but multiple effects can be created in a single room.
3. Shift-drag the handle you desire to move independently.
4. The upper-left diagonal line in the Vectorscope.
5. Use two secondary operations.
6. The Saturation controls in the Basic tab affect all colors uniformly.
7. There is no limit to the number of control points on a custom shape.

8. In the Geometry room, points can be added by opening the end, but can't be added between two existing points. Points cannot be deleted.

9. The Geometry room preview allows you to drag the softness points independently. This requires first increasing the mask softness control.

10. Masks can't be combined in this manner.

11. Ascending.

12. No. Curves ignore keys and vignettes.

8

Lesson Files   Color Book Files > Lesson Files > Lesson 08 > Color_FX.colorproj

Time   This lesson takes approximately 75 minutes to complete.

Goals   Add individual nodes to create special effects

Combine nodes to create unique or custom looks

Understand node-based effects flows

Save node trees as preset effects

Reapply saved presets to other clips

Apply and customize preset effects

Learn how to deconstruct a preset

Color Effects

If you're like most colorists, the more comfortable you are with manipulating the various aspects of an image, the more likely it is that you'll start dreaming of the unlimited possibilities of such manipulation. Color correction can mean so much more than fixing skin tones and creating beautiful sunsets. You can make radical changes to your footage, not only affecting mood and tone, but changing the story itself.

From transforming footage that was shot during the day to appear as if it was shot at night, to creating period looks, to simulating various film acquisition, processing, and presentation techniques, Color can facilitate a wide range of effects that greatly expand your ability to tell your story more effectively.

Using the Color Effects Room

Color has a special place for building and exploring such effects: a playground where you can combine and manipulate a set of building blocks that affect your images in myriad ways. The building blocks are called *nodes* and the playground is the Color Effects room (or *Color FX* room).

Nearly all of the elements in the Color Effects room could be replicated through sophisticated manipulations in the Primary or Secondaries rooms, but in many instances it's far quicker and simpler to apply a pre-baked color effect and adjust a few parameters instead.

1   Open Lesson Files > Lesson 08 > **Color_FX.colorproj.**

2   If your media does not appear in the Timeline, the media is offline. Choose File > Reconnect Media and navigate to Lesson Files > Lesson 08 > Media. Click Choose..

3   Press the spacebar to play the first clip (**19_33A-2(A).mov**).

The clip shows a close-up from the Leverage scene you worked with in earlier lessons.

NOTE ▶ The Color FX room uses the results of the Primary In and Secondaries rooms, so any corrections applied in those rooms will be visible when viewing a clip in the Color FX room.

Using the effects in the Color FX room, you can quickly make radical changes to the look of the shot and, by extension, to the feel of the show.

4   Click the Color FX tab or press Command-4 to open the Color Effects room.

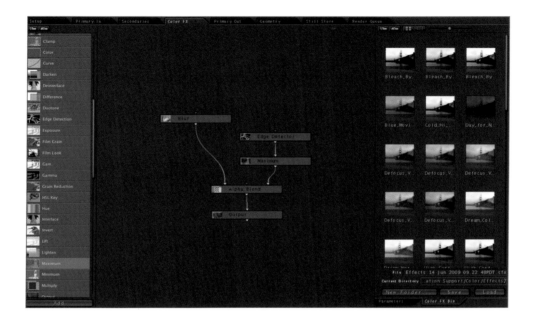

NOTE ▶ Your screen will not have any nodes in the Node View area in the middle of the screen until you complete this lesson.

The Color FX room is divided into four main areas. On the left, the Node List displays all the available effects. The middle area, where you construct your custom effects by dragging and connecting various nodes, is called the Node View. The right side has two tabs: Parameters, where you set the values for each node, and the Color FX bin, which contains a collection of preset node trees that perform specific effects.

Applying Nodes

There are several different types of nodes. Some apply specific effects, such as adding blur or noise to an image. Some allow you to limit how other nodes are applied. For example, a node may allow you to apply an effect to just the red channel, or to a masked area of the image, or to only one field of interlaced footage. Other nodes affect how different components are combined, so if you have a masked area with one effect on it, and the rest of the image has a different effect, you can choose to recombine the two areas using different blending modes. Finally, there are nodes that perform these recombinations, so if you've separated, say, the red, green, and blue channels to perform discrete effects in each channel, there are nodes to put the image back together.

TIP ▶ For a detailed description of each node and how to use it, consult the Color User Manual.

Applying individual nodes to a clip is simple, and sometimes one node may be all you need to create the desired effect.

NOTE ▶ An Output node is required in order for any effect to be rendered.

1   Drag the Blur node from the Node List into the Node View.

When you drag a node the node is added and, as a bonus, an Output node is added as well. The two are connected by a white line commonly called a *noodle*.

The Output node is required in order for Color to incorporate your effect into the render pipeline. It's the result of the Output that gets sent to the Geometry room. Any nodes not connected to the Output node will be ignored.

The effect of the Blur node is applied to the clip and the amount of blur is controlled by the settings in the Parameters tab.

2   Click the Parameters tab (if that tab isn't already showing).

3   Middle-click the Spread parameter and drag to the right to increase the blur amount to 3.

TIP ▶ Holding down the Option key while dragging with the middle-click allows you to make faster adjustments.

Although simply blurring an entire image this way is not common or practical, this node can be an essential element of more complex effects, as you'll learn in the next exercise.

Building Color Effects

Individual nodes can be useful, but the real power of the Color FX room emerges when you combine multiple nodes to create more complex effects. In this next section you'll build a skin-softening effect that can be very useful when working with the potentially unflattering resolution of HD cameras.

1   Drag the Edge Detector node to the Node View.

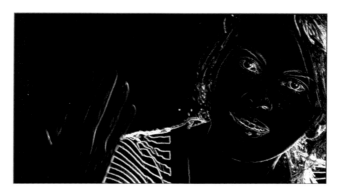

2   In the Parameters tab, customize the settings of your edge detector effect. Select the B&W checkbox, and set the Scale to 10.

3   Middle-click the Bias slider and drag to the left until the image is totally black, and then slowly drag back to the right, until the edges of the woman's face and hair are visible, but the majority of her face is still black (approximately –0.007). The more texture you see in her skin, the less dramatic the skin-softening effect will be.

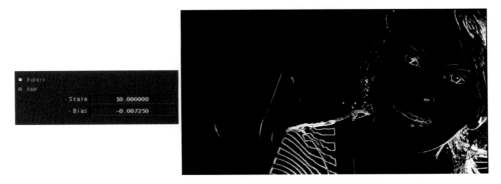

Whichever node is selected determines what is displayed in the Viewer and which parameters are displayed in the Parameters tab.

4   Click the Blur node, and then click the Edge Detector node again. Notice that the Viewer updates to display the effect of each node as you select it.

Because no noodles connect the two nodes, you can see only one effect or the other. To combine their effects, you must create a noodle to join them.

Input port

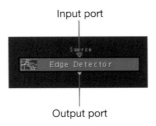

Output port

Each node has small triangular Input and Output ports on its top and bottom edges. You can control how the various nodes interact by the way these ports are connected.

5   Drag the Output port on the bottom of the Blur node to the Input port on the Edge Detector node.

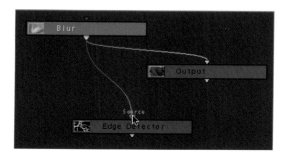

TIP ▶ Do not release the mouse button until after the Input port lights up. Otherwise the noodle will not successfully link the two nodes.

The nodes are connected with a noodle, but you'll notice that your Viewer shows only the Blur effect. You selected that node when you clicked the Output port, so even though the two nodes are connected, you're only monitoring the selected node.

6   Click the Edge Detector node to select it.

Because the nodes are now connected, the Edge Detector node now displays the combined effect of the two nodes. The blur is applied first, and the edge detector after that. Because the blur removes the edges from the image, the Edge Detector node doesn't show many edges.

7   Click the Input port on the top of the Edge Detector node.

This disconnects the nodes, and the Viewer now displays the edge detector without the Blur effect.

NOTE ▶ Notice that when you move your pointer over a node's Input port, a tiny display indicates the source currently feeding that node.

8   Drag a noodle from the Output port of the Blur node to the Input port of the Edge Detector node to reconnect them.

9   Click the Output node.

The Output node shows only the Blur effect, because even though the edge detector is visible in the node tree and connected to the Blur effect, it isn't connected to the Output node. The Output node controls the final result of the Color FX room, so leaving a node disconnected from it means that node won't actually be included in the final render of this shot.

10 Drag a noodle from the Output port of the Edge Detector node to the Input port on the Output node.

TIP ▶ Although not required, it's helpful to drag your nodes in a way that lets you easily understand the natural flow of data from one node to the next. You can lasso around multiple nodes to select more than one at a time to move them or even delete them.

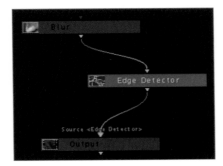

Each Input port can accept only one source, so by dragging the edge detector to the Output node, you replace the noodle from the Blur node.

NOTE ▶ Some nodes do accept multiple sources. Such nodes contain more than one Input port.

Controlling Node Order

The nodes in your Node View construct a sort of flowchart. The image goes in at the top and comes out on the bottom. The noodles connecting the nodes' inputs and outputs determine the order in which the effects are applied. This order can have a significant impact on the resulting image. For example, currently the Blur node is feeding the Edge Detector node, but what would happen if you reversed that order?

1   Drag the Output port of the Edge Detector node to the Input port of the Blur node.

Color won't let you make this link, because you can't create circular references in your node trees.

2   Click the Input port on the Edge Detector node to disconnect the Blur node.

3   Repeat step 1.

The figure shows the result of the Blur node.

The output of the Edge Detector node becomes the source of the Blur node.

4   Drag the nodes to rearrange them and tidy up your Node View.

5   Drag a noodle from the Output port of the Blur node to the Input port of the Output node.

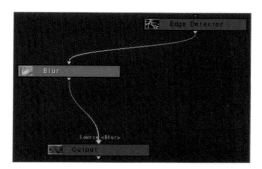

6 Click the Output node to make it active.

By reordering the nodes, you can create two different looks. In one case, the edge detection is applied to the blur, and in the other, the blur is applied to the edge detection.

Blur first   Edge detector first

7 Rearrange the nodes so the Blur node is feeding the Edge Detector node, and the Edge Detector node is feeding the Output node.

Bypassing Nodes

Occasionally, you may want to temporarily disable a node to observe how that one element is affecting your overall effect. Each node has a Bypass checkbox that allows you to turn off the effect without resetting the parameters.

1 Select the Edge Detector node and click the Bypass checkbox at the top of the Parameters tab.

This disables the effect of that node.

2 Deselect the Bypass checkbox to reactivate the node.

Monitoring Unselected Nodes

The selected node determines which effect is displayed in the Viewer and which settings are accessible in the Parameters tab. However, sometimes you may want to monitor one node while changing parameters on another. For example, you may want to make an adjustment to the edge detection scale while observing the output of the duotone. This lets you see how one node affects another later in the chain.

1 Double-click the Edge Detector node.

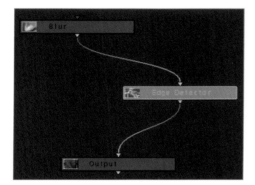

The node turns beige. This indicates that it's controlling the display in the Viewer. By default, it also activates the node, so its parameters are displayed in the Parameters tab.

2 Single-click the Blur node.

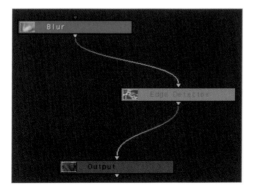

The node turns blue, and the controls in the Parameter tab are updated, but the Viewer continues to display the output of the beige node.

Now you can adjust the blur settings while observing how they affect the combined effect of the two nodes.

3   Lower the Spread value to 1.

4   Double-click any empty spot in the Node View area to deselect the beige node.

Adding Nodes to Existing Trees

Once you've begun building a node tree, you can add new effects without disconnecting and reconnecting all your noodles.

1   Drag the Maximum node to the noodle connecting the Edge Detector node to the Output node. When the noodle turns blue, release the mouse button.

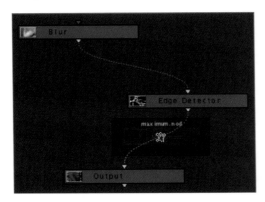

The node is inserted between the two existing nodes, automatically connected to both. It's also automatically made active.

2   Increase the brush size parameter to about 1.25.

This parameter fattens the lines created in the edge detector node.

Next, we're going to use the fattened edge detector as a mask. The blurred version of the clip will appear in the black areas, and the original unblurred version of the clip will shine through the white areas. To do this, we'll need to use another kind of node, one with multiple inputs.

3   Click the Input port on the top of the Edge Detector node to disconnect the Blur node.

4   Connect the Output port of the Blur node to the Output node.

5   Drag the Alpha Blend node onto the noodle between the Blur and Output nodes. When the noodle turns blue, release the mouse button.

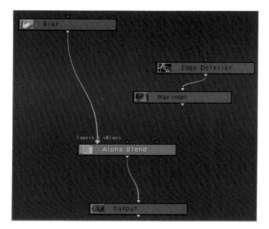

The Blur is mapped to the first input of the Alpha Blend.

6   Drag the Output port of the Maximum node to the rightmost Input port of the Alpha Blend mode.

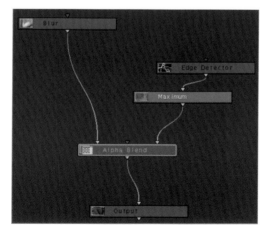

The input of this third port determines how the inputs from the first two ports are mixed. Any black pixels will be taken from the first Input port, and any white pixels will be taken from the second port.

Because nothing is plugged into the second port, Color will just use an unaffected version of the source clip.

7   Double-click the Alpha Blend node, and then single-click the Blur node.

8   In the Parameters tab, toggle the Bypass checkbox to see the effect turn on and off.

9   Adjust the Spread value until the image doesn't look blurry, but a subtle softening still occurs on the woman's skin (the final value should be about 0.8).

Original

Effect applied

As you can see, creating color effects using node trees is both easy and fun. You'll likely employ a fair amount of trial and error as you learn the uses of the various nodes, and soon you'll be creating your own complex effects with multiple branches and more nodes than you can imagine.

Saving and Reapplying Effects as Presets

Now that you've created this useful effect, you probably want to apply the same effect to other clips in your show. Perhaps you may even want to save it to apply to clips in other shows, or to email to your friends to prove just how masterful a colorist you are.

Fortunately, Color allows you to save Color Effects settings as presets.

1 Click the Color FX Bin tab.

2 Click the Icon view button to see a preview of each effect.

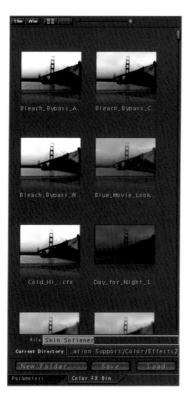

For now, you'll ignore the existing presets, and save your own.

3 In the File field, type *Skin Softener*. Click Save.

The custom preset is saved and appears among the other presets in the window.

4 Click the Directory field to see a pop-up revealing the folder on the disk where the effect file was saved.

By default it's saved in the Home > Library > Application Support > Color > Effects folder.

NOTE ▶ If you select a different folder when clicking the Directory field, you can always return to the home folder by clicking the Home button at the top of the Color FX bin.

5   In the Timeline, press the Down Arrow key to move to the next clip (**18-33B-3-v.mov**).

6   Press Shift-Command-A to deselect all clips and ensure that the effect is applied to the clip under the playhead.

7   Locate the Skin Softener preset in the Color FX preset bin, and double-click it or drag it to the Node View.

The saved effect is applied to the new clip.

Modifying an Applied Preset

In this case, the blur appears a little too obvious. Once the effect is applied to your new clip, you can modify the individual parameters however you like. The saved preset will not be affected.

1   Double-click the Output node so that your Viewer always displays the finished image.

2   Click the Blur node.

3   Click the Parameters tab to access the Blur parameters.

4   Lower the Spread parameter to .65.

These settings are only a suggestion, and you'll likely want to adjust the edge detector settings too, especially when applying this effect to a variety of different shots. In some cases you may need to use other nodes to artificially boost the contrast of the image prior to applying the edge detector, or replace the blur with a more subtle smoothing effect, such as the Grain Reduction node.

Feel free to experiment to create different effects and different combinations. Add or remove nodes as you see fit. If at some point you come up with a new effect you'd like to save, return to the Presets bin, type a name for your effect, and click Save.

Working with Preset Color Effects

Color ships with a collection of useful and versatile preset color effects. Some are simple two- or three-node combinations with a few well-chosen parameter settings. Others are so complex that many colorists would be loath to build them themselves.

In either case, applying them couldn't be easier.

1   In the Timeline, press the Down Arrow key to move to the next clip (**04_warplane**).

2   In the Color FX bin, switch to list view.

3   Press Shift-Command-A to deselect all clips and ensure that the effect is applied to the clip under the playhead.

4   Double-click the Bleach_Bypass_Adjustable preset.

> **NOTE** ► Applying a preset replaces any nodes currently in the Node View.

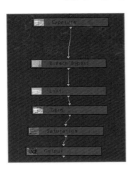 

The preset is applied to the clip.

5   In the Node View, double-click the Output node to display it in the Viewer.

6   Single-click the Saturation node to access its parameters.

7   Click the Parameters tab.

8   Adjust the Saturation parameter to 1.

This adds a bit more color to the airplane without overriding the general effect. Any of the nodes can be adjusted this way to customize and finesse the effect to the needs of your particular shot.

▶ **What Is Bleach Bypass?**

Bleach bypass is the photographic technique of skipping the step in the development process that removes the silver from the film. This effectively renders a black-and-white version of the image on top of the color image, albeit in an organic, integrated way. (Technicolor's ENR and Deluxe Labs' ACE are proprietary variants of this technique that allow the film to be only partially bleached.)

The resulting images typically have increased contrast and grain and lowered saturation, especially in certain hues. This creates a harsh, cool, metallic look that has been wildly overused in recent years in commercials, television shows, music videos, and even feature films (such as *Saving Private Ryan*, *Three Kings*, and *Fight Club*).

Projects intending to employ this process typically make adjustments during production to retain extra detail in the bright areas (by underexposing slightly) and increase saturation (typically through production design and film-stock choices), as the process generally blows out whites and removes saturation. If your source footage wasn't shot with this intention, you may find the results undesirable (or you may have to deliberately step down various parameter values to achieve the desired result).

Despite its overuse, the look remains remarkably popular, so you can count on clients requesting it for many years to come. Fortunately, Color provides several simulated varieties of the effect as presets, so you can be trendy without breaking a sweat.

Analyzing Presets

There are several other bleach bypass presets for you to experiment with. Naturally, different footage will respond to the filters differently, and your desired result may require further manipulation of the various parameters.

1   Click the Color FX Bin tab.

2   Double-click the Warm_glo preset.

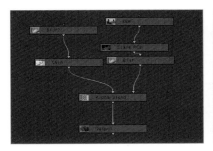 

The Bleach_Bypass_Adjustable preset is replaced with the Warm Glo effect.

The Color FX room is particularly useful for glow effects, which are another of the most popular types of effects at the colorist's disposal. Glows typically require the application of some blur to at least portions of the image, and there are no glow functions in the Primary or Secondaries rooms.

To see how this particular effect is created, you can view each step of the process by clicking the nodes in the tree. It's helpful to start at the bottom.

3 Click the Alpha Blend node.

This node takes three inputs, combining the first two based on the transparency defined by the third. This means that the image feeding into Input 3 is only used as a grayscale matte to limit which portions of Input 2 are visible.

Input 1 is empty, which means it automatically takes a clean copy of the video, so the nodes feeding into Input 2 are being mixed with the clean video.

4 Click the Gain node.

This is the blurred version of the image. The Gain node is used to add the "warm" color that gives this preset its name.

5   Click the Blur2 node.

This node shows the blurred version before the color effect is added.

Next, examine the matte.

6   Click the B&W node.

This takes a copy of the original video and strips the chrominance. Mattes work by making black areas transparent (you'll see the version from Input 1), white areas opaque (you'll see the version from Input 2), and gray areas semi-transparent (you'll see a mix of both).

By creating a black-and-white version of the image, you create a mask based on the contrast of the image itself. However, the image is mostly gray, so to give the matte a clear edge, you must bifurcate the gray values, creating a high-contrast version.

7 Click the Scale RGB node.

This node does just that, making the plane itself opaque, while the sky is transparent.

8 Click the Blur node.

This node adds a bit of softness to the matte, so the edge between Input 1 and Input 2 is gradual. The amount of this blur (combined with the blur in the other branch) controls the amount of apparent "glow" in the final image.

9 Click the Alpha Blend node again.

By understanding the components that make up an effect like this, you can more effectively customize them or even create your own versions of similar effects.

Observing Bypassed Nodes

Every node has a Bypass checkbox that allows you to temporarily examine how an effect looks when one of the nodes is removed from the tree, without having to delete the node or reset its parameters.

For example, let's say you liked almost everything about this glow effect, but didn't like the "warming" effect created by the Gain node.

1   Double-click the Output node to view the final result of the effect.

2   Click the Gain node to access its parameters.

3   In the Parameters tab, select the Bypass checkbox.

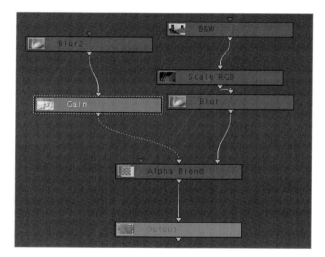

The Gain node is ignored, and a dotted orange outline surrounds the node and its noodles to indicate this in the Node View.

TIP ▶ This is another useful way to see how each node is contributing to the final result. By viewing the output, and turning the Bypass checkbox on and off for each of the other nodes, you can observe the effect of each node.

Although the presets provided with Color are powerful effects that can be used in a wide range of circumstances, you should always look at them as a starting point, or a suggested recipe. By customizing them or recreating similar effects tailored to your specific needs, you can quickly create masterful effects that are truly unique.

Best of all, you can save your creations and share them with other Color users. And finally, it's a good idea to get involved in one of the many online forums where colorists share tips and swap color FX scripts. Before you know it, you'll have more preset effects than you know what to do with!

Lesson Review

1. What is a node?
2. What is a noodle?
3. How do you customize a node?
4. True or false: Changing node order has no effect.
5. How can you monitor one node, and modify another?
6. What happens if an Input port is empty?
7. Can an Input port have more than one source?
8. Can nodes be added between existing nodes?
9. How can a node tree be saved?
10. What happens to existing nodes when a preset is applied?

Answers

1. An individual effect element.
2. A line indicating the flow of data from node to node.
3. By changing settings in the Parameters tab.
4. False. Node order is critical to achieving desired results.
5. Double-click the node you want to view, and then single-click the node you want to modify.
6. The source image is used as the input.
7. No. A node requiring more than one input will have multiple Input ports.

8.   Yes, by dragging directly to the noodle that connects them.

9.   Node trees can be saved as preset effects in the Color FX bin.

10. All existing nodes are replaced.

9

Lesson Files   Color Book Files > Lesson Files > Lesson 09 > GradeMgmt.colorproj

Time   This lesson takes approximately 120 minutes to complete.

Goals   Utilize multiple grades on individual clips

Switch between saved grades to compare looks

Add and delete grades from shots and groups

Save and restore both individual corrections and grades

Move grades from one clip to another in different ways

Create and manage groups of clips to consolidate work

Move grades to and from groups and individual clips

Grade Management

Effective grading is a subtle and subjective art. The fickle client who requests endless changes (often ending up right where you started) is so common, he's almost a cliché. A good colorist knows this and plans ahead, storing different versions of each shot's corrections so she can easily compare looks, make changes procedurally, and when needed, quickly revert to an earlier grade.

Additionally, most shows repeat shots within each scene. The most common example of this is a typical dialogue scene in which the editor cuts back and forth frequently between similar camera setups and angles. These repeated shots will most likely require the exact same color adjustments, so once you've graded one, you can simply reapply that same grade to the other similar shots.

And finally, long-form documentary and drama programs frequently repeat locations, which may or may not have been shot on the same day under similar lighting conditions. It's a critical part of the colorist's job to make these scenes appear consistent. Although this might seem a straightforward task, you can quickly work yourself into a frenzy by tweaking shot two to match shot one, then going back and adjusting shot one to match shot two, and so on.

Color is designed to assist colorists who find themselves in any of these situations. It provides a variety of ways to streamline and simplify what could otherwise be cumbersome and complicated project management tasks. This lesson will familiarize you with many of the most common grade management tasks.

Managing Grades on a Single Shot

No matter what type of shot you're correcting, you'll likely want to experiment with some alternative grades before committing to a final choice. In Color, each shot can have four grades stored at any one time, and you can switch between them with a simple keystroke.

1 Quit and restart Color before proceeding with this lesson. Do not open any other projects before opening the one you're instructed to in the next step.

2 Open Lesson Files > Lesson 09 > **GradeMgmt.colorproj**.

3 If your media does not appear in the Timeline, the media is offline. Choose File > Reconnect Media and navigate to Lesson Files > Lesson 09 > Media. Click Choose.

This project contains a full scene from a sample movie. The first few shots have already been graded.

4 Right-click the Timeline ruler (or pinch open on a multi-touch trackpad) and drag to zoom in on the first few clips.

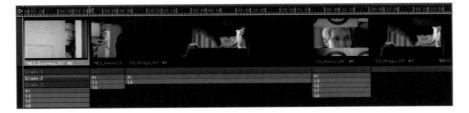

The grade track beneath the clips displays the different grades applied to each clip. The first clip has three different grades applied, and grade 2 is active. Grade 2 contains a Primary In (PI) and three secondaries. Each of these corrections appears as a colored bar in the grade track area beneath the three grades.

5 Press Command-2 to make the Primary In room active.

It might not be obvious from looking at the Viewer what settings have been adjusted, but in the Primary In room you can see that the Luma curve has some points added, and the Highlight Sat. and Shadow Sat. controls in the Basic tab have numerical values in yellow (indicating that they're not at their default settings).

6   Press Command-3 to open the Secondaries room.

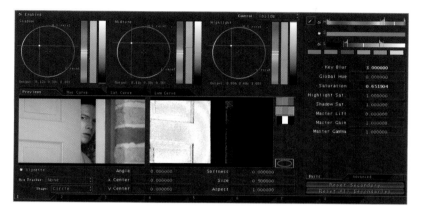

From the green bars in the Timeline grade track, you can see which Secondaries rooms are in use (1, 2, and 8).

7   Click Secondaries tab 1 (if it isn't already active).

8   Click Preview tab.

9   Click the Final Image button (red-green-blue) to display the results of the secondary correction in the Viewer.

10 Select the Enable checkbox, and then deselect it again.

This allows you to see exactly how Secondary 1 is affecting the image. In this case, a key is applied to select the door and the color balance controls are adjusted to shade the door a yellow color.

11 Click Secondaries tab 2.

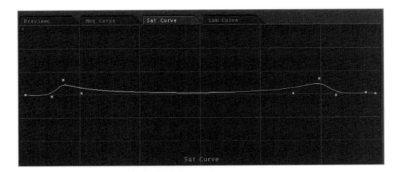

This secondary is employing a Sat curve to boost the saturation of the character's face.

12 Toggle the Enable checkbox and watch the Vectorscope to see this secondary's impact.

13 Click Secondaries tab 8.

This secondary has the Vignette checkbox selected, and a simple shape is being used to limit the effect on the bricks.

If you don't see any settings that seem to be active, be sure to check both the Inside and the Outside control areas.

14 Set the Control pop-up to Outside.

The color balance controls update to display the settings that are affecting the bricks.

15 Press Control-G to turn the whole grade on and off.

Overall, this is a very heavy grade, using a variety of controls to manipulate the image in numerous ways.

Switching Between Grades

When you have a shot with more than one grade applied to it, you can quickly switch between the grades to compare their effects. This is an essential and powerful tool that enables you to effectively evaluate a variety of grading options before settling on your final choice.

Color has four grade settings for each clip.

1 Choose Grade > Grade 1 or press Control-1 to switch to grade 1.

Grade 1 has a very different look. Observing the grade track also indicates that it contains one primary and two secondaries. The grade track changes contents depending on what kind of corrections are used in the currently active grade.

You can also change grades directly in the grade track.

2   Click grade 3 in the grade track to switch to that grade.

This grade has only the primary and one secondary grade applied to it.

3   Press Control-1, Control-2, and Control-3 to switch between the different looks.

Switching between grades does not affect the settings within those grades. Any changes you make in the various rooms will automatically be saved as part of the currently active grade. For this reason, when working with multiple grades, it's important to keep track of which grade is currently active.

4   Drag the grade track divider (the gray line beneath the grade track in the Timeline) upward until the track is at its minimum height.

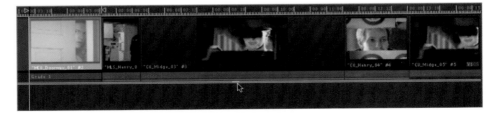

When the grade track is collapsed in this way, you won't be able to see which grade is currently active.

5   Drag the grade track divider back down to expand the track and reveal all the grades and corrections.

NOTE ▶ In some situations, Color will not update the contents of the grade track as you add or remove corrections. To force the grade track display to update, switch back and forth to another grade.

Adding and Deleting Grades

When you begin working on a clip in Color, any corrections you make are saved in grade 1. If you want to leave the grade 1 settings alone and make changes to another grade instead, you must first add that grade.

This first clip already has three grades applied, so there's only one more possible grade to add.

1 Choose Grade > Grade 4 or press Control-4.

A fourth grade bar appears in the grade track and is made active.

2 Press Command-2 to open the Primary In room and make some adjustments to the clip.

3 Press Control-2 to switch to grade 2.

The clip reverts to the setting saved in grade 2. The changes you just made haven't been lost, however; they've been saved in grade 4.

4 Press Control-4 to switch back to grade 4.

Your custom settings are restored.

5 Right-click grade 4 in the grade track and choose Remove Grade 4 from the shortcut menu.

The grade is removed, and grade 1 is automatically set as active.

TIP ▶ Rather than deleting the grade, you could also have chosen Reset Grade 4, which would clear any corrections you may have applied, while leaving the grade intact in the grade track.

NOTE ▶ If there's only one grade applied to a clip, it can't be removed.

Duplicating a Grade

One of the most common workflows employing multiple grades is to create a grade, and then make an alternative version that is mostly the same but with some modifications. For example, in this first shot of the man answering the door, you might set the overall contrast to your liking, but then want to experiment with different colors for the door.

Once you get grade 1 set, you don't want to have to recreate it in grade 2; you simply want to duplicate it into grade 2, and then make modifications to that duplicate. Although Color doesn't have a specific command for this common task, you can accomplish it very easily employing a special type of copy and paste.

In addition to the four grades assignable to each clip, Color has five "memory banks" specifically for grades. By copying your grade into one of those banks, you can paste it into another grade on the same clip, creating the duplicate you desire.

TIP ▶ You can also paste it onto another clip, but we'll get to that later in this lesson.

1 Press Control-2 to make grade 2 the active grade.

2 Choose Grade > Copy Grade > Mem-bank 1 or press Control-Shift-Option-1.

All aspects of the grade are saved into the memory bank. This memory bank will store your grade until you copy a new grade into that slot, or until you quit Color.

3 Press Control-4 to create grade 4.

4 Choose Grade > Paste Grade > Mem-bank 1 or press Shift-Option-1.

Grade 2 is "duplicated" into grade 4. Now you can make changes to that grade, and at any point switch back to grade 2 to revisit your original settings.

Setting the Beauty Grade

In this example the looks you're choosing between are dramatically different from one another. But in the real world, often your different grades may have only subtle differences, and it's fairly easy to lose track of your preference.

Color has a way to keep track of your current "favorite," regardless of which grade is currently active. It's called the *beauty grade*.

1   Press Control-3 to activate grade 3.

2   Choose Grade > Set Beauty Grade or press Shift-Control-B.

Grade 3 turns orange in the grade track.

NOTE ▶ The beauty grade is nothing more than a marker. It has no impact on the image whatsoever, and does not affect which grade is currently active.

3   Press Control-2 to switch back to grade 2.

The active grade appears blue, and the beauty grade remains orange. When the beauty grade is active, it stays orange. There can be only one beauty grade per clip.

You can remove the beauty grade on the selected clips, or on all clips in the sequence.

4   Make sure the clip is selected in the Timeline and choose Grade > Clear Selected Beauty Grades.

The beauty grade is cleared.

> **TIP** ▶ The beauty grade doesn't have to be active in order to clear it.

Saving Corrections and Grades

All the work you do grading shots is valuable time spent, and most shows will require very similar corrections across many different clips. Furthermore, some settings can even be used across multiple projects. For these reasons, Color allows you to save both individual corrections and whole grades to files on your hard disk, so you can reuse them in other projects, bring them with you when moving to a new workstation, or even share them with other colorists.

These saved settings are easily accessible from within Color and can be quickly applied to other shots in a variety of ways.

> ### ▶ Corrections Versus Grades
>
> At the end of Lesson 1 you learned about the terms *color correcting* and *color grading* and how the terms are frequently used interchangeably. In Color, the noun forms of these terms (*corrections* and *grades*) have specific, non-interchangeable meanings, with an important distinction.
>
> Settings made in an individual room (Primary In, Secondary 3, and so forth) are called corrections, whereas the combination of corrections created across multiple rooms on a single clip is called a grade.
>
> Both corrections and grades can be saved as files, and in fact, if you peek inside a saved grade (which is actually a folder), you'll find multiple correction files that correspond to the rooms that had active settings when the grade was originally saved.

1   Position the Timeline playhead over the second clip in the Timeline (**MLS_Henry_02**).

This clip has one grade applied, containing a Primary In correction and two secondaries.

2 Press Command-2 to open the Primary In room.

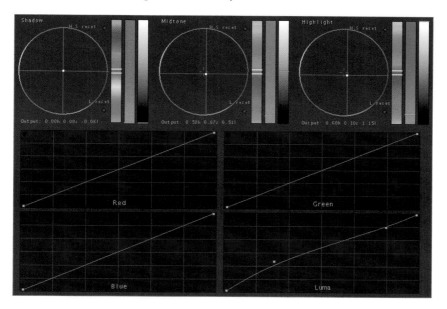

A variety of settings have been adjusted, and for the purpose of the lesson, assume the correction is exactly the way you want it.

Up until this point, we've basically ignored the file list area (called the *bin*) on the left side of the Primary In room. This area is specifically for storing Primary In corrections.

3   In the File field in the lower-left corner of the Primary In room, type *MSHenry Correction_01* and press Return.

4   Leave the Directory setting to the default value (which is Home > Library > Application Support > Color > Primary).

5   Click the Save button.

The correction is saved as a file, and an item appears in the file list area, representing the saved correction.

6   If your file view area isn't displaying icons, click the Icon View button.

NOTE ▸ You can choose to save your corrections to any directory you like, but by selecting another location, you'll need to navigate there manually to recall the saved correction.

7   Use the slider at the top of the file list area to adjust the size of the thumbnail.

8   Click the List View button to change the view to a list.

Reapplying a saved correction is simple and straightforward. As you might expect, you can apply it to other clips (which you'll do in the next exercise) or you can reapply it to a different grade on the same clip.

9   Press Control-2 to add a second grade to the clip.

10 Double-click the saved grade in the file list.

Those settings are applied to the Primary In room of grade 2.

Now you can make adjustments to that grade, and easily return to the saved state if you change your mind.

11 Adjust the Blue curve to cool the overall balance of the shot.

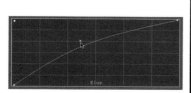

This modification changes the look of the shot. If you're happy with this as an alternative grade, you can keep it (keep in mind that you already have the old Primary In settings stored in grade 1). However, if you don't like the changes, you can easily revert to the saved state.

12 Double-click the saved correction in the file list (or select it and click the Load button).

The room is restored to the saved state.

TIP Color doesn't have a multiple undo feature, so saving your corrections frequently as you work allows you to step backwards through your work, almost like a manual "history palette."

13 Switch the file list back to icon view.

Deleting Saved Corrections

The file list area simply looks for certain file types on your hard disk. Because these are saved files, they'll be available to different projects and can even be moved around. The downside to this is that you can quickly build up quite a few saved corrections that clutter your file list.

Deleting saved corrections can be done directly in the file list in Color, or manually in the Finder. In order to demonstrate deleting them, it will be helpful to create a few new saved corrections.

1 Make any change to the Primary In controls and click the Save button.

2 Repeat step 1.

Two new corrections are added to the file list.

NOTE ▶ If you don't add a custom name prior to saving, the date and time are used as the filename. These names are not editable in Color once the file has been saved.

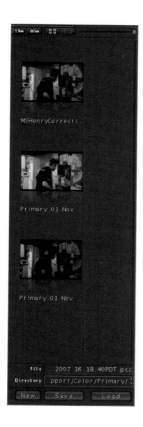

3 Select one of the new grades in the file list and press Delete (or Forward Delete).

Color warns you that deleting saved corrections is not undoable.

4 Click Yes.

The correction is deleted forever.

Organizing Corrections

Another approach to managing your saved corrections is to organize them into subfolders. Color allows you to create new folders directly in the file list. However, you must plan ahead: Corrections can't be moved from one folder to another (inside Color) once they've been created.

1   Click the New Folder button (at the bottom of the file list area).

> **NOTE** ► On lower-resolution monitors, this button name may be truncated to "New."

A dialog appears asking you to name the new folder.

2   Type *Henry Primaries* and click Create.

A new folder is added, and the file list displays the contents of that new folder (which is empty).

3   Type a name in the File field and click Save.

Your correction is saved in the new folder.

4   Click the Parent Directory button (the leftmost button at the top of the file list).

The file list displays the directory containing the folder you created in step 1.

Although organizing your corrections into folders and subfolders (typically named for each project, and then each shot, respectively) is smart, in practice, it's hard to anticipate your corrections well enough to get everything in the right folders, especially because Color won't allow you to rename or rearrange the corrections once they've all been created.

Fortunately, because they're all just files and folders on your hard disk, you can easily clean them up in the Finder.

5   Switch to the Finder.

6   Navigate to Home > Library > Application Support > Color > Primary.

Here you can freely rename and rearrange your corrections, adding folders and sub-folders however you wish. Each correction is saved as a pair of files. The .lsi file is the thumbnail and the .pcc file is the correction settings. You should always move them together.

7   Create a new folder, name it *Alternate Henry Looks*, and drag some of the correction files into it.

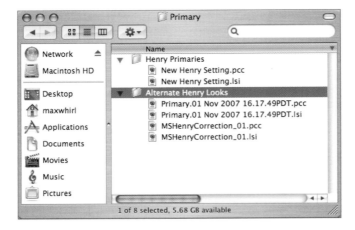

8 Switch back to Color.

9 In the file list, click the Home button (the second button from the top left).

NOTE ▶ If the Home button returns you to a different folder, you can click the Parent directory button to navigate to the Color > Primary folder.

The file list is refreshed to display the folder you just created in the Finder.

Saving Secondary Corrections

All of the techniques you used in saving Primary corrections can be applied in the Secondaries room as well. The only difference is that you must remember that saving a secondary correction actually saves the exact state of *all eight* secondary rooms. Even if some of the rooms are disabled or unused, all of their settings will be saved—and replaced—if you apply a saved secondary to a clip.

1   In the Timeline, press the Down Arrow key to move the selection to the third clip (**CU_Midge_03**).

    This clip has two secondaries applied, rooms 1 and 8.

2   Press Command-3 to switch to the Secondaries room, and click through the tabs to see the effects applied.

3   Triple-click the default name in the File field to select all of it and then type *Midge_ Look1* and click Save to save this Secondary.

    The secondary corrections are saved as a file.

4   Click the Secondary 2 tab to make that room active.

5   Select the Enable checkbox and click the preview tab if it's not already selected.

6   Select the Vignette checkbox, set the shape to Circle, and mask the area of the striped wall on the left side of the frame (use the figure below as a guide).

7   Make sure Control is set to Inside and lower the Highlight contrast slider until the stripes (visible as the staggered white dots) are lowered to about 40% in the Waveform Monitor.

This helps direct the viewer's point of focus toward the woman's face.

8   Type *DimStripes* in the File field and click Save.

The correction is saved in the file list.

9   Click the Reset All Secondaries button in the lower-right corner of the room.

All secondaries are reset and disabled.

10   Double-click the Midge Look 1 correction.

Secondaries 1 and 8 are turned on, and restored to the saved settings.

11   Double-click the DimStripes correction.

That saved state is applied to the shot.

Saving Grades

So far you've saved and reapplied corrections in the Primary In and Secondaries rooms individually. Color also has a way to save all of the corrections across all the rooms into a single grade. Because these saved grades are not tied to one particular type of correction, they're managed in the Setup room.

1   Press Command-1 to open the Setup room.

2   Click the Grades tab. The Grades tab contains a file list nearly identical to the file lists in the Primary In and Secondaries rooms. The only difference is that this one stores whole grades rather than individual corrections.

3 Position the playhead over the first clip in the sequence, and click it to select it.

4 Click the New Folder button in the Grades tab of the Setup room.

5 Name the folder *Lesson 09* and click the Create button.

6 Type *Shot 1 Custom Grade* in the File field and click the Save button.

The grade is saved.

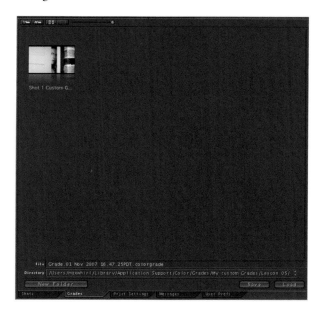

NOTE ▶ Applying a saved grade to a new clip will obliterate any existing corrections on that clip in any room.

Removing Grades in the Finder

Saved grades actually contain saved corrections within them. If for any reason you want to extract one of the individual corrections, you can do so in one of two ways. First of all, once the grade is applied to a clip, you can always go to the room for the corrections you want to save (Primary In, Secondaries, Color FX, and so on) and save the correction there using the steps from the previous lesson.

Alternatively, you can remove the grades in the Finder.

1 Switch to the Finder.

2 Navigate to Home > Library > Application Support > Color > Grades > Lesson 09.

3 Right-click the **Shot 1 Custom Grade.colorgrade** file and choose Show Package Contents.

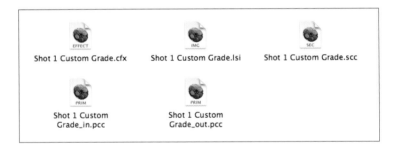

The "file" opens as if it were a folder, and the individual grades are contained inside. You can manually copy one of these grades into another folder (along with a copy of the .lsi thumbnail file) and navigate to that folder from within the Primary In or another room's file list. If you do this, be sure to include a copy of the .lsi file with each of the other grades you extract. Otherwise, there will be no thumbnail visible in the Color file lists.

TIP Your Color projects are also packages that can be opened in the Finder to expose all of the corrections, thumbnails, and other elements used in your project. Although this procedure is not always for the faint of heart, it's good to know all those elements are accessible if you need them.

Moving Grades from Clip to Clip

All of this grade and correction management is useful for single clips, but it becomes downright essential when dealing with shows that repeat similar clips across scenes and sequences—and what show doesn't?

Like most aspects of Color, there are many ways to accomplish this common task, and you'll likely apply different ones in different situations. First of all, you can use the grade memory banks to copy and paste grades from one shot to another, just like you did to move corrections between grades on the same shot earlier.

Also, by saving corrections or grades into files as you did in the previous exercises, you can easily apply those saved settings to new clips.

1   In Color, make sure the Setup room is open and the Grades tab is displayed.

2   In the Timeline, press the Down Arrow key until you reach the next instance of the doorway clip (clip 10).

3   In the Grades tab, drag the grade you saved in the previous exercise to the clip's grade track in the Timeline.

The settings stored in the saved grade are applied to the selected clip. If there were previously any corrections applied to the clip (in the current grade) they'll be replaced.

Applying Saved Settings to a New Grade

Alternatively, you can choose to apply the settings to a new grade (rather than replacing the contents of the existing grade). You might do this if you want to see how the grade looks on a different clip, without necessarily removing the existing grade you've already created.

1   Double-click the third clip in the Timeline (**CU_Midge_03**).

This clip already has a grade applied, but perhaps you want to see how the grade from the doorway shot looks on it.

2   Press Control-2 to activate grade 2 on this shot.

3   Drag the saved grade from the Grades tab to the clip.

TIP ▶ If you drag to the main clip in the Timeline, the settings will be applied to the currently active grade. Alternatively, you can drag directly to one of the grade bars in the grade track to apply it to a different grade.

The settings are applied to grade 2.

Applying individual corrections from one clip to another can also be accomplished by following this same procedure. The only difference is that you drag the saved correction from the file list in the Primary In or Secondaries room instead of from the Grades tab. Corrections will be applied to the corresponding room of the current grade, replacing any existing settings in that room.

Using the Copy To Buttons

The Primary In and Out rooms have a built-in way to copy their settings to other clips—either to selected clips or to every clip in your project. There are two buttons in the lower-right corner of the room (below the Auto Balance button).

This makes sense because many scenes are shot in a single location under similar circumstances, and the basic "balancing" you apply will likely be the same or very similar for all of those shots.

1   Double-click the fourth shot (**CU_Henry_04**) to make it active.

2   Press Command-2 to open the Primary In room.

The primary corrections applied to this clip are already done, so you're ready to copy them to other similar clips in your show. But can you apply these settings to every clip? Or should you copy them to only some of the clips?

3   Press Shift-Command-M to toggle your Timeline playback to Movie mode.

4   Press the spacebar to play the sequence.

Although many of the clips are from the same location and in similar lighting conditions, some of them are clearly different. There is no way you'd want to use the same settings on the outside doorway shot as the inside pizza box shots. This rules out using the Copy To All button. But clearly you might choose to copy these settings to some of the other clips.

5   Again position the Timeline playhead over the fourth clip to make it active.

6   Press Shift-Command-M to return to clip-based playback.

7   Click once to select the sixth clip (another copy of the same shot).

The blue highlight indicates that the clip is selected, and the gray highlight on the fourth clip indicates that it's the active clip. (Its settings are the ones displayed in the Primary In room above.)

8 In the Primary In room, click the Copy To Selected button.

9 Position the playhead over the sixth clip to verify that the primary settings have been applied there.

Dragging and Dropping Grades

Another way to move corrections from one clip to another is to drag them right in the grade track of the Timeline. You can drag entire grades or individual corrections.

1 Move and/or zoom the Timeline so you can clearly see shots 3 through 10 in the Timeline. (It's easy to spot clip 10, because you applied corrections to it earlier and none of the surrounding clips have any corrections applied.)

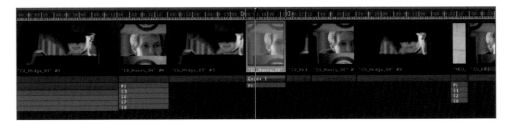

You can see by looking at the thumbnails in the Timeline that there are several instances of both the CU_Henry and the CU_Midge shots. In the last exercise, you copied just the primary correction from shot 4 to shot 6, but in this case you want the whole grade (containing both primary and secondary corrections).

2   Drag the grade 1 from shot 4 onto grade 1 of shot 6.

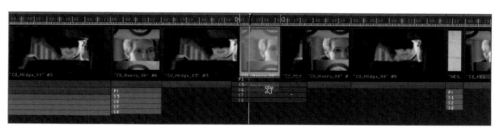

The grade is copied from one clip to the other. You can also use this technique to copy the contents of one grade to another grade on the same clip.

TIP To preserve any existing settings in grade 1 on shot 6, you could have enabled grade 2 on shot 6, and then dragged grade 1 from shot 4 onto that new grade.

Dragging Individual Corrections

You can drag individual corrections from one clip to another or one grade to another. Primary corrections will replace any Primary settings in the destination grade. Secondaries will replace only settings in the same Secondaries room. If no such secondary exists, it will be added.

It's unlikely that you'd move a secondary from one shot to another containing different footage (secondaries are too specifically tied to the contents of the scene). But when dragging between two instances of the same shot, or from one grade to another on the same shot, it can be a great time saver.

1   Position the playhead over the fourth shot (the first instance of **CU_Henry**) to make it active and click it once to select it.

This shot currently has one grade, containing a primary and four secondaries. You might be happy with some aspects of the grade but not others. Rather than changing the grade itself, you can create a new one containing some, but not all, of the grade 1 corrections.

2   Press Control-2 to add a second grade to the shot.

This makes grade 2 active, but to move corrections out of grade 1, grade 1 must be selected.

3   Click grade 1 in the grade track to make it active.

4   Drag S5 from grade 1 to grade 2.

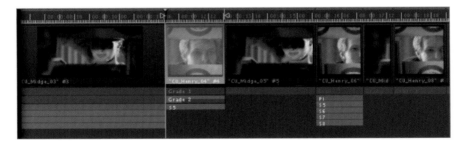

Grade 2 now contains only that secondary.

Although all this dragging and dropping is quick and easy and has its place in your work-flow, it's not without peril. Rather than doing your work by looking at the Viewer and making unique adjustments in the rooms on each shot, you're hoping that part-and-parcel moving from one place to another will do the job. In some cases it very well might, but don't forget to watch every shot and make sure the grade works.

Grouping Shots

Of course, in many shows you can safely copy grades from one shot to another because the shots are from the exact same footage. To accommodate this common situation, Color has a shot-grouping feature that allows you to apply a grade to every instance of a shot in one step.

To begin grouping, you must first identify all the shots you want to group. Rather than doing that in the Timeline, it's often easier to use the Shots browser in the Setup room.

1   Press Command-1 to open the Setup room.

2   Click the Shots tab to open the Shots browser.

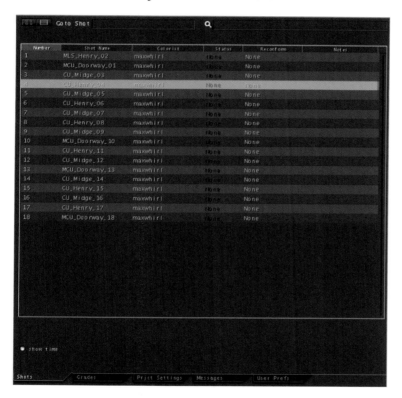

Just like the file viewer and grades, the Shots browser can be displayed in either icon or list view.

3   If list view isn't already displayed, click the List View button.

The clips are displayed in a list. You can sort the list by any of the columns by clicking the header area.

4   Click the Shot Name header to sort the clips by that column.

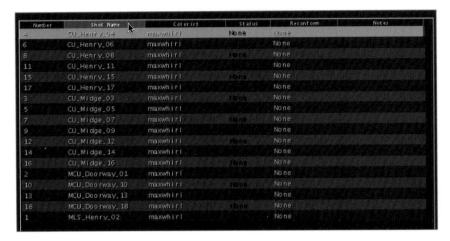

Now it's easy to see which shots are from the same source media.

5   Shift-select all of the CU_Henry shots.

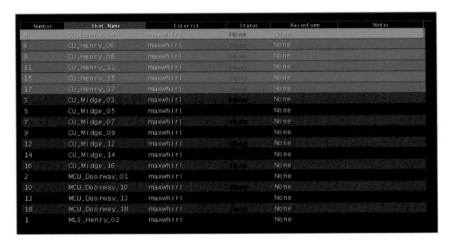

With all the clips selected you're ready to define those clips as a group. However, grouping can be done only in icon view.

6   Click the Icon View button.

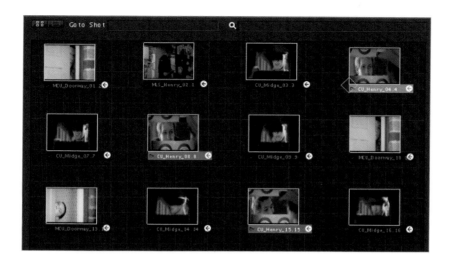

The clips remain selected, as indicated by the cyan highlight on the clip names. The cyan diamond indicates the currently active clip.

7 Right-click and drag any blank space in the window to zoom in and out. Zoom the view out until you can see all the clips.

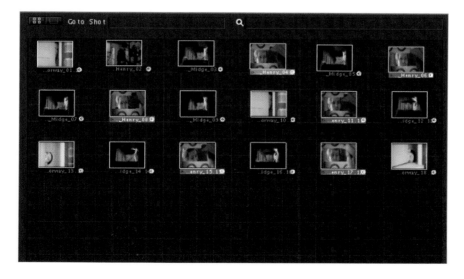

The Henry clips remain selected.

8 Press G to group the clips.

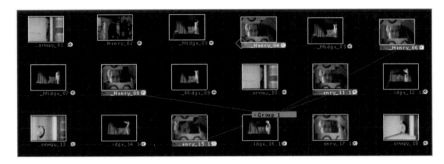

A new object is added to the icon view: a bar without an icon that represents the group. All of the grouped clips are tethered to the group by blue lines.

9 Drag the group icon to separate it visually from the other clips.

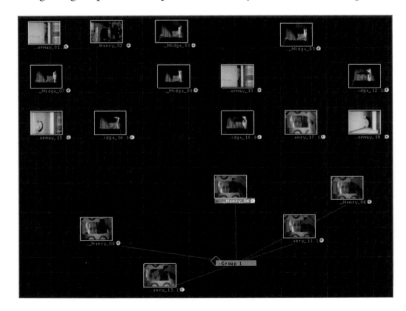

The remaining shots can also be grouped.

10 Zoom out to give yourself some more workspace, and then drag the four shots of the doorway into a row, away from the other clips.

NOTE ▶ You can drag clips only by their names, not by the icons themselves.

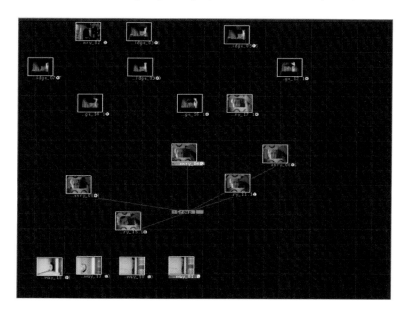

11 Shift-click to select all four clips and press G to create a second group.

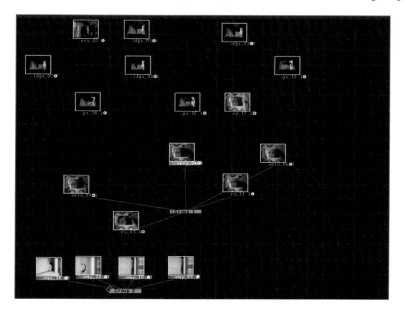

Almost all of the remaining clips are of Midge, and so can be grouped together. However, Shift-clicking all the remaining icons can be tedious. It's much quicker to select the clips in list view.

12 Click the List View button.

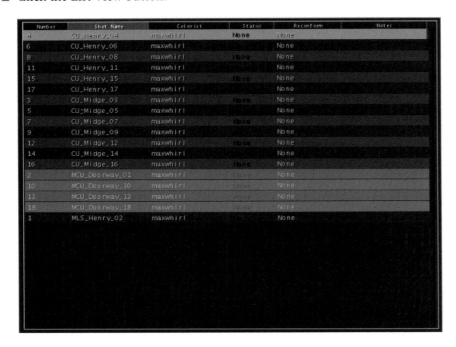

The clips should remain sorted the same way they were last time you used this view, and the four doorway clips are selected because they were selected in the icon view.

13 Select the seven CU_Midge clips.

14 Switch back to icon view and press Command-G to make a group of the Midge clips.

The only clip not included in any group is the MS_Henry shot. There's no reason every clip must be included in a group, but because this is another shot of Henry, in the same setting, perhaps it might benefit from sharing the same grade settings as the rest of the Henry shots. You can add and remove clips from a group directly in the icon view.

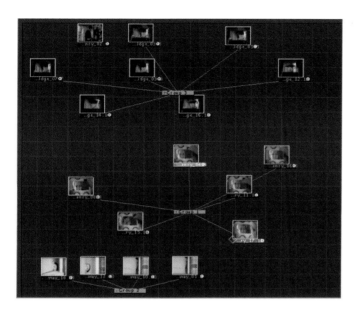

15 Drag the MS_Henry shot until it's near the other Henry shots.

16 Right-click the name and drag to add a blue line to the clip. Drag the blue line to connect it with the CU_Henry group icon.

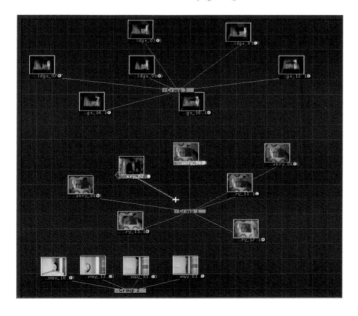

If at any point you change your mind about a grouping, and want to remove a clip from the group, that's easily done as well.

17 Right-click and drag from the name of MS_Henry to any blank place in the window.

The clip is removed from the group.

If you like, you can clean up your icon view by moving the clips and the groups around to prevent confusing overlapping objects or grouping lines.

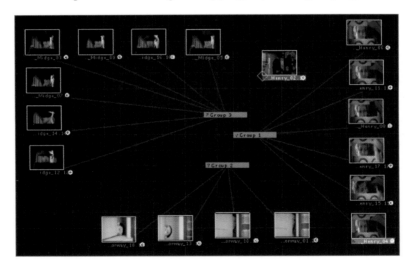

Putting clips into groups doesn't have any impact on their grades. If the shots previously had grades applied to them, adding or removing them from a group won't affect those existing grades. Grouping merely provides a way for you to apply a grade to multiple clips simultaneously.

Furthermore, once you've applied a grade to a group, any adjustments you make on any single clip will have no effect on the other clips in its group. This is good in that it allows you to use the group to apply a base and grade, and then tweak each clip individually to optimize its look.

Applying Grades to Groups

Now that you've successfully grouped your clips, it's time to apply some grades to those clips. Grades can be applied to groups only by dragging a grade that has already been applied to a clip from the Timeline to the group icon in the icon view of the Shots browser.

That means that before you can apply a grade to a group, you must first create or apply that grade to a clip (probably one in the group). For this lesson, all the grades have already been created, and have been applied to at least one of the clips for each group.

1   In the Timeline, drag the grade 1 bar from the first CU_Midge shot to the group icon in the Shots browser. CU_Midge doesn't need to be selected or active.

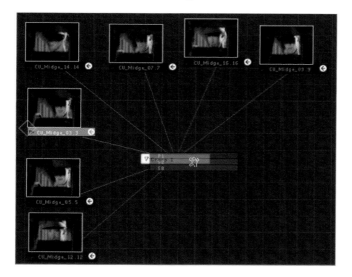

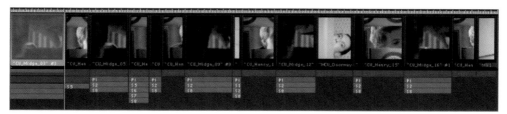

The grade is instantly applied to all the clips in the group. Any grade 1 settings on any clip within the group (in any room) will be replaced with the settings from the grade you just dragged.

If you want to change the grade for that shot, you must repeat this process.

2   Position the Timeline playhead over any of the CU_Midge clips.

> **TIP** ▶ Because all the clips now have the exact same grade settings, it doesn't matter which one you activate.

3   Press Command-2 to open the Primary In room.

4   Drag the Midtone color balance control toward red-orange to add a little more warmth to the shot.

This one shot is updated, but none of the others in the group have been affected. If your intention was to make the correction on this one shot, you're done. If, however, you want to update this change across all the shots in the group, you must do one more step.

5   Press Command-1 to return to the Setup room. The Shots browser should still be open and in icon view.

6   Drag the grade 1 bar from the active clip in the Timeline to the group icon for CU_Midge in the Shots browser.

The new grade is reapplied to each of the other clips of the group.

Working with Multiple Grades

If you include clips containing more than one grade in a group, or if you want to apply more than one grade to a group, you must ensure that the source and destination grade numbers are consistent.

For example, if you drag grade 2 from the first doorway shot onto the doorway group, and the other instances of the doorway shot only have one active grade, the grade 2 settings will be applied to the grade 1 setting on those other clips. This may or may not be your intention.

1   Drag the grade 2 bar from the first clip in the Timeline to the group icon for the doorway shots in the Shots browser.

Not only have you just replaced any grade 1 settings on the other three instances of that shot, but on the first shot, the grade was reapplied to grade 2, leaving grade 1 alone.

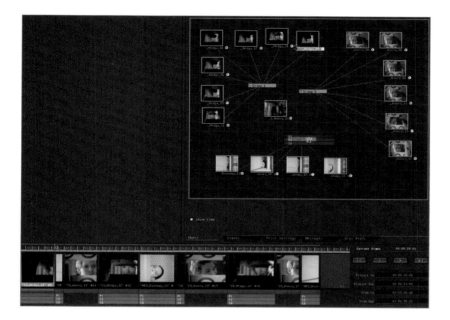

2   To apply multiple grades to a group, manually apply additional (empty) grades to each item in the group, and then drag grades to each of those slots.

Resetting Grades

If you ever go so far down the wrong path that you simply want to reset your entire grade to default settings, there is a quick and easy way to do it.

1   Right-click the grade 1 bar for the last doorway shot in the sequence.

2   Choose Reset Grade 1 from the shortcut menu.

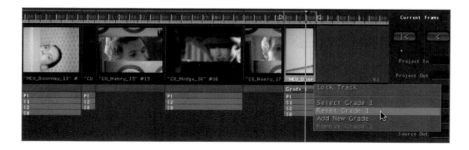

NOTE ▶ The playhead must be over the clip for the Reset Grade to work.

All settings in all rooms are reset to their default values.

This resets only the one instance of the clip. If you want to reset the grade for all items in the group, use the newly reset grade to do so.

3   Drag grade 1 on the last clip to the group icon in the Shots tab in the Setup room.

NOTE ▶ You can safely ignore the Grade Copy Error. It's simply informing you that you're trying to copy a "blank" grade.

Grade 1 is now reset for all instances of that clip, including the first instance, from which you dragged the settings to the group in the first place.

Be aware that this operation is not undoable.

Color's grade management tools make short work of the complex job colorists face when dealing with real-world projects that include many similar or identical shots in the course of each sequence.

Because you can save and restore grades within a session using the memory banks, or across sessions using saved grade and correction files, you never have to recreate looks from scratch. This not only saves you time, but ensures consistency across your whole show.

Lesson Review

1. How many grades can each clip contain?
2. Can you duplicate a grade on a single clip?
3. Where are saved corrections and grades stored?
4. How do you switch between grades on a single clip?
5. How do you delete a grade?
6. Do corrections contain grades or do grades contain corrections?
7. What does an orange grade bar in the grade track mean?
8. Can clips be grouped in the Timeline?
9. How do you remove a clip from a group?
10. True or false: Modifying one clip's grade in a group automatically updates the rest of the clips in that group.

Answers

1. Each clip has four possible grades.

2. You can effectively duplicate a grade by copying and pasting—or dragging—from one grade to another.

3. Home > Library > Application Support > Color, and then in individual folders for each type of saved setting.

4. By selecting the grade number in the menu or Timeline, or by pressing Control + the grade number.

5. Right-click the grade and choose Remove Grade from the shortcut menu.

6. Grades contain corrections.

7. Orange indicates the user-selected *beauty grade*.

8. No.

9. Right-click and drag from the name to an empty space in the Shots browser.

10. False.

10

Lesson Files   Color Book Files > Lesson Files > Lesson 10 > Keyframing.colorproj

Time   This lesson takes approximately 60 minutes to complete.

Goals   Create dynamic corrections and effects in any room

Add, delete, move, and navigate to keyframes

Control Color's interpolation methods

Animate user shapes over time to track objects

Finesse animations by adding and removing keyframes

Keyframing Effects

So far, all of the corrections, grades, and effects you've created in Color have been static—that is, the settings you've applied have remained constant across the duration of the clip. Although static color modifications are adequate for many shots, video is a dynamic medium, and just as often there are changes that occur during a shot that require animated adjustments to your settings.

Color allows such changes for nearly every aspect and parameter in the program through a simple and easy-to-understand keyframing mechanism. This means that everything from basic contrast changes in the Primary In room to the shape and size of custom shapes in the Geometry room can change over time to accommodate changes in your video image. Just be aware that curves (in either the Primary or Secondaries rooms) can't be keyframed.

Animating Effects in Color

Color's Timeline contains a special track just for viewing and manipulating keyframes. Each room's keyframes appear on the room's own bar, so you can compare their relative positions and align keyframes from different rooms as needed.

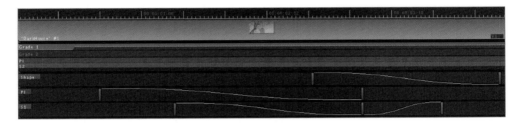

The only significant limitation in Color's keyframing architecture is that individual parameters can't be keyframed independently. Each room stores all of its settings at each keyframe position. However, this is a satisfactory alternative to having individual keyframes for each of the hundreds of parameters in the program. In most cases, you're animating the entire state of the room, anyway.

The other tricky aspect of Color's animation system is that the buttons and onscreen controls aren't adjustable until your keyframes have been added. You must use menu items or keyboard shortcuts to add, remove, or manipulate keyframes, so getting started can be a little intimidating. Never fear; once you get started, you'll find animating effects to be one of the easiest and most straightforward aspects of Color's many features.

1   Open Lesson Files > Lesson 10 > **Keyframing.colorproj.**

2   If your media does not appear in the Timeline, the media is offline. Choose File > Reconnect Media and navigate to Lesson Files > Lesson 10 > Media. Click Choose.

This project contains three clips, each of which can benefit from animating keyframes in different rooms.

3   Play the first clip (**Leverage_Danger.mov**).

This clip illustrates a very common problem you're likely to encounter in your own footage. As the camera pans across from the "HIGH VOLTAGE" sign to the workman, the exposure changes undesirably. The cinematographer set the exposure to be correct for the sign, but that meant it was too dark for the man. Fortunately, this can be corrected easily using a couple of keyframes in the Primary In room.

4   Press the Up Arrow key to make sure the playhead is parked on the first frame of the clip.

You can do a little bit to improve the beginning of the shot, and this particular shot provides an opportunity to use the 3D Color Space Scope.

5   Press Command-2 to open the Primary In room.

6   Click the Luma button at the top of the Waveform monitor in the Scopes window.

7   Lower the Shadow contrast slider to bring the blacks in the sign down to 0 IRE.

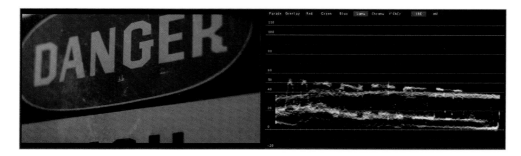

8   Raise the Highlight contrast slider to bring the white traces representing the letter D to about 80 IRE.

Traces for the letter "D"

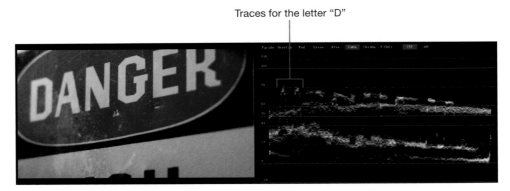

You may notice that the shadows have a reddish cast to them. This can be remedied in a number of ways.

9   Right-click the Vectorscope and choose 3D Color Space from the shortcut menu.

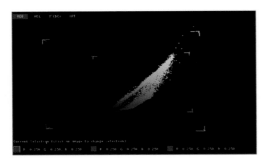

The 3D Color Space Scope appears.

NOTE ▸ The 3D Color Space Scope is like a Vectorscope extruded into three dimensions. One of the things it's most useful for is seeing saturation in the highlights and shadows of your image. Our eyes aren't particularly good at recognizing hue in very dark or very bright images, so this scope can help you identify the specific hue you need to remove to make the black in the sign true black.

10   Click the HSL label at the top of the 3D Color Space Scope.

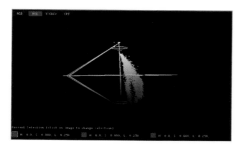

This sets the scope to a slightly different view that will be helpful in this example.

11 Drag around in the scope to change your orientation, so that the black target is on the top, and the band of traces is parallel to the screen, as shown in the image below.

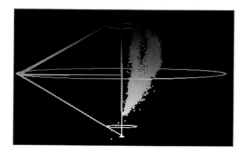

NOTE ▶ It may take some practice to manipulate the 3D scope view effectively. Rest assured that once you've spent more time with it, you'll eventually get the hang of it.

What the scope reveals is that there are no traces inside the circle of color that indicate the black target—in other words, there is no true black in this image. All of the darkest pixels are skewed toward the red/orange hue.

12 Rotate the scope again so you're looking straight down at the black target.

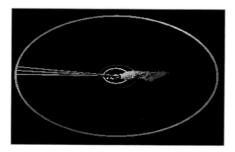

13 Drag the handle of the Shadow color balance control, and watching the 3D Color Space Scope, begin dragging slowly. Keep the traces on the same axis and continue until some of the traces move into the black target and turn black.

If you're really good, you can perform this operation without even looking at the Shadow color balance control. However, if you do use the color balance control, you'll find that you'll need to drag toward 5 o'clock (or 165°). Don't go too far and bring all the traces into the black—remember that there is a large part of this image that's supposed to remain red.

In fact, when you're done removing the red from the shadows, you've removed quite a bit of it from the midtones as well. Now you can add those back in.

14 Drag the Midtone color balance handle straight up toward red.

You can continue to tweak the color of the shot until you're satisfied. But remember you're only getting it right for the beginning of the shot.

15 Play the clip to see how the second half of the shot looks.

Unfortunately, this part of the shot looks unacceptably dark. This shot is a perfect candidate for using keyframes.

Adding Keyframes

Color's keyframe controls are very simplistic, but that doesn't mean they're not effective. In this case you should be able to get the shot just right using only two keyframes.

1   Click the Timeline, press the Up Arrow key to return to the beginning of the shot, and choose Timeline > Add Key Frame or press Control-9.

A new track appears in the Timeline labeled PI (for Primary In) and a keyframe is added on the current frame.

2   Move the Timeline playhead until you can see the workman clearly in the shot.

NOTE ▶ Once you add a keyframe to a clip, you can't make changes to the controls in that room unless you you're parked on a keyframe.

3   Press Control-9 to add a keyframe on the current frame.

4   Adjust the three contrast sliders (Shadow, Midtone, and Highlight) to increase the overall brightness of the clip until you can clearly see the texture of the pillars in the foreground, while keeping the blacks black, and raising the highlights to your liking.

5   Play the clip.

The beginning looks great, and the end looks great, but in between you can see Color interpolating the change, which makes the transition between the keyframes visible. You can solve this problem by carefully choosing where the keyframes occur in time.

Manipulating Keyframes

The Timeline always displays the keyframes for each room, and in the Timeline you can adjust the keyframes' positions and the interpolation method that Color employs to determine the settings on the in-between frames.

TIP▶ Keyframes are saved in the grade in which they were created. Switching to a different grade will update the keyframe track to show the keyframes for that new grade (if any exist).

In most cases, the keyframed effect should be subtle and invisible to the viewer. Depending on the specifics of the shot, you may need to finesse the keyframes directly to achieve that subtle effect.

1   Drag the bar beneath the keyframes down to give more room to the keyframe track in the Timeline.

2   Drag the left keyframe to the right to begin the change as the camera pans across the black wall.

TIP ▶ Command-drag a keyframe to see a preview in the Viewer while you're adjusting its position.

3 Command-drag the right keyframe to the left to end the animation well before we ever see the workman.

4 Play the clip.

By delaying the beginning of the animation, you retain the original settings the whole time the Danger sign is visible. However, if you move the keyframe too far to the right, the animation happens too quickly and the effect becomes more visible as the image appears to brighten suddenly.

This is a very simple example of keyframing. You can add as many keyframes as you have frames of video in your shot. Any settings that change values from one keyframe to the next will be interpolated for the interim frames.

Navigating to Keyframes

Once you begin using keyframes, it's important to make sure that you're parked exactly on a keyframe before making additional adjustments. (Color won't let you make any adjustments if you're not parked on a keyframe.) Fortunately, Color provides a quick and easy way to navigate directly to keyframes.

1 Right-click (or Control-click) the track.

2   From the shortcut menu, choose Next Keyframe.

The playhead jumps to the next keyframe for the current clip in the current room.

TIP ▸ You can also press Option–Left Arrow key or Option–Right Arrow key to navigate to keyframes from the keyboard.

NOTE ▸ Keyframes in other rooms or other clips are ignored.

When you're parked on a keyframe, it lights up with a blue highlight. Always check that a keyframe is highlighted before making additional adjustments.

Deleting Keyframes

If you don't like the results of your animation, you have a variety of possible solutions. First, you can reset the room while parked on a particular keyframe. This allows you to keep your keyframes in place while creating new settings for that particular frame.

Another option is to remove an individual keyframe, which can be helpful when you have many keyframes and want to smooth the interpolation.

1   Navigate to the second keyframe.

2   Choose Timeline > Remove Keyframe or press Control-0.

The selected keyframe is deleted, leaving the other keyframe intact. Alternatively, you can just delete all keyframes using the Timeline shortcut menu.

3   Press Command-Z to undo step 2.

4   Right-click the keyframe track in the Timeline, and choose Delete All Keyframes.

A warning dialog appears asking you to confirm the deletion. This operation cannot be undone, so be careful when choosing this option.

NOTE ▶ This operation removes only keyframes in the current room.

5   Press Cancel to prevent your keyframes from being deleted.

Keyframing Other Rooms

The basics of keyframing work exactly the same in all of Color's rooms, but it will be helpful to explore some other keyframing examples to familiarize yourself with all of the various settings and controls.

Although keyframing can be used to compensate for dynamic exposure or other problems in your source footage, it can also be used to create dramatic and exciting special effects.

1   Press the Down Arrow key to move to the second clip.

This is a shot of a flame blowing out of a factory. You can keyframe a Secondary correction to perform a selective desaturation over the duration of the shot.

2   Press Command-3 to open the Secondaries room.

3   Click the eyedropper and drag across the flame in the Viewer.

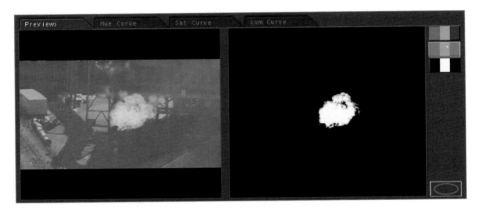

The yellow-orange color of the flame is selected as a key.

4   Adjust the HSL qualifiers as needed, and increase the key blur parameter to about .3 to soften the edge of the key.

5   Press Control-9 to add a keyframe for the current room.

6   Press the Right Arrow key to move about two-thirds of the way through the clip.

> **NOTE** ▶ You may wish to adjust the track heights in the Timeline to see the Secondaries keyframe track better.

7   Press Control-9 to add a second keyframe.

8   Set the Matte Preview Control to Final (red-green-blue).

9   Set the Control pop-up menu to Outside, so that your adjustments affect the area outside of the flame.

10 Lower the Saturation control to 0.

Because you set the two keyframes, Color will automate the transformation, slowly draining out the color (except for the flame) over the course of the shot.

11 Play the clip.

12 To speed up the change, drag the keyframes closer together in the Timeline. To slow it down, drag them farther apart.

> **TIP** Each Secondary room has its own set of keyframes that will appear on its own track in the Timeline.

Changing Interpolation Settings

Whenever you create multiple keyframes, Color must calculate the proper settings for the frames between them. This is called *interpolation*. You can control the way Color interpolates your settings by choosing one of three modes:

Smooth: The parameters begin and end by changing slowly, creating an organic easing effect that helps to hide the precise locations of the keyframes. This is the default interpolation method.

Linear: The parameters make a steady, uniform progression from the starting value to the ending value. This can be useful when an effect begins and ends on the first and last frames of a clip, but otherwise it may draw attention to the keyframe positions by causing a sudden value change.

Constant: The value from the previous keyframe is applied to all interim frames. Effectively, this setting disables interpolation, allowing you to create an effect in which a value changes suddenly on a precise frame.

The interpolation method can be changed for the range between any two keyframes. For example, you can create an effect where the values stay constant between the first two keyframes, then move smoothly to the third, and so on. To change the interpolation method, you must park on the left keyframe, and then toggle through the three methods.

1   Play the clip and observe the way the desaturation effect occurs.

2   Press Option–Left Arrow key or Option–Right Arrow key to move the playhead to the left keyframe.

3   Choose Timeline > Change Keyframe or press Control-8.

    The interpolation switches from Smooth to Linear.

4   Play the clip.

    In this instance the difference between smooth and linear is somewhat subtle, but it is observable, especially when watching the scopes.

5   Repeat steps 2 and 3.

    The interpolation switches to Constant.

6   Play the clip.

Now the values don't change at all until the second keyframe is reached, creating a very different effect, and not one you would likely use in this case.

7   Repeat steps 2 and 3 again to return the interpolation to Smooth.

Animating User Shapes

One of the most powerful uses for keyframing in Color is in modifying the shape and position of a mask over time to accommodate movement in the frame.

1   In the Timeline, press the Down Arrow key to move to the next clip.

2   Play the clip.

This clip shows a group of people running along the beach. There is some camera movement to keep the people centered in the frame.

Creating a vignette around the ocean would allow you to enhance the color of the water; however, because of the camera movement, the vignette would have to be animated to stay aligned with the image. This is a perfect time to employ keyframing.

3   Press Command-3 to open the Secondaries room (if it's not already open).

4   Select the Enable checkbox to turn on Secondary 1.

For the sake of simplifying the lesson, some settings have already been applied to both the Inside and Outside for this secondary. Color is just waiting for you to draw a shape around the ocean.

5   Select the Vignette checkbox, and from the Shape pop-up menu, choose User Shape.

The Geometry room is automatically opened.

6 Create a shape that outlines the ocean. You can use the figure below as a guide.

TIP ▶ To zoom in and out on the Geometry room preview area, right-click and drag left or right.

NOTE ▶ In the real world, you would likely soften the edges of such a shape, but for the sake of this keyframing exercise, leave the mask with a hard edge. This makes it much easier to see how effective your keyframing is, and you can always add the softness later.

7 Click Attach.

This connects the shape to the secondary and enables it for keyframing.

8 Making sure you're parked on frame 1, press Control-9 to add your first keyframe.

9 In the Timeline, press End to move to the last frame of the clip.

Drag handle

10 Press Control-9 to add a second keyframe.

11 Drag the green box at the center of the shape (called the *drag handle*) to realign the shape with the new position of the ocean. You'll also need to adjust some of the control points on the upper-right corner of the shape to account for the new camera position.

12 In the Timeline, step through the clip, frame by frame, and watch the shape position.

Adding Intermediary Keyframes

Although the beginning and end of the shot now look correct, unfortunately the camera move doesn't line up very well with the automatic interpolation between the first and last frames. This effect is going to require more than two keyframes.

There is no limit to the number of keyframes you can create, other than the number of frames in your clip. However, in most cases, the fewer keyframes you use, the smoother your effect will be. This shot obviously requires some additional keyframes, but for optimal results, you should try to determine the best places to put them so that you can create as few as possible.

1 Use the arrow keys to step through the shot frame by frame.

About midway through the shot (at approximately 17:00), the camera tilt levels off momentarily and the mask position becomes misaligned.

2   Press Control-9 to add a new keyframe at that point, and drag the shape to realign it with the ocean.

Adding a new keyframe automatically forces new interpolation between the first keyframe and this one, and between this one and the ending frame.

3   Step through the entire clip again.

Now the first half seems pretty well aligned, but the second half still seems a bit disconnected.

4   Move the playhead approximately halfway between the second set of keyframes, and press Control-9 to add a new keyframe at that point.

5 Adjust the shape's position (and its control points, if necessary) to align it with the ocean on the current frame.

6 Once again, step through the entire clip.

Repeat these steps as needed until the mask accurately follows the camera move.

This method works well for simple movement such as the example above. For more complex movement, you can employ Color's motion tracking tool (covered in Lesson 11).

Keyframing Color Effects

Just like these other rooms, Color FX can be keyframed, and as in the other rooms you get only one keyframe track—regardless of how many nodes are applied, or how many parameters each node contains. However, each individual node can be keyframed independently.

When a node is selected, the Color FX keyframe track displays only keyframes for that one node. Selecting a different node replaces the contents of the keyframe track with the keyframes for the newly selected node. Understanding this will help prevent you from panicking when you see keyframes appearing and disappearing while you work in the Color FX room.

Adding keyframing skills to your mastery of the myriad grading tools in each of Color's rooms will take you beyond the beginner stage and prepares you to tackle many of the real-world challenges that colorists face on a daily basis.

Lesson Review

1. Which rooms can be keyframed?
2. Can individual parameters be keyframed?
3. What are keyframes for?
4. How are keyframes added?
5. Do you set the value before adding a keyframe, or add a keyframe before setting values?
6. How do you delete an individual keyframe?
7. Name and describe each of Color's interpolation modes.
8. How do you make a shape keyframeable?
9. How many keyframes can be added to a clip?
10. Can Color FX nodes be keyframed individually?

Answers

1. All rooms can be keyframed.
2. No.
3. Keyframes allow you to animate effects over time.
4. By choosing Timeline > Add Keyframe or pressing Control-9.
5. Always add a keyframe first.
6. Park on that keyframe and choose Timeline > Remove Keyframe.

7. Smooth: Creates gradual organic transitions between keyframes. Linear: Creates uniform progression between keyframes. Constant: Holds the value of the previous keyframe.

8. It must be attached to a secondary correction.

9. One per frame, per room, per grade.

10. Yes.

11

Lesson Files   Color Book Files > Lesson Files > Lesson 11 > Geometry.colorproj

Time   This lesson takes approximately 75 minutes to complete.

Goals   Recompose shots to correct framing errors or redefine the focus of a shot

Animate pan and scan effects to add simulated camera movement or accommodate a smaller screen size than the source footage

Track motion within a frame

Attach trackers to vignettes to animate secondary corrections

Manually track objects that can't be automatically tracked

Control tracking smoothness to finesse an animation path

Lesson **11**

Recomposing and Tracking

Although Color is primarily a color correction tool, for many projects it falls in the category of "finishing" software. Color's output is often the last stop before exhibition, so it offers a few critical features in the Geometry room to perform last-minute motion effects such as reframing a shot, and it also has full-fledged pan and scan tools. This can be essential if you're preparing a show for an output method other than the acquisition format, such as outputting a 4:3 version of a 16:9 show, or an SD version of an HD show, and so on.

The Geometry room is also where you perform motion tracking for shots where a mask or correction needs to move around the frame to follow a particular object. Color's tracking mechanism is simplistic, which makes it easy to employ, and its usefulness is limited to straightforward tracking applications. Remember, Color is not a full-fledged compositing tool; for nearly all color-correction tasks, its tracker is perfectly adequate, but if you have a shot requiring multipoint tracking, try Motion or Shake.

Using the Geometry Room

The Geometry room is where you perform any physical manipulation that you need to apply to your shots, such as panning and scanning, creating user shapes (which you've done in several previous lessons), and tracking object movement within the frame.

The large preview area gives ample space for performing these manipulations and changes dynamically depending on the active mode. The three tabs on the right (Pan&Scan, Shapes, and Tracking) control which mode is active and contain the different settings each mode requires.

You can almost think of these as three different rooms. In fact, Pan&Scan and Shapes each have their own keyframe tracks. (Tracking is a sort of keyframing operation, so it doesn't require a keyframe track in the Timeline.)

Recomposing Shots

The Pan&Scan tab facilitates zooming in and out and rotating and manipulating your clips in space, much like Final Cut Pro's Motion tab. You can perform a single, static operation, such as enlarging a two-shot to turn it into a single, or you can perform dynamic effects using keyframes, such as adding a zoom during a shot.

1   Open Lesson Files > Lesson 11 > **Geometry.colorproj**.

2   If your media does not appear in the Timeline, the media is offline. Choose File > Reconnect Media and navigate to Lesson Files > Lesson 11 > Media, and then click Choose.

3   Press Command-6 to open the Geometry room.

4   Click the Pan&Scan tab if it isn't already selected.

Although this room allows you to manipulate clips with results similar to what you get using motion effects in Final Cut Pro, the interface works in almost the opposite way. Be aware that moving from one application to the other requires a bit of a mental readjustment.

For example, in Final Cut Pro, you drag clips and position them in a static Canvas. To zoom in on a clip, you enlarge the clip so that it appears bigger in the frame.

In Color's Geometry room, the clip never changes size or position. Instead, you adjust the size and position of the *frame*. To zoom in on a clip, you shrink the frame so that it displays only a limited portion of the original image.

TIP ▶ The red outer frame indicates the actual frame boundary. The two inner white frames indicate action-safe and title-safe boundaries to aid in your framing decisions.

Although Final Cut Pro users might find that Color's approach takes a little getting used to, it's very intuitive in its own right. Plus, you always have the Viewer right there to show you what your final frame is going to look like.

TIP ▶ The settings in Final Cut Pro's Motion tab and Color's Pan&Scan tab are actually linked together: If you send a clip to Color containing Motion settings (including keyframes), the Geometry room will automatically display those same settings, and if you send a clip from Color back to FCP, any pan and scan work will be translated to Motion settings.

The size of the frame is determined by the Resolution setting in the Project Settings tab of the Setup room.

5   Press Command-1 to open the Setup room.

6   Click the Project Settings tab.

7   Examine the Resolution Presets.

This project is set to 720 x 486 NTSC SD, although the source footage is all HD.

8   Press Command-6 to return to the Geometry room.

The HD footage used in this lesson is larger than these new project settings, so the frame boundaries in the Geometry room appear smaller than the source clip. While the Geometry room preview shows the whole clip, the Viewer shows the output as determined by the size and position of the frame.

9   Click anywhere inside the frame boundary, and drag to reposition it and change the portion of the source clip that's displayed in the Viewer.

10   Drag the frame so that the man is nicely framed in the right third of the screen.

You can also enlarge or shrink the frame to zoom in or out on the image, or rotate the frame to rotate the image (in the opposite direction).

11 Drag any corner of the frame and enlarge it as far as you can without exceeding the edges of the source video.

This image also has a slight clockwise tilt to it.

12 Drag any edge of the frame to rotate it counterclockwise to make the horizon appear level in the Viewer.

TIP Be sure to watch the image in the Viewer and not in the Geometry room to see when the horizon looks level.

You may have to shrink the frame slightly to ensure that there's no black edge visible in the corners of the frame, which would reveal the artificial frame manipulations you've created.

TIP Zooming in on an image (by shrinking the frame beyond its default size) will soften the image and may reveal image noise, blockiness, or other artifacts. The size and compression format of the source image, and the amount of enlargement you perform, determine the degree of these undesirable effects.

Animating Pan and Scan Effects

In addition to simply reframing shots, you can use keyframes to create a wide variety of motion effects in the Geometry room, from subtle corrections to radical new camera movement.

1 In the Timeline, press the Down Arrow key to move to the next shot.

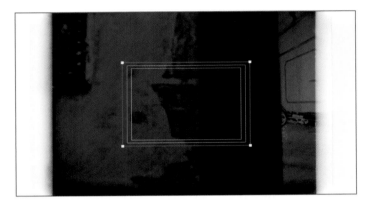

2 Drag the playhead through the Timeline to view the whole clip while watching the Geometry preview area.

This show was transferred from film (telecined) at full frame, specifically to allow for reframing in post. It was also captured at a full 1920 x 1080 frame size, so it can be safely resized, even in a 1280 x 720 project. The white bars on the left and right of the image are artifacts from the telecine process and are not intended to be seen in any situation.

The source footage contains a horizontal dolly move, revealing the chandelier through the doorway as the camera passes by. In this example, you'll add another movement, offsetting the dolly move somewhat (to keep the chandelier in frame as long as possible) and creating a vertical "boom" movement to emphasize the fact that the chandelier is on the floor, where it's not supposed to be.

3   Press the Up Arrow key to move the playhead to the first frame of the clip.

4   Press Control-9 to add a keyframe.

5   Position the frame in the Geometry preview area at the upper-right corner of the visible part of the frame.

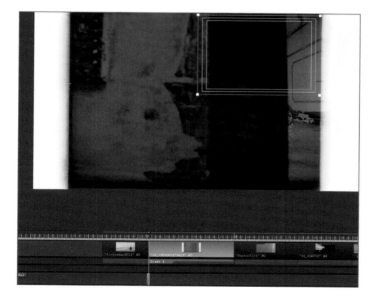

6   Press the Down Arrow key, and then the Left Arrow key once to move to the last frame of the clip.

7   Press Control-9 to add a second keyframe.

8   Drag the frame to the lower-left corner of the visible area in the Geometry preview area.

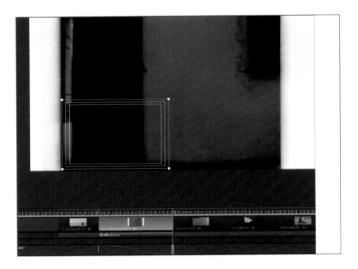

9 Play the clip.

The overall effect is good, but if you stop halfway through, you can see that the chandelier is not quite fully visible in the frame.

By adding a third keyframe midway through, you can improve the overall move.

10 Position the playhead midway through the clip, and press Control-9 to add a keyframe.

11 Position the frame to contain more of the chandelier.

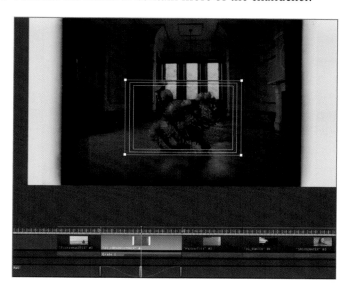

12 Play the clip.

Although this solved one problem, it created another. Now the camera move appears to stall midway through the shot, undermining the momentum of the original material. This is because of Color's default keyframe interpolation, which adds an "ease in/ ease out" effect at each keyframe.

In this case, changing the interpolation to Linear will give a more desirable effect. Interpolation can be set only on the leftmost keyframe for each section.

13 Press Option–Left Arrow to move the playhead to the first keyframe.

14 Choose Timeline > Change Keyframe (or press Control-8) to set the interpolation to Linear.

15 Press Option–Right Arrow to move to the middle keyframe.

16 Press Control-8 to change this keyframe to Linear as well.

17 Play the clip.

Now the animated pan and scan effect doesn't pause midway through the shot.

This shot can be recomposed in a wide variety of ways. Experiment on your own with different ways of displaying the shot. Remember that you can zoom in and out, rotate the image, and use the different interpolation settings to create linear, smooth, or constant (which will pause the movement between two keyframes) motion effects.

NOTE ▶ Animated Pan and Scan settings will not be sent to Final Cut Pro. However, if you're outputting to DPX files, the animated effect will be "baked" into the final output. For more about exporting to DPX, see Appendix A.

Tracking Objects

Moving shots always provide additional challenges for colorists, especially when using secondaries that operate on specific objects within the frame. When an object can be isolated based on a specific color, you can use keyframes to follow any movement within the shot. When keys won't work, you can employ Color's tracking tool to follow objects that move in the frame.

1 Press the Down Arrow key to move to the next shot and play it.

This shot already has some primary corrections to improve the overall contrast, but it could be greatly improved by adding a vignette to give some more sunset color and blue to the sky.

2   Press Command-3 to open the Secondaries room.

3   Move the playhead midway through the clip so that the buildings are visible in the frame.

4   Enable Secondary #1, and select the Vignette checkbox.

5   Set the Vignette shape to Square. In the preview area, enlarge, position, and soften the mask to cover the top half of the frame as pictured below.

6   Set the Matte Preview control to Final.

7   Click the Display Vignette button in the lower right corner of the preview area to turn off the yellow vignette in the Scopes window.

8   With the Control pop-up menu set to Inside, lower the Shadow contrast slider to bring out more detail in the buildings (until the blacks on the left of the frame hit 0% in the Waveform Monitor), and move the Midtone color balance control toward orange to add more saturation to the masked area.

9   Set the Control pop-up menu to Outside, and move the Shadow, Midtone, and Highlight color balance controls toward blue to add a touch more color to the water.

10 Play the clip.

Oops! The correction sure looked good on that one frame, but it needs to follow the camera move to be useful in this shot. Enter the tracker.

11 Press Command-6 to open the Geometry room, and click the Tracking tab to access the motion tracker controls.

12   Make sure the playhead is on the first frame of the clip, and click the New button.

A new tracker is added and appears in the list at the top of the tab. (You can have many trackers applied to each clip.)

The inner box of the tracker identifies the specific object in the image you want Color to track, and the outer box provides the range where Color will search for that object in the subsequent frames. You can move and resize both boxes directly in the preview area. If the object's movement is fast, you will likely need a larger search box.

Tracking is most effective on high-contrast areas and video noise reduces its efficacy, so you must choose your tracking target carefully. In this image, there's not very much to choose from at all.

13   Reposition and resize the tracker so that the tip of the island is in the inner box and the outer box surrounds it with a small search area.

TIP ► If the outer (search) box is too small and the tracked object moves too far, too fast, the tracker may not be able to find it, and your tracking operation will fail. On the other hand, if the search box is too large, it might intersect another similar object in the frame, and the tracker might start following the wrong object. Additionally, the larger the outer box is, the more time the processing will take.

14 Click the Process button.

Color steps through the clip frame by frame and tracks the object. A progress bar is displayed in the Tracker tab, and as the growing green bar in the Tracker area of the Timeline.

NOTE ▶ Although in this example you track the entire clip from the first to last frame, trackers can have In and Out points to limit their action to a subsection of a clip.

Applying Tracking Data to Corrections

Of course, just tracking an object doesn't have any effect on the image. In order to use that information, you must attach it to a correction. In this case, you'll attach it to the secondary vignette you created earlier.

1 Press Command-3 to open the Secondaries room.

2 In the Vignette section, select Tracker 1 from the Use Tracker pop-up menu.

TIP ▶ To disconnect a tracker from the vignette, select "none" from the Use Tracker pop-up menu.

The vignette position is linked to the tracker data.

3   Play the clip.

The effect now moves along with the camera move.

Offsetting the Vignette

This is a deceptively easy example because the object you tracked is in nearly the exact same position as the center of the vignette. Often this won't be the case. You can track any high-contrast object in the image and manually offset the position of the vignette to affect a different part of the image.

In this case, the vignette can be offset slightly to better align it with the horizon.

> **NOTE** ▸ In actuality, this example would benefit from replacing the square shape with a custom-drawn shape that could include the bluff on the left side of the frame. Because this is a lesson on tracking and not on masks, we're using the simple square to reduce the overall number of steps.

1   In the Secondaries preview area, drag the mask to a new position so that the yellow line (indicating the center of the soft edge) lines up more closely with the horizon.

2   Play the clip.

The vignette still moves along with the tracker data, but it's offset by the amount you dragged. You can do this on any frame in the clip, and the offset will automatically be calculated forward and backward. Just note that every time you move the vignette, you're resetting the offset value.

Manual Tracking

In many instances, tracking can't be done automatically. Something else in the frame obscures the tracked object, or the object moves off the edge of the screen, or sometimes there just isn't an object with high enough contrast to track at all.

1   Press the Down Arrow key to move to the next clip.

2   Play the clip.

This clip presents a very challenging tracking case. If you wanted to change the color of the boat, or add a tint to the windshield, or do any number of other corrections that would rely on following the boat's movement in the frame, you would first need to track that movement. However, any of the obvious points for tracking become obscured by splashing water or by the boat moving off the edge of the frame. This means automatic tracking won't work.

Fortunately, Color has a well-implemented "manual" tracking mechanism. In the next exercise, you'll track the boat's movement.

Before you begin tracking, think about what object in the frame will be a good target. Look for any spot that will be easy to recognize, and that remains visible throughout the duration of the clip.

For this clip, the right edge of the dark blue line on the boat's hull is a pretty good target. It stays mostly above the water and is a clear enough edge that it should be relatively easy to keep track of (literally).

3   Position the playhead on the first frame of the clip.

4   In the Tracking tab of the Geometry room, click New.

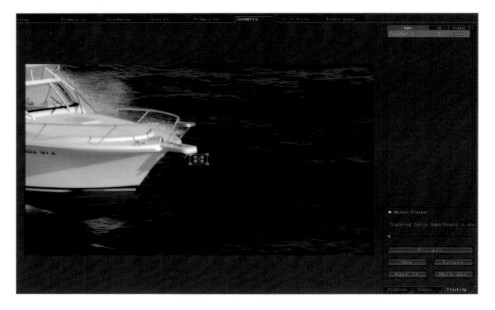

A new tracker is added to the preview area.

5   Select the Manual Tracker checkbox.

The tracker disappears, which indicates that Color is awaiting your input for where the tracker should begin.

The next time you click, you'll define the starting position of the tracker, so don't click carelessly!

6   Click the right edge of the dark blue line on the boat's hull.

When you make that click, several things happen. A red square appears, identifying the tracker's position for that frame. Then, Color automatically advances the video by one frame and awaits your next click.

At first this can be confusing, but it actually makes the manual tracking procedure easy.

7   Click the new position of the right edge of the dark blue line.

Again, the clip is advanced one frame.

8   Continue clicking the blue line, frame after frame.

NOTE ▸ There are some frames where it will be difficult to see the exact position of the target. First of all, you can zoom in on the preview area by right-clicking (Control-clicking) and dragging left or right, and if you still can't see it, guess. Don't worry about getting everything perfect. You can always go back and clean up an errant frame position if necessary.

TIP If you have a few individual tracking points that appear to be out of place, you can fix them by moving the playhead to that particular frame and clicking a new position (not dragging the point) in the tracking preview area.

Once you've reached the last frame, "Tracker 1" will appear in green text. Then you can smooth the overall motion path.

9   Drag the Tracking Curve Smoothness slider.

If you go too far, the tracker may no longer follow your target precisely, but a small bit of smoothing can greatly improve the overall effect of the tracker.

Now it's up to you to come up with a vignette to attach to this tracker. Perhaps you want to tint the windshield of the boat, or even apply a user-drawn shape to turn the white deck blue. Whatever you choose to do, you won't be able to judge its effectiveness until you attempt to use the tracker to perform an effect. And beware, this is an extremely difficult shot. You may need to add keyframes to the vignette shape to achieve your desired effect.

Now that you've tracked the moving boat, you can use that data to attach a secondary, a custom shape, or even control the movement of the pan and scan box.

Extra Credit

Finally, there is one more shot in the project: the swimming woman.

Add a tracker to her lips or nostrils (or any other high-contrast area), and create a tracked vignette to turn her face bluish (to suggest that the water is cold).

Although many projects never need such tools, mastering these effects in the Geometry room broadens your capabilities as a colorist and expands the types of projects and clients you'll be ready to take on. As you get more comfortable with these effects, you'll undoubtedly find many new and unexpected uses for them, beyond even their intended purpose.

Lesson Review

1. What does the red outline in the Pan&Scan preview area represent?

2. When zooming in on a shot, should the red outline get bigger or smaller?

3. How can pan and scan effects be changed over time?

4. What does a Constant keyframe interpolation do to a pan and scan move?

5. Describe an ideal tracking target.

6. What will make automatic tracking impossible?

7. How does adding a tracker change the image?

8. How is manual tracking done?

9. Can manual tracking points be corrected after they're created?

10. How can a track be smoothed once it has been created?

Answers

1. The frame boundary.

2. Smaller.

3. Using keyframes.

4. It freezes the movement for the duration between the two keyframes.

5. A small high-contrast object that is visible for the duration of the shot.

6. If the target becomes obscured or moves beyond the frame boundary.

7. Adding a tracker by itself has no effect on the image.

8. By clicking once per frame on a target object, which automatically creates a path.

9. Yes, by positioning the playhead on a particular frame and clicking to create a new tracking point.

10. By using the Tracking Curve Smoothness slider in the Tracking tab of the Geometry room.

12

Rendering & Output

Once all your grading work is done, it's time to render your work and return to Final Cut Pro where any transitions, titles, still images, and other special effects are reintegrated into the project and you can export or share your finished movie.

Color never exports a single file containing your entire movie. Instead, it renders new copies of each of the clips in your movie. Because color grading is intended to be a finishing step, it's common to render these movies in the highest possible quality.

You can export multiple versions of your clips, either by using multiple grades or by making changes and re-rendering a clip. This allows your client to delay his decisions about which look to go with until the last possible minute. Annoying? Yes, but flexibility is never a bad thing.

Preparing for Rendering

For this lesson, you'll begin in Final Cut Pro, send a sequence to Color, apply some pre-
pared grades and then proceed with the rendering process. This will allow you to experience the same workflow you'll employ on your own projects, but without having to take
the time to do any actual grading.

1   Open Lesson Files > Lesson 12 > **Rendering.fcp**.

2   If your media does not appear in the Timeline, the media is offline. Choose File >
Reconnect Media and navigate to Lesson Files > Lesson 12 > Media. Click Choose.

The project contains one sequence called Leverage Edit.

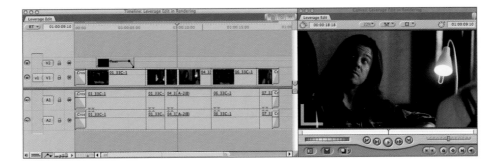

3   Select the sequence in the Browser and choose File > Send To > Color.

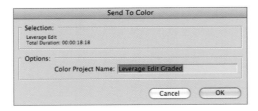

4   Name the Color project *Leverage Edit Graded* and click OK.

Color launches, and the new project is loaded.

Rather than manually grading the project, you'll use some saved grades specifically designed for this project.

5   Press Command-1 to open the Setup room and click the Grades tab.

6   Click the Up Directory button and navigate to Lesson Files > Lesson 12 > Saved Grades.

In this folder are saved grades for this project.

7   In the Timeline, press Shift-Z, and then double-click the first clip in the sequence.

8   In the Grades tab, select **shot1_G1** and click the Load button to apply that preset to the current grade.

9 Drag the divider bar to expand the grade track in the Timeline and expose the corrections applied to each grade.

10 Press Control-2 to add another grade to the clip.

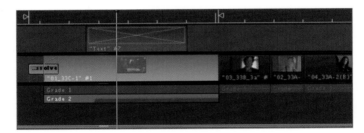

11 Double-click **shot1_G2** to load that alternate grade into grade 2.

12 Press Control-3 to add a third grade to the clip.

13 In the Grades tab, double-click shot1_G3 to load a third look into the shot.

14 Press Control-1, Control-2, and Control-3 in sequence to see the three different looks for the shot.

15 Press Control-G twice to briefly disable the grade and compare the clip to the original.

16 Double-click the second clip in the Timeline, and then double-click the shot2_G1 grade to apply it.

17 Double-click the third clip in the Timeline, and then double-click the shot3_G1 grade in the Grades tab to apply it.

18 Double-click the fourth clip in the Timeline, and then double-click the shot4_G1 grade.

19 Double-click the fifth clip in the Timeline.

This clip is exactly the same as the first clip, so you can use the same grade.

20 Double-click shot1_G1 to add that grade to the shot.

21 Double-click the last clip in the Timeline, and then double-click shot6_G1 in the Grades tab.

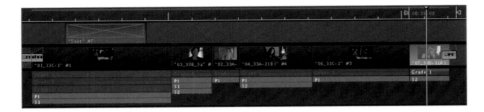

Now all the clips have their grades applied. Obviously you could go in and continue to tweak these shots or create new, alternative grades for many of them. To keep this lesson focused on rendering and output, you can just work with these preset grades.

Checking the Output Settings

Once your clips have all been graded, you're ready to output the files. But first you must confirm that the render settings are configured correctly.

1　In the Setup room, click the Project Settings tab.

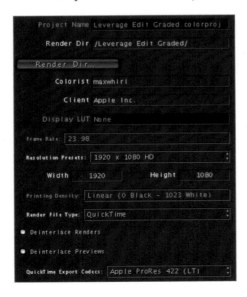

2　Make sure the Render File Type pop-up menu is set to QuickTime.

3　Set the QuickTime Export Codec to ProRes 422 (LT).

This is a versatile and attractive version of the ProRes 422 codec with relatively low data rate requirements.

NOTE ▸ Some third-party video cards may provide additional export codec options such as AJA Kona 10-bit RGB.

4   Set the Handles value to 00:00:00:00.

Color renders only the portion of the clip that's used in the Timeline. If you want to be able to do minor edits to the corrected sequence once it's back in Final Cut Pro, you can add handles to each clip. Keep in mind that doing so will increase rendering time and file sizes.

Now you must set the directory on your disk where the new files will be stored.

5   Click the Render Directory button at the top of the window.

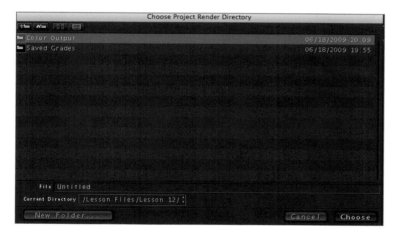

6   Navigate to Lesson Files > Lesson 12 and click the New Folder button.

7   Name the new folder *Color Output* and click Create.

8   Click Choose to select that new folder as the destination directory.

> **TIP** ▸ Always set the Render directory before adding any shots to the Render Queue to ensure all shots are rendered to the same location.

9   Click the User Prefs tab.

10 Click the Internal Pixel Format pop-up menu and choose Floating Point.

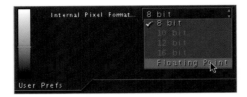

The settings available in this menu depend on the graphics processor (GPU) in your Mac.

TIP ▸ Disabling Video Output in the User Prefs will speed up rendering performance.

Queuing the Render

Finally, with all your settings double-checked, it's time to actually begin the rendering process!

1 Click the Render Queue tab (or press Command-8) to open that room.

Double-click the first clip in the Timeline and press Control-1 to activate Grade 1.

2 Click Add All to add all the clips to the queue.

A yellow bar is added to the grade bar for each clip in the Timeline to show that it's in the queue.

3   Select the first clip in the Timeline, and then press Control-2 to change the first clip to activate Grade 2.

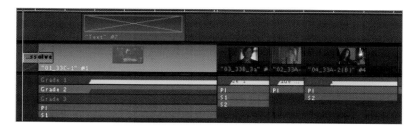

Grade 2 is selected in the Timeline, and no yellow bar appears on that grade.

4   Click Add Selected to add the current clip again.

The clip is added again, but this time with Grade 2 active, and that grade now also has a yellow bar. When you click Start Render, both versions of the clip will be rendered out.

5   Press Control-1 to activate Grade 1 and click Add Selected again.

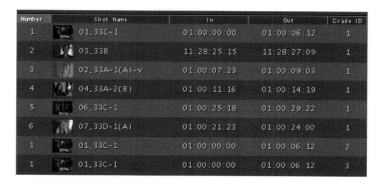

Now three versions of that first clip are added to the queue.

6   Click Start Render.

Color begins rendering your files.

The Viewer displays the frames as they're written to disk. In the Timeline grade track, the yellow line turns pink while the clip is being rendered, and it turns green once the clip has been successfully rendered.

Sending to Final Cut Pro

Now that all your files are rendered, it's time to return to Final Cut Pro.

1   Choose File > Send To > Final Cut Pro.

A warning appears saying that not all of your clips are rendered. This warning can be helpful when the unrendered clips are video clips you forgot to render in Color, but in this case, it's just referring to the offline title on track V2.

2   Click Yes.

Another warning explains that the clips that are unrendered will link to the original media in your Final Cut Pro Timeline. This is exactly what you want to happen.

3   Click OK.

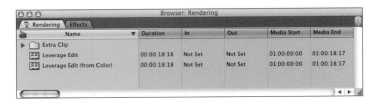

Color exports the sequence XML data, which is automatically imported into Final Cut Pro, using the same sequence name, but with the text (from Color) appended.

If you have an existing Final Cut Pro project open, the new sequence will be placed into that sequence. If Final Cut Pro is not running, it will launch and a new project will be created to receive the sequence from Color.

4   Double-click the new sequence and play it.

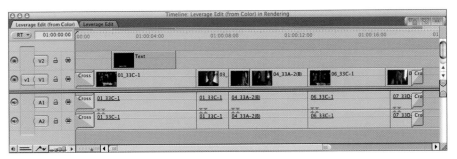

The sequence should look exactly like the original sequence. Any sound clips, titles, effects, transitions, Motion projects, and generators will be placed back into the sequence, even if they were hidden or offline when working in Color.

In this case, there is a title on track V2, fade In and Out effects at the beginning and end of the sequence, and of course, audio clips associated with each of the video clips.

One very important change, however, is that the video clips in the sequence show the same names as the clips in the original sequence but they point to different files on the disk. They point to the new exported media created in Color.

5   Right-click the second clip in the sequence (**01-33C-1**), and from the shortcut menu choose Reveal in Finder.

A Finder window opens showing the source file. The file (and its enclosing folder) are named using the clip order in the Color sequence (2), and the grade number (grade 1).

6   In the Finder, press Command-3 to switch the window to column view.

You can see the path used to store the newly rendered files, based on the Render directory you set earlier in the lesson.

7   Select the 1 folder.

Inside this folder, there are three files because you exported three different versions (based on the three different grades) in Color.

If you decided you wanted to switch to a different grade, you could manually relink to a different version in Final Cut Pro, but there's an easier way.

8   Switch back to Final Cut Pro.

9   Rename the Leverage Edit (from Color) sequence to: *Leverage Edit (from Color) Grade 1*.

10   Switch back to Color.

11   Double-click the first clip, and press Control-2 to apply Grade 2 to the shot.

12   Choose File > Send To > Final Cut Pro.

13   Again, say Yes and OK to the dialogs that appear.

A new version of the Color sequence is sent to Final Cut Pro, but now the first clip is pointing to Grade 2.

14   Rename the new version of the sequence *Leverage Edit (from Color) Grade 2*.

Making Changes in Color

You can continue to change your grading decision in Color even after sending it back to Final Cut Pro. As long as you re-render the clips, the changes will be transparently updated in Final Cut Pro.

1   Return to Color.

2   Double-click the second clip (**03-33C-1**).

3   Click the Secondaries tab or press Command-3 to open the Secondaries room.

This clip has two secondaries applied, Secondary 1 and Secondary 2.

4   Click the 2 tab to activate that secondary.

This secondary was intended to enhance the blue color of the actor's eyes. It uses a combination of a key and a mask, but the shot needs a tracker applied so the mask can follow his movement.

You learned all about how to use trackers in Lesson 11. Here's another chance to put that knowledge to use.

5   Press Command-6 to open the Geometry room.

6   Click the Tracking tab.

7   Press the Up Arrow key to ensure that you begin on the first frame of the clip.

8   Click the New button in the Tracking tab.

A tracker is added to the preview area.

9   Position the inside box of the tracker on the right side of the actor's right eye. Set the outside box to about twice the size of the inside box.

10   Click the Process button.

11 Press Command-3 to return to the Secondaries room.

12 Set the Use Tracker pop-up menu to tracker.1 and position the shape in the preview area so the center point is on the bridge of the man's nose.

13 Play the clip to ensure that the blue is affecting only the man's eyes.

If you're happy with the secondary, you're ready to re-render this shot.

14 Click the Render Queue tab, or press Command-8 to open the Render Queue room.

15 Click the Add Unrendered button.

Number		Shot Name	In	Out	Grade ID	Progress
1		01_33C-1	01:00:00:00	01:00:06:12	1	Completed
3		02_33A-1(A)-v	01:00:07:23	01:00:09:03	1	Completed
4		04_33A-2(B)	01:00:11:16	01:00:14:19	1	Completed
5		06_33C-1	01:00:25:18	01:00:29:22	1	Completed
6		07_33D-1(A)	01:00:21:23	01:00:24:00	1	Completed
1		01_33C-1	01:00:00:00	01:00:06:12	2	Completed
1		01_33C-1	01:00:00:00	01:00:06:12	3	Completed
2		03_33B	11:28:25:15	11:28:27:09	1	Queued

Clip 3 is added to the list again.

16 Click Start Render.

The changed clip is re-rendered. You don't need to re-send to Final Cut Pro. Because you re-rendered the same clip in the same grade, the file will automatically be updated in Final Cut Pro.

17 Switch back to Final Cut Pro.

The sequence is updated with the new version of the clip.

Color doesn't throw out the original file; it simply renames it. Later on, if you change your mind, you can get back to the original look without having to use Color.

18 In Final Cut Pro, right-click the second clip (**01-33C-1**) and from the shortcut menu, choose Reveal in Finder.

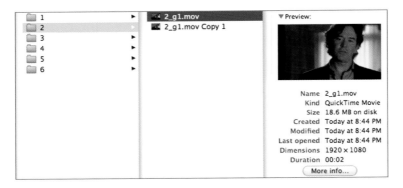

The first version of the clip has been renamed **2_g1.mov Copy 1**. The newly rendered one is named **2_g1.mov**.

Making Changes in Final Cut Pro

As you can see, it's very easy to continue working in Color after you've sent the sequence to Final Cut Pro, but what about the other way around? What happens if you thought your picture was locked, you sent the sequence to Color, and then you get that dreaded phone call—the director has notes?

Don't panic. Although it's never ideal to have to make changes after you've locked picture, it's not the end of the world either. Color has a special mechanism for incorporating changes to the edited sequence.

One warning, however: You must work from the exact same Final Cut Pro sequence that was originally sent to Color. If you make a duplicate and make your new edits there, when you try to update the project in Color you'll run into problems.

1   In Final Cut Pro, open the Leverage Edit sequence (or bring it to the front if multiple sequences are open).

2   In the toolbar, click the Ripple tool, and drag the left edge of the second clip to the right to shorten the clip by about 7 frames.

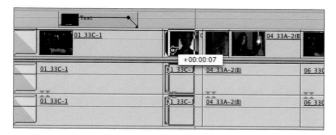

3   Open the Extra_Clip bin in the Browser and double-click the clip inside to open it into the Viewer.

In and Out marks have already been chosen.

4   In the sequence, set an Out point at the beginning of the second-to-last clip
     (**06-33C-1**).

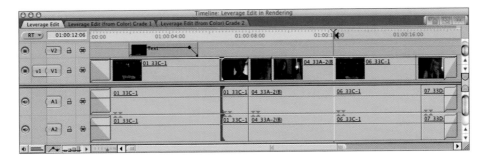

5   Perform an Overwrite edit to add the new clip to the sequence.

6   Play the newly edited sequence.

     You can make a wide range of changes to your sequence, but for this example, these
     two edits are enough to demonstrate this workflow.

7   Select the Leverage Edit sequence in the Browser and choose File > Export >XML.

     The Export XML dialog appears.

8   Leave the settings at their defaults and click OK.

9   Navigate to Lesson Files > Lesson 12.

10   Name the XML file *Leverage Edit _Revision1*, and click Save.

11   Switch to Color.

12 Choose File > Reconform.

13 Navigate to the same location (Lesson Files > Lesson 12) and choose the XML file you just exported.

14 Click Load.

Color compares the data in the current project and in the XML.

With a flick of its wrist it updates the sequence in the Color project to reflect the changes made in Final Cut Pro.

In this case, the first change, the trimming of the second shot, requires no modification in Color, but the second change added a new shot to the sequence, which needs to be graded.

Because it's from the same camera angle as shot 3, you can just copy the grade from that shot to this one.

15 Drag the grade from shot 3 to the newly added shot.

Because that's the only change needed, you're now ready to render and send back to Final Cut Pro.

16 Press Command-8 to open the Render Queue.

17 Click the Add Unrendered button, and then click Start Render.

18 When the render is complete, choose File > Send To > Final Cut Pro.

A new sequence is generated in Final Cut Pro.

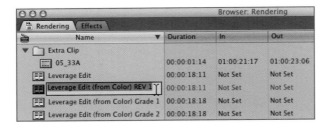

19 Immediately rename the new sequence *Leverage Edit (from Color) REV 1*.

20 Open and play the new sequence.

The updated sequence incorporates the edits made in Final Cut Pro, as well as all the grading done in Color. You are now ready to output your final version.

Wait, what's that? The phone ringing again? The director wants to go back to the way things were before?

No problem. You've still got the old ("from Color") sequences right there, ready to go instead. But be sure to bill an extra hour anyway.

Using Color's Archive Feature

An archive is a compressed duplicate of a project that's stored within the project bundle itself. Whenever you manually save your project, an archive is automatically created, and it's named with the date and time at which it was saved.

Unlike Final Cut Pro, when Color auto-saves a copy of the project, it doesn't create an archive. Archives are created only when you save manually or choose Save Archive As.

The project bundle is a special kind of folder, called a *bundle*. Normally, it appears as a single file, but if you right-click a project file, you can choose Show Package Contents to reveal the bundle contents. Inside the project bundle is a folder named Archive, where archive files are stored.

1   Open Lesson Files > Lesson 12 > **Archive_Example.colorproj.**

2   Choose File > Reconnect Media and navigate to Lesson Files > Lesson 12 > Media, and then click Choose.

3   Choose File > Open Archive.

A list of archive files is displayed.

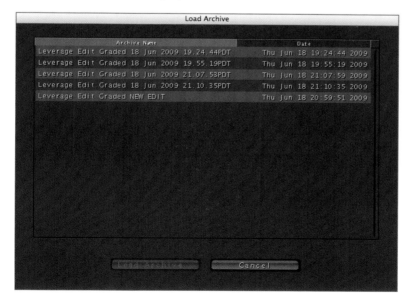

By default, the filenames are based on the name of the project and time of day, but you can customize the name when you choose Save Archive as.

NOTE ▸ If the Color project was renamed, the archive names may not match the current name.

If you open an archived file, the current Color project is completely overwritten with the archived file.

Before you load an older archive, it's a good idea to archive the current Color project.

4   Click Cancel to dismiss the Load Archive dialog.

5   Choose File > Save Archive As.

The default name is the current project name plus the date and time. You can edit the archive name to give it a more descriptive name.

6   Name the archive *Safety Copy of Leverage Edit.*

7   Click the Archive button.

8   To see the newly created archive, repeat step 2.

TIP ▸ Using archive files is a great way to be able to step back in time to a prior state of your project. Whenever you've completed an especially time-consuming grade, it's a good idea to manually save the project to create an archive that you can return to later if the project goes haywire.

Lesson Review

1.   How do you render two different grades for the same shot?

2.   What room has controls for setting the Render Directory and the Export Codec?

3.   Name two ways to create an archive file.

4.   True or false? Rendered clips replace the original source footage on the hard drive.

5.   True or false? Color renders the entire clip, regardless of the portion used by the Timeline, when rendering grades.

Answers

1. Add the clip to the Render Queue with the first grade active, and then make the second grade active and add the clip to the queue again.

2. The Setup room.

3. Archive files are created every time you do a manual save, or use the Save Archive As command.

4. False.

5. False. Color renders only the portion of the clip marked by the In and Out points on the Timeline, plus any handles specified in the Project Settings tab of the Setup room.

Bonus Lesson

Lesson Files	Color Book Files > Lesson Files > Bonus Lesson > CommonRecipes.colorproj
Time	This lesson takes approximately 60 minutes to complete.
Goals	Create a *Black Hawk Down/Mogadishu* look
	Create a *CSI: Miami* look
	Create a *Schindler's List* color isolation look
	Create a flashback/dream look
	Create a "Saturated Sunrise" look

Common Recipes

Now it's time to have some fun and mimic the masters. In addition to coming up with your own color effects, there are times when you may want to "borrow" someone else's signature look—drawn, perhaps, from a specific film or a genre of films. In this lesson, we've put together recipes for some useful and interesting looks you might be familiar with, along with some handy techniques for dealing with skin tone correction. (Please note that all of these looks were created with Broadcast Safe on.)

Let's start cooking!

Black Hawk Down/Mogadishu Look

Our aim here is to turn some fairly flat-looking HD footage into a typical Hollywood depiction of "Africa." This footage was shot in Rwanda, so we aren't trying to fake the location. We're merely trying to produce an image that will look familiar to audiences who, through long exposure to television and film, have come to associate a certain film look with that continent.

1   Open Lesson Files > Bonus Lesson > **CommonRecipes.colorproj**.

There are seven shots in the Timeline grouped into a Before section at left, and an After section at right. We'll start with the first one, showing a security guard holding an AK-47 machine gun.

2   Right-click and drag the Timeline ruler (or pinch open on a multi-touch trackpad) to zoom in on the first few clips.

We're starting fresh with this shot; no initial corrections have been made.

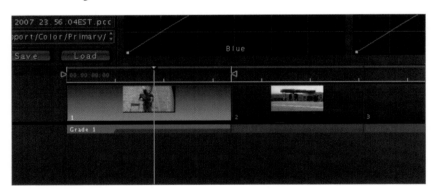

3   Press Command-2 to activate the Primary In room.

4   To make sure your clip is active, double-click it.

The next step is to increase the overall contrast of the clip, using Luma in the Waveform Monitor as a guide.

5   First, use the Highlight contrast slider to increase the highlights by approximately 15%.

6   Then, using the Shadow contrast slider, reduce the black level to about 1% black until the highlights touch 100% in the Waveform Monitor.

Again, using the Waveform Monitor as a guide, be careful not to crush the shadows too much initially.

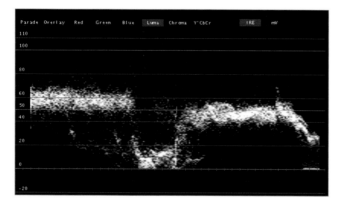

7   In the Basic tab on the right side of the frame, next to the color balance controls, type *0.9* in the Saturation field to reduce the saturation to 0.90 and press Return.

8   Press Command-3 to open the Secondaries room, and click Secondaries tab 1 (if it isn't already active).

9 Select the Enabled checkbox to enable the first Secondary (S1).

10 Using the Midtone color balance control, slowly introduce a yellow tone across the entire image.

> **NOTE ▸** The exact amount of yellow you add is your choice, but be careful not to push it too far or it will overpower the final look you're going for.

11 Next, we need to reduce saturation in the shadows. In the Basic tab next to the color balance controls, reduce Shadow Saturation to *0.30*.

12 Click Secondaries tab 2. Use the secondary Sat Curve to increase the warmer tones and reduce the blues and aquas, until your Sat Curve resembles the one shown here.

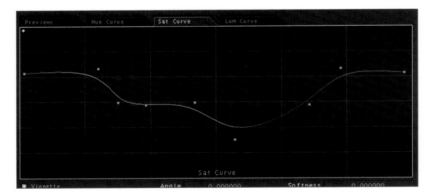

13 Select and deselect the Enabled checkbox while watching the Vectorscope to see the impact of this secondary correction.

14 Press Command-5 to bring up the Primary Out room.

Increasing Color Density

Now we'll manipulate the curves to increase the richness of the colors. Use the image below as reference for adjusting the curves to achieve the desired look.

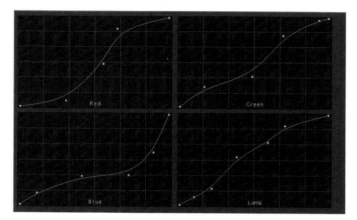

1 Toggle the grade on and off by pressing Control-G to compare the original shot with the graded one.

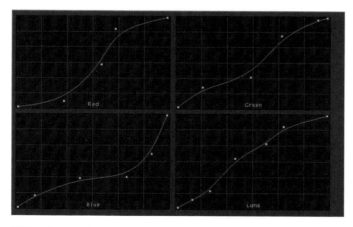

2   The next step is to make slight tweaks in the Primary Out room to ensure that you don't crush (lower) the shadow levels too much. Otherwise, you'll be in danger of losing the image detail in both the shadows and darker midtones.

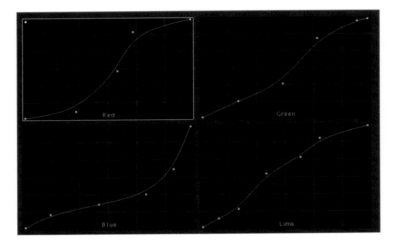

TIP ▶ After you've established this look you could drag this grade to other clips (as shown below), but another easy way is to save this look as a grade in the Setup room that you can then reuse later. Additionally, you could use groups, as discussed in Lesson 9, to make applying this grade to comparable clips even easier.

CSI: Miami Look

Now it's time to make a fairly overcast day in Sydney look like a warm, cloud-free day in Miami. We also have a vintage car in the shot, which we'll dress up to help make the scene look more convincing.

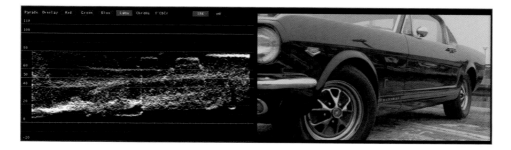

1   Proceed to shot 3 (**03CITYCAR**) on the Timeline.

2   Press Command-2 to make the Primary In room active. Double-click the clip to ensure that it's active.

3   The next step is to boost the overall contrast of the clip. First, move the playhead in the Timeline past the halfway mark in the clip until the frame you see matches the image below. Next, increase the highlights by approximately 95% white using the Highlight contrast slider, and then reduce the black level to about 1% using the Shadow contrast slider, being careful not to crush the shadows too much initially.

At all times, keep an eye on the Waveform Monitor as your guide.

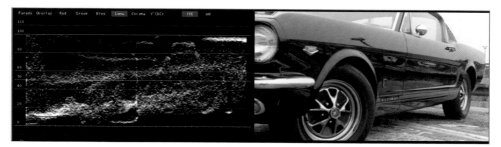

4   Increase the saturation to 1.33 by typing *1.33* in the Saturation field or middle-clicking and dragging until you reach the desired value.

5   Press Command-3 to open the Secondaries room.

6   Click Secondaries tab 1 (if it isn't already active).

7   Select the Enabled and Vignette checkboxes.

8   Choose a square vignette and stretch it out in the preview area until it covers the top 20% of the screen.

9 Type *0.8* in the Softness field. If necessary, toggle the Control pop-up menu to ensure that you're switched to Inside control.

10 Ensure that you're set to Final View in the Secondaries preview area, and push the Midtone color balance control into the orange-red direction until your clip resembles the screen below.

> **NOTE** ▶ Be careful when adjusting the midtones. Because you're working with Broadcast Safe on, if you push the midtones too far into the orange-reds, the color will clip.

11 Click Secondaries tab 2.

We now need to use the secondary Sat Curve to increase reds, blues, and yellows, and reduce the greens.

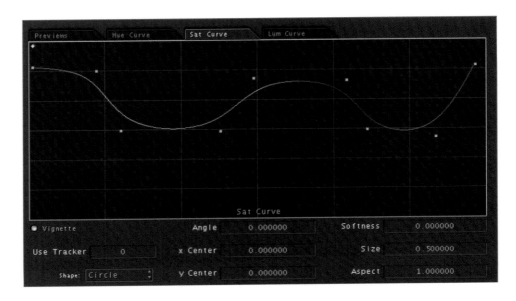

12 Use the third secondary (S3) to create an additional vignette in the top half of the frame as shown below. Set the vignette shape to Circle and approximate the settings shown in yellow in the screenshot.

Next, we'll bring down the outside shadow levels to darken the road.

13 Ensure that the Control pop-up menu is set to Outside, and use the Shadow contrast slider to crush the shadows by about 19–22%.

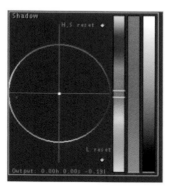

Using Your Grade on a New Clip

Now it's time to move on to the next clip and drag the entire grade over. We'll try to modify this look for the building. Initially, it looks good, but to be safe, let's rotate the "grad" (as in gradient) in the sky.

NOTE ▶ Gradient filters (grads) are thin layers of glass used by cinematographers and DPs around the world to filter light frequency out of an image prior to acquisition to film or digital. Only recently have tools like Color allowed us to simulate this effect digitally by positioning square vignettes in a frame, like dropping a glass grad in front of a camera lens. Camera matte boxes allow an operator to rotate glass grads. In Color, we can simulate this effect by rotating a vignette.

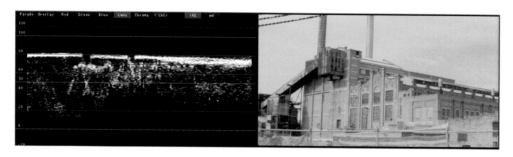

It's very common to start with a base grade that generally works and then copy this to all the clips that are similar in framing. You can then proceed to each shot independently and make minor tweaks without affecting the neighbors on the Timeline, as you'll do now.

1   Press the Down Arrow key to move to shot 4.

     In this shot the sky is pretty flat and cool. You can warm it up quite a bit by going back to the Secondaries room and using the adjustments from the previous clip and tweaking them slightly.

2   Drag grade 1 from shot 3 (**03CITYCAR**) onto grade 1 of shot 4 (**04CITYFACTORY**).

3   Increase the reds and saturation in the sky, adjusting the color balance controls as shown below.

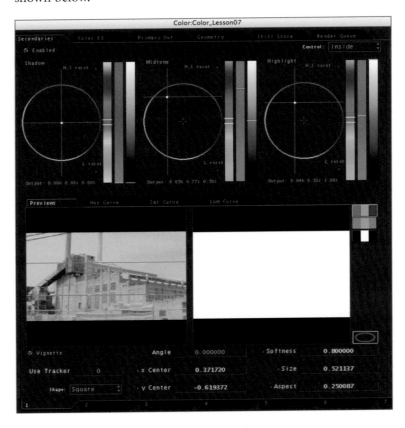

4   Increase the softness so that the sky gradient is not too over the top.

5   Toggle Control-G to compare the graded image to the original.

Schindler's List **Look**

You can create an interesting look by simply reducing the color levels in the image and relying on just black, white, and a single color hue. This popular effect was perhaps used most memorably in Steven Spielberg's *Schindler's List*, to draw attention to a girl's red coat in an otherwise black-and-white setting during the liquidation of the Krakow ghetto. In this exercise, we'll recreate the effect using a shot of a prisoner in a cell, as shown below (this is the final version—yours should look like this at the end of the exercise).

1   Proceed to shot 5 (**09JAILORANGE**) on the Timeline, and double-click it to make it active.

2 Press Command-2 to make the Primary In room active.

3 Next, boost the overall contrast of the clip by increasing the highlights by approximately 10%, and reducing the black level to about 5% black using the Waveform Monitor as a guide. Use the Shadow and Highlight contrast sliders to make these adjustments.

We still need black detail for this shot.

4 Press Command-3 to open the Secondaries room.

5 Click Secondaries tab 1 (if it isn't already active).

6 Click the eyedropper, and in the Viewer, drag the red crosshairs across the figure's orange jumpsuit. The eyedropper should auto-enable the Secondary.

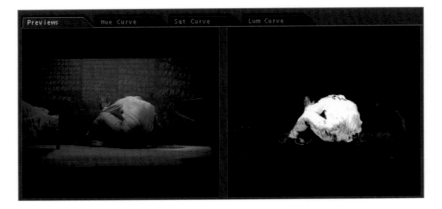

7 Now you'll improve the key by extending the tolerance handles outward to feather the edges and setting the Key Blur to 3.0.

8 Continue to enhance the matte using the HSL qualifiers, adjusting them so the settings resemble the screen below.

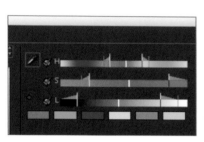 

9 If necessary, check the Control pop-up menu to ensure that you're switched to Inside control, and then proceed to move all the color balance controls toward orange.

10 Toggle the Control pop-up menu to select the outside controls of the key and then reduce the saturation to 0.

Now let's add more contrast to the black-and-white walls.

11 Using the Shadow and Highlight contrast sliders, reduce the shadows by 12% and increase the highlights by 40%.

12 Click Secondaries tab 2.

The next step is to create a vignette and give the lighting more downward direction.

13 Select the Vignette checkbox and then select a circle vignette. Place the circle around the man and soften the edges.

In the next few steps you'll try to create a pool of light on him, similar to that of a downward-facing lamp.

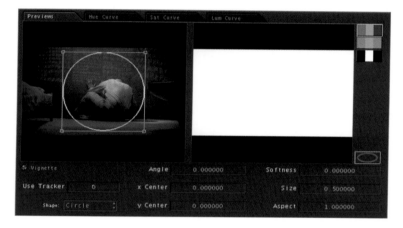

14 Switch to Outside control using the Control pop-up menu; then reduce the shadows by a further 15%. If it looks too harsh, increase the softness of the vignette using the Softness field.

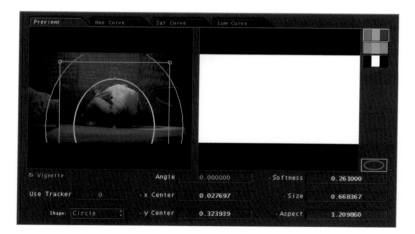

15 Now compare before and after!

Flashback Look

Since the first "talkies," soft-focus effects have been used to evoke flashbacks, dream sequences, and romantic moments that occur somehow outside of everyday time. In this exercise, we'll give a fallen chandelier the full '40s flashback treatment.

1 Proceed to shot 6 (**05EMPTYHOUSE**) on the Timeline.

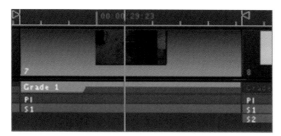

2   Press Command-2 to make the Primary In room active, and double-click the clip to make sure that it's active.

3   Increase the overall contrast of the clip using the Luma curve. Plot the points as shown below.

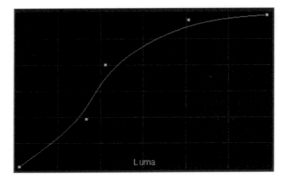

4   Press Command-3 to open the Secondaries room.

5   Click Secondaries tab 1 (if it isn't already active).

6   Advance the playhead until you're in the middle of the shot as pictured below.

7   Click the eyedropper, and in the Viewer, drag the red crosshairs across the white windows.

Your key should look like the image below.

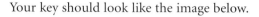

8 Now extend the key by deselecting the H (Hue) and S (Saturation) sliders. Shift-click the left range handle of the Lightness slider and drag it to the left to feather.

9 Set your Key Blur to 9.0.

10 Make sure you have Inside control selected and push the highlight levels to 2.671 and the shadows to 0.51.

11 Increase the feather on the Lightness slider by adjusting the tolerance handles until you begin to see a white glow.

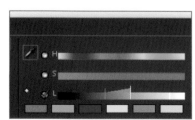
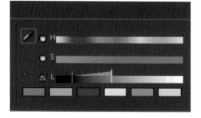

The key will increase and begin to blow out the highlights.

NOTE ▸ It's especially important to have Broadcast Safe on when you're creating this look.

12 Save the grade for later use.

"Saturated Sunrise" Look

"Saturated Sunrise" is an extremely useful effect when the shooting conditions don't measure up to the full drama of the scene. Here we'll take a very flat-looking shot of a World War II plane flying in gray skies and give it a more stylized and saturated look.

Original

Graded

1 Select shot 9 in the Timeline, **07WARPLANE**. Right-click the Timeline ruler and drag to zoom in.

2 Press Command-2 to make the Primary In room active, and double-click the clip to make sure it's active.

3 Now it's time to warm up the shot overall by giving the midtones and shadows a healthy orange push as shown below.

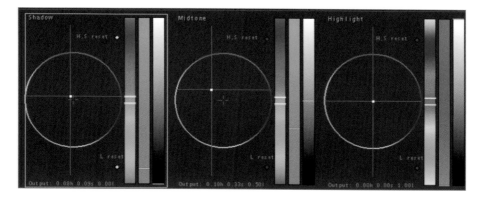

4 Next, create a few points on the Primary Luma curve as shown below.

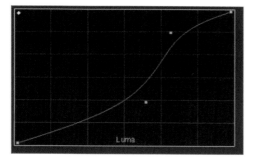

5 Increase the saturation to approximately 1.07–1.1, and then reduce highlight and shadow saturation in the Highlight Sat. and Shadow Sat. fields to 0.92 and 0.9, as shown below.

6 Press Command-3 to open the Secondaries room.

7 Click Secondaries tab 1 and select Enabled.

8 Now pull a key using only the Lightness slider in the HSL qualifiers. Follow the screenshots for guidance on settings.

The key should look like the screenshot below.

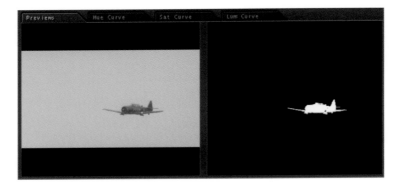

9 Increase the Key Blur to 0.5, select Inside control in the Control pop-up menu, and
then reduce shadow saturation to 0.00.

10 Now proceed to add some green tones to the plane in the midtones.

11 Click the 2 tab to activate the second secondary to work with the sky.

12 Select the Enable and Vignette checkboxes and set the Shape pop-up to Circle.

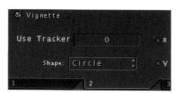

13 Match the shape settings to those shown in the screenshot below.

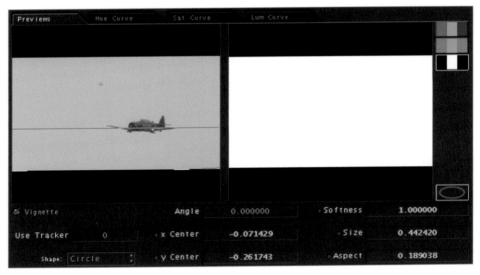

NOTE ▶ You can switch the Matte Preview mode buttons to Matte Only to see the gradient you've created in the Viewer.

14 Switch to Outside control mode and add orange tones to the midtones and highlights in this part of the shape, as shown below.

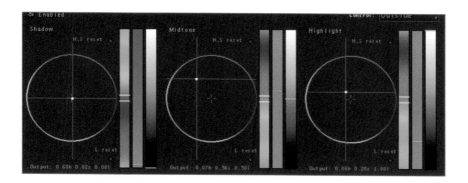

15 Switch over to Inside control and add blue tones to the shadows, midtones, and highlights.

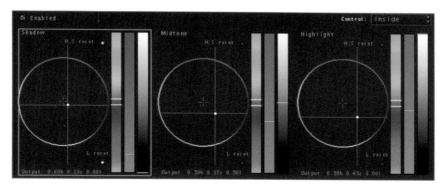

16 Switch to Final and your image should now look like the screenshot below.

TIP ▶ This would be a good time to head to the Color FX room and try some effects presets, especially the bleach bypass looks, on this shot. You should be able to achieve some really great looks by adding Color FX at this stage.

Lesson Review

1. How do you gauge the impact of changes you make to the Sat. Curve to warm up the tones of an image?

2. True or false: If you push the midtones too far into the orange-reds, the color in your image will clip.

3. When using the vignette controls to create a pool of light around a portion of an image, how can you correct when the light becomes too harsh?

4. How can you preview a gradient you've created in the Viewer?

Answers

1. Select and deselect the Enabled checkbox while watching the Vectorscope.

2. True—if Broadcast Safe is on.

3. Increase the softness of the vignette using the Softness field.

4. By enabling the Matte Only button, the third button in the Matte Preview Mode controls.

2K, 4K, RED, and Alternate Workflows

In addition to the standard workflows used throughout this book, Color lends itself to a number of less common—and often more advanced— workflows used for film and video projects. This appendix gives you a brief overview of some of the alternate workflows you may encounter. It covers the following:

▶ Importing Clips to the Timeline

▶ Importing EDLs

▶ Slicing the Timeline (*notching*)

▶ Using the Timeline Edit Tools

▶ Working with RED

Importing Clips to the Timeline

In addition to Final Cut Pro roundtrips, you also have the option of importing media files directly to the Color Timeline. This can be useful in specific situations, such as when you're converting Cineon and DPX source media into QuickTime offline or online media. When doing such conversions, the reel number and timecode from the source media are cloned to the converted media. It also can make sense if you're setting up a project for a demonstration or classroom situation and don't want to depend on Final Cut Pro round trips.

> **NOTE ▸** Although the methods outlined in this appendix are great for 2K or 4K workflows, it should be noted that these techniques pertain specifically to Cineon and DPX workflows.

1   Click the Setup tab to bring up the Setup room.

2   Navigate to the media you want to import into the Timeline.

3   Click a media file to bring up additional information about the shot.

4   Double-click the clip you want to add to the Timeline.

The clip will be placed after any other shots that already exist in the Timeline.

NOTE ▶ You can also select the clip in the Setup room and click the Import button in the Timeline.

You can also import an entire directory of clips.

5 Select a directory in the File Browser and click the Import Dir button.

When importing a directory, Color will scan all subdirectories and import all Color-compatible media files, QuickTime movies, or image sequences.

Importing EDLs

An Edit Decision List, or EDL, is a way of representing a film or video edit. It contains an ordered list of reel and timecode data, which indicates where each video clip can be obtained in order to conform the final cut. Color imports the following frequently used EDL formats (the most common of which is CMX 3600):

▶ Generic

▶ CMX 340

▶ CMX 3600

▶ GVG 4 Plus

The steps for importing an EDL into Color are fairly straightforward, and there are several reasons to use this approach. The first is to use as a cut list to cut up a master video file for purposes of color correction. In this way, you can use an EDL and the master file to simulate tape-to-tape workflow. What's more, using EDLs is the only way to reconform a project from Final Cut Pro to Cineon or DPX image sequences as part of a 2K or 4K workflow. This can be very useful for programs that have been previously mastered, or effects-heavy sequences that would take too much time to prepare for an ordinary roundtrip workflow.

1 Open Color, and choose File > Import > EDL.

2 Choose an EDL file from the Projects window.

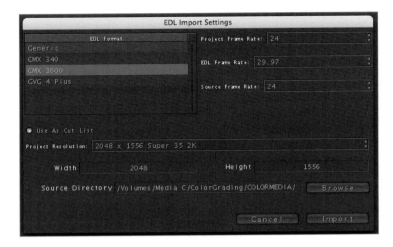

The EDL Import Settings dialog opens, containing the following controls:

EDL Format: Select the format of the EDL file you're importing.

Project Frame Rate: Select the frame rate of the Color project you're about to create, which, in most cases, should match the EDL format.

EDL Frame Rate: Choose the frame rate of the EDL you're importing.

Source Frame Rate: Choose the frame rate of the source media.

NOTE ▸ In most cases, all three of these frame rates should match.

Use As Cut List: This checkbox lets you specify that this EDL should be used as a cut list to automatically conform a matching video master file.

Once imported, the master video file is automatically broken into individual clips (sometimes called *notching*) based on the information in the EDL.

The whole movie imported as a single clip

The Timeline has been notched at every edit

Project Resolution: Select the resolution of the Color project you're creating. With rare exceptions, this should be set to the same resolution as your source clips.

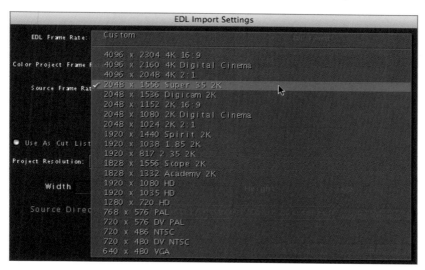

3   Specify the location of the source media you wish to link the project to. Use the Source Directory dialog to browse and select the correct directory and source media.

> **NOTE ►** Keep in mind that the source media files with matching timecode must first be ingested using Final Cut Pro.

4   After choosing all the necessary settings listed above, click Import.

A new Color project is created, and the Timeline will now contain the media nicely sliced up into shots.

Slicing in the Timeline and Using the Timeline Edit Tools

From time to time, it's useful to be able to manually override the Timeline and create your own edits. Here are some simple ways to do this.

> **NOTE ►** Be very careful, because Color is not designed primarily as an editing application, and therefore should not be treated as one. Also, note that these tools are not intended for FCP-based projects; you will ruin an FCP roundtrip this way.

Repositioning a Shot in the Timeline

1   Right-click (or Control-click) in the Timeline, and choose Unlock Track to unlock the track in the Timeline.

2   Choose Timeline > Select Tools. (Select Tools is the default state of the pointer in Color.)

3   Drag the shot to another position in the Timeline.

> **TIP** ▶ You can't mistakenly overwrite other media; in Color, dragging a clip on top of another clip will automatically position the new clip before or after that clip.

Deleting a Shot in the Timeline

1   Using the Select Tools, click to select one or multiple shots in the Timeline.

2   Press either Delete (lift delete) or Forward Delete (ripple delete), depending on the desired result.

Using the Timeline Edit Tools

In addition to the Select Tools, Color offers a selection of standard trimming tools:

Roll Tool: Takes the Out point of clip 1 and the In point of clip 2 and moves them in tandem. If you roll to the right you'll make clip 1 longer and clip 2 shorter.

Slip Tool: Lets you adjust the In and Out point of a shot without affecting its duration.

Split Tool: Lets you add an edit point to a shot by cutting it into two pieces. Click the ruler above the clip to split a clip.

Splice Tool: Occasionally, you might accidentally have created a cut, or would prefer to rejoin two shots that have been split for convenience. The splice tool joins cuts together.

Working with RED

Footage shot in the RED format (R3D) has certain metadata that can be added in-camera, or after the fact using the Red Alert! software provided by the camera manufacturer.

This metadata is of significant interest to the colorist, as it provides access to the original display characteristics of each clip from color balance to gamma to the colorspace the footage was recorded in.

> **NOTE ►** Regardless of what these parameters were originally set to, the original camera data is always retrievable. These parameters simply provide a baseline grade for decoding the native REDCODE image data.

Using this information, you can see what the DP or video tech in the field had in mind, or you can also completely override that, and create an entirely new look.

In order to use RED footage in Color, you must install the RED Final Cut Studio tools (available for free from RED).

With that software installed, a new tab is added to the Primary In room, called the RED tab.

If you import native RED files into Color (using any of the methods described earlier), these fields will automatically be populated with the metadata stored in the files.

> **NOTE** ▶ Very often, footage originally shot on RED is transcoded to one of the Apple ProRes codecs during Log and Transfer or other ingest methods. Once converted out of the native RED format, the footage loses the RED Metadata and the clips act exactly like any other QuickTime clips.

Once imported, you can grade RED clips just like any other footage, including making changes to the settings in this tab. Like the rest of the Primary In room, all the settings interact. So the Blue Gain in the RED tab and the Blue Gain in the Advanced tab (as well as the Blue Curve, and so on) will compound or counteract each other.

For more details on the specific controls in this tab, consult the Color Help, the RED Final Cut Studio Whitepaper, or the Red software documentation.

Outputting from RED

Once color grading is done, RED projects intended for video or online exhibition should be output as QuickTime movies in the ProRes 422 codec. (You may choose the ProRes 422 (HQ) or ProRes 4444, depending on the device to which you're outputting.) The instructions for this workflow are exactly the same as in Lesson 12.

If you're sending your project to be printed to film you can either export as QuickTime: ProRes 4444, or another common workflow is to export the clips as DPX (Digital Picture eXchange) files.

Choosing this format will create folders full of numbered still images (in the DPX format) that make up the footage in your clips. DPX files are uncompressed, and the data is stored in a 10-bit logarithmic format that best preserves the gamma of the original image, making DPX files ideal for use on a film scanner.

Once you've chosen DPX as the output format, Color allows you to choose from three different options in the Printing Density pop-up menu in the Project Settings tab of the Setup room.

This workflow can be used for any footage that you intend to print to film using a film scanner or similar equipment. As always, check with the facility performing your transfer to confirm the exact settings they prefer before performing your final render.

RED media can be decoded to any resolution, but if you render to another codec or media format, the resolution is determined by the values in the Resolution Preset.

The Render Proxy setting in the User Prefs allows you to automatically scale the rendered output to quarter, half, or full resolution. This scaling is done based on the resolution of the source media, not the Resolution Preset. Because 4K REDCODE media can take a long time to render, you may want to set the Render Proxy setting to Half Resolution to generate 2K output.

Similarly, setting the Grading Proxy and Playback Proxy settings to Quarter Resolution will significantly improve performance while you're grading. Proxies are generated on the fly for RED media.

> **NOTE** ▶ Pan & Scan settings for 2K REDCODE files are passed back to Final Cut Pro's Motion tab when the Send to Final Cut Pro command is chosen. However, 4K REDCODE media will always have the Pan & Scan settings baked into the output files.

Glossary

2K An image resolution in the RGB color space, usually 2048 x 1556 pixels for a 1.33:1 aspect ratio (Native 2K). The minimum bit depth is 10 bits (linear or log). Other 2K formats include Academy 2K (1828 x 1332, 1.37:1) and Digital Cinema 2K (2048 x 858, 2.39:1 or 1998 x 1080, 1.85:1).

3D Color Space Scope A video scope displaying chroma and luma in a single view that you can manipulate in 3D space.

archive A compressed duplicate of the project, stored within the project bundle itself. The archive file lacks the thumbnail and Still Store image files of the full version, saving only the state of the internal project file, Timeline, shot settings, grades, corrections, keyframes, and pan and scan settings. Whenever you manually save your project, Color automatically creates an archive.

beauty grade The grade you like best for each shot, indicated by a red marker in the Timeline. The beauty grade does not have to be the currently selected grade.

bit depth The number of bits in a color channel; that is, the total number of values used to display the range of color by every pixel of an image. Color supports bit depths of 8-bit, 10-bit (linear and log), and 16-bit.

black level An analog video signal's voltage level for the color black, represented by IRE units. Absolute black, or *setup*, is represented by 7.5 IRE for NTSC in the United States. Video sent digitally has no setup: The Y′C$_B$C$_R$ black level remains at the appropriate digital value corresponding to the bit depth of the video signal (represented by 0 percent on a Waveform Monitor). Modern I/O devices will insert setup for analog devices where appropriate.

broadcast safe Describes luma and chroma within the Federal Communications Commission's legal limits for broadcasting. Color has built-in Broadcast Safe settings that automatically prevent video levels from exceeding user-defined limits.

B-spline A method of editing curves. You define the shape of the curve by dragging control points to "pull" it, like a magnet pulling a thin wire.

C

chroma (chrominance) The color information in a video signal, ranging from the absence of color to the maximum levels of color that can be represented. Specific chroma values are described using two properties, *hue* and *saturation*.

Chroma subsampling Since our eyes can perceive variations in brightness more than variations in color, chroma subsampling is used to compress the color data required to save an image. Chroma subsampling is described as a ratio of how much color data exists (Cb and Cr) relative to the amount of brightness data (Y). Common chroma subsampling ratios in Y′C$_B$C$_R$-encoded video are 4:4:4 (the highest), 4:2:2, 4:1:1, and 4:2:0.

Cineon A high-quality RGB-encoded image format developed by Kodak for digitally scanning, manipulating, and printing images originated on film. Color supports 8-bit and 10-bit log Cineon image files.

clipping The loss of luma and chroma information in an image. The Enable Clipping button in the Basic tab of the Primary Out room lets you set ceiling values for the red, green, and blue channels. This lets you prevent illegal broadcast values in shots to which you're applying extreme primary, secondary, or Color FX corrections.

color balance Refers to the overall mix of red, green, and blue for the highlights (brightest), midtones, and shadow (darkest) areas in a clip.

Composer A window in the Color interface that contains the Timeline as well as all the color-correction controls, which are divided into eight tabs called *rooms*.

contrast The distribution of dark, medium, and light tones in an image. An image's *contrast ratio* is the difference between the darkest and lightest tonal values within that image. Typically, a higher contrast ratio, where the difference between the two is greater, is preferable to a lower one.

control surface A color-correction device. Control surfaces typically include three trackballs that correspond to the three overlapping tonal zones of the primary and secondary color balance controls (shadows, midtones, and highlights), three rotary controls for the three contrast controls (black level, gamma, and white point), and other rotary controls and buttons.

correction In Color, an adjustment made within a single room. Once saved, corrections can be applied to one or more shots in your project without changing the settings of any other rooms.

curves A method of performing corrections, in which chroma and luma values are represented as diagonal lines, and their values are modified by reshaping their lines.

D

DPX Stands for *Digital Picture eXchange*. An RGB-encoded image format derived from the Cineon format, it is similarly used for high-quality uncompressed digital intermediate workflows. Color supports 8-bit and 10-bit log DPX image files.

E

EDL (Edit Decision List) A text file that sequentially lists all of the edits and transitions that make up a program. EDLs are used to move a project from one editing application to another, or to coordinate the assembly of a program in an online editing facility.

G

gain The amount by which the luma of an image's white point is raised. In Color, the master gain control found in the Basic tab of the primary rooms controls overall white level. Individual RGB gain adjustments can be made in the Advanced tab of the primary rooms and secondaries room.

gamma (1) A curve that describes how the middle tones of an image appear. Gamma is a nonlinear function often confused with "brightness" or "contrast." Changing the value of the gamma affects the middle tones while leaving the whites and blacks of the image essentially unaltered. Gamma adjustment is often used to compensate for differences between Macintosh and Windows video graphics cards and displays. (2) The nonlinear representation of luminance in a picture on a broadcast monitor or computer display. Applying a gamma adjustment while recording an image maximizes the perceptible recorded detail in video signals with limited bandwidth.

grade A group of primary, secondary, and Color FX corrections saved across several rooms as a single unit.

H

highlights The lightest values in an image; one of the three overlapping tonal zones (along with shadows and midtones). The white point of an image is the lightest pixel in the highlights.

histogram A video scope that displays the relative strength of all color or luma values in an image by plotting a bar graph that shows the number of pixels at each percentage.

HSL (hue, saturation, lightness) A color model.

hue An attribute of color perception. Red, blue, yellow, and green are examples of hues. Hue is measured as an angle on a color wheel.

I

Internal Pixel Format A pop-up menu whose options determine the bit depth used for internal processing.

K

keyframe A visual and mathematical representation of a parameter's value(s) at a given point in time. Interpolating images between two keyframes results in the animation of color corrections, vignettes, Color FX nodes, pan and scan effects, and user shapes.

L

LUT (lookup table) A file containing information typically used to adjust the colors generated by a display. LUTs can be used to calibrate your display with hardware probes, and they also let you match your display to other imaging mediums, including digital projection systems and film printing devices.

lift The amount by which an image's luma value is adjusted. In Color the master lift control, found in the Basic tab of the primary rooms, controls overall luma level. Individual RGB lift adjustments can be made in the Advanced tab of the primary rooms and secondaries room.

luma Luma describes the exposure of a video shot, from absolute black (0 in Color) through the gray tones to the brightest white (100). Because luma and color are separate qualities, the grayscale result of a complete desaturation can be called the image's luma.

Merge Edits A splicing command in the Timeline menu. It rejoins two shots separated by a through edit at the current playhead position.

M

midtones (1) The distribution of all tonal values in between the black and white points of an image. (2) One of the three overlapping tonal zones of an image (along with shadows and highlights). Nonlinear adjustments to the distribution of midtones are often referred to as *gamma* adjustments.

node An image-processing operation used in the Color FX room. Combinations of nodes are called *node trees*. Nodes can apply different types of effects to different channels or parts of an image.

N

noodle The link between the output of one node and the input of another.

playback mode The method by which you set the Timeline In and Out points of a video for playback. The default method is the shot mode: Whenever the playhead moves to a new shot, the Timeline In and Out points automatically change to match the shot's Project In and Project Out points, and playback is constrained to that shot. In movie mode, the Timeline In and Out points are the first and last frames of the project, respectively.

P

primary color correction A correction that affects the entire image at once. Generally, such corrections comprise three-way adjustments of the color balance, contrast, and saturation of an image for the three ranges of tonality (shadows, midtones, and highlights.)

printer points Controls in Color meant to digitally recreate the optical process of light shining through a camera film negative for purposes of color correction. Color uses 50 discrete increments for red, green, and blue. Each point is a fraction of an f-stop.

proxy Lower-resolution substitute used in place of the source media file in your project. Using proxies increases playback, grading, and rendering performance. Proxies are only available when working with Cineon and DPX image sequences.

R **Reconform** A command that enables an XML- or EDL-based Color project to match the editorial changes made to an original Final Cut Pro sequence.

Render Queue A tab containing a list of shots in the program that you want to render. Once you've finished color-correcting your program, the controls in the Render Queue let you render the appropriate set of media files for the final output of your program, either to Final Cut Pro or to other compatible systems.

RGB (red, green, blue) A color model comprising the three primary additive colors used in computer displays, scanners, video monitors, and other devices.

ripple An edit that adjusts a shot's In or Out point, making the shot longer or shorter, without leaving a gap in the Timeline. The edit ripples through the rest of the program, moving shots to the right of the one you adjusted either earlier or later in the Timeline.

roll An edit that adjusts the Out point and In point (the cut point) of two adjacent shots simultaneously. No shots move in the Timeline as a result; only the edit point between the two shots moves.

round trip In Color, the importing of a project from Final Cut Pro for color correction and the exporting of the color-corrected project back to Final Cut Pro.

S **saturation** The intensity of a color. A completely desaturated image has no color and becomes a grayscale image. Like hue, saturation is also measured on a color wheel: It describes the distance from the center of the wheel to the edge.

secondary color correction Adjusting specific elements of an image separately. Changing the color of an object in an image is an example of secondary color correction. Each shot can have up to 16 secondary operations (including Inside and Outside controls), which are made in the Secondaries room.

shadows The darkest values in an image; one of the three overlapping tonal zones (along with highlights and midtones). The black point of an image is the darkest pixel in the shadows.

slip An edit that adjusts a shot's In and Out points simultaneously, thereby changing the portion of the shot that appears in the Timeline. A slip edit does not change a shot's position or duration in the Timeline.

splice To rejoin two shots that have been split by a through edit.

split To add an edit point to a shot by cutting the shot into two pieces.

Still Store A tab in which you can save freeze frames of shots and use a split-screen display to compare them with other shots in the Timeline.

superwhite (1) In Color, luma levels from 101 to 109 percent, where 100 represents absolute white. (2) White that is brighter than 100 IRE. Although many cameras record video at these levels, superwhite video levels are not considered broadcast safe.

tracker An onscreen control that follows an element or adjustment from frame to frame. Trackers can be used to animate primary and secondary corrections, user shapes, and pan and scan settings. There are two types of trackers in Color (auto and manual), both of which are created in the Tracking tab of the Geometry room.

T

Vectorscope A video scope that shows the overall distribution of color in an image. The video image is represented by a graph consisting of a series of connected points that fall about the center of a circular scale. The angle around the scale indicates a point's hue, and the distance from the center represents the saturation.

V

Viewer A window in the Color interface that contains your video images as well as the video scopes.

vignette In Color, a mask used to isolate an area of an image. Vignettes can be adjusted to highlight a foreground subject or to shade background features, thereby focusing viewer attention. You can control the shape, softness, and placement of vignettes.

W **Waveform Monitor** A video scope that shows different analyses of luma and chroma using waveforms that are plotted left to right on a scale called the graticule. The Waveform Monitor in Color can display luma only, chroma only, Y'C$_B$C$_R$, red only, green only, blue only, RGB (Overlay), and RGB Parade.

white level (1) An analog video signal's amplitude for the lightest white in a picture, represented by IRE units. (2) In digital video the representation for the lightest white in a picture, measured in percent. White levels brighter than 100 IRE/100 percent are not broadcast safe.

Y **Y'C$_B$C$_R$** The color model in which component digital video is typically recorded. The Y' component represents the luma, or black-and-white portion, of an image's tonal range. C$_B$ and C$_R$ represent the two color-difference components.

Index

Apple Certification
Fuel your mind.
Reach your potential.

Stand out from the crowd. Differentiate yourself and gain recognition for your expertise by earning Apple Certified Pro status to validate your color correction skills.

This book prepares you to earn Apple Certified Pro—Color Level One. Level One certification attests to essential operational knowledge of the application. Level Two certification demonstrates mastery of advanced features and a deeper understanding of the application. Take it one step further and earn Master Pro certification.

Three Steps to Certification

1 Choose your certification path.
   More info: training.apple.com/certification.

2 Select a location:

   Apple Authorized Training Centers (AATCs) offer all exams (Mac OS X, Pro Apps, iLife, iWork, and Xsan). AATC locations: training.apple.com/locations

   Prometric Testing Centers (1-888-275-3926) offer all Mac OS X exams, and the Final Cut Pro Level One exam. Prometric centers: www.prometric.com/apple

3 Register for and take your exam(s).

"Now when I go out to do corporate videos and I let them know that I'm certified, I get job after job after job."

—Chip McAllister, Final Cut Pro Editor and Winner of The Amazing Race 2004

Reasons to Become an Apple Certified Pro

- **Raise your earning potential.** Studies show that certified professionals can earn more than their non-certified peers.

- **Distinguish yourself from others in your industry.** Proven mastery of an application helps you stand out from the crowd.

- **Display your Apple Certification logo.** Each certification provides a logo to display on business cards, resumes and websites.

- **Publicize your Certifications.** Publish your certifications on the Apple Certified Professionals Registry to connect with schools, clients and employers.

Training Options

Apple's comprehensive curriculum addresses your needs, whether you're an IT or creative professional, educator, or service technician. Hands-on training is available through a worldwide network of Apple Authorized Training Centers (AATCs) or in a self-paced format through the Apple Training Series and Apple Pro Training Series. Learn more about Apple's curriculum and find an AATC near you at training.apple.com.

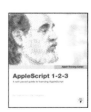

ONE SIX RIGHT
THE ROMANCE OF FLYING

Learn more about this independent film's journey from conception to distribution at:
www.apple.com/pro/profiles/terwilliger